FOR ME
TO LIVE

Essays in Honor of
James Leon Kelso

Dr. James Leon Kelso

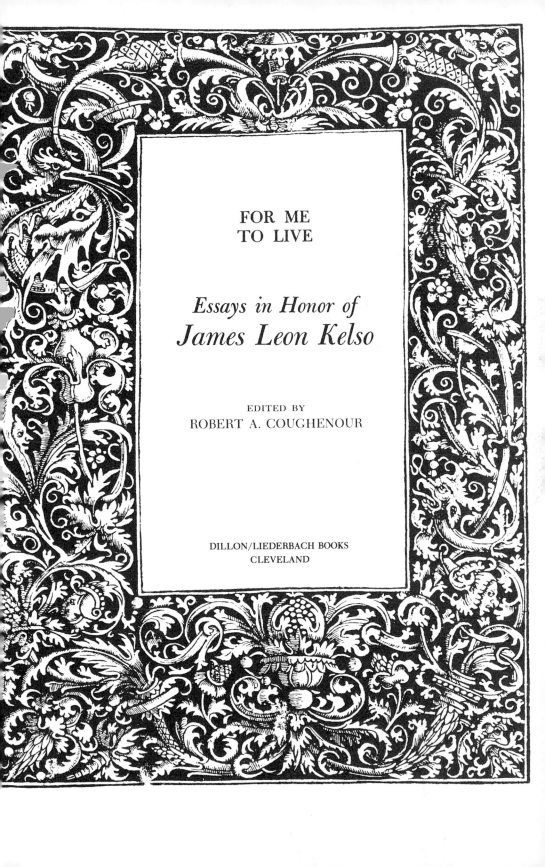

FOR ME
TO LIVE

Essays in Honor of
James Leon Kelso

EDITED BY
ROBERT A. COUGHENOUR

DILLON/LIEDERBACH BOOKS
CLEVELAND

For Me To Live: Essays in Honor of James Leon Kelso
Edited by Robert A. Coughenour

Published by Dillon/Liederbach, Inc.
14591 Madison Avenue
Cleveland, Ohio 44107

Library of Congress Card Number: 72-89962
International Standard Book Number: 0913228-05-2

"Books should to one of these four ends conduce:
For wisdom, piety, delight, or use."

—Sir John Denham

Manufactured in the United States of America

Benson Printing Company
Nashville, Tennessee

Above: Jordanian Scene—Robert A. Coughenour photo

Below: Dr. and Mrs. Kelso catalogue ancient pottery of Bethel (Jerusalem, 1960)   W. H. Brownlee photo

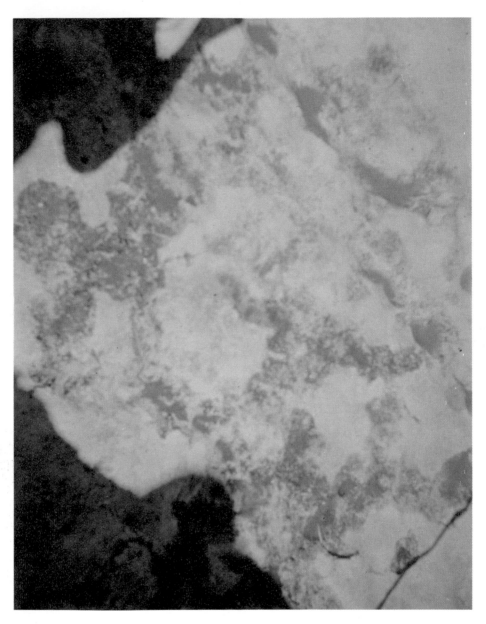

Blood streaks on bedrock at Bethel,
July, 1960
[Dark portions, upper left and lower
left are shadows.]

W. H. Brownlee photo

Testing for blood on bedrock at
Bethel. July, 1960

[Purplish color shows presence of blood. To left of tested area is
small "pool of blood," water stained with blood in the cavity.]

W. H. Brownlee photo

Bethel Excavation Staff, 1960, Beitin, Jordan
(A portion of the 1960 Bethel Excavation staff, the largest directed by Dr. Kelso. Professor Kelso is fourth from left standing; two contributors to this volume are pictured: William H. Brownlee, third from left standing; and Theophilus M. Taylor, second from right standing.

FOR ME
TO LIVE

Essays in Honor of
James Leon Kelso

Foreword

THE NATIONAL GEOGRAPHIC recently produced a cultural map of the Middle East. Appropriately, the accompanying text is titled, "Where Water Sets the Pace." As the article says, ". . . the magic touch of water [is] the key to existence in the arid Middle East." James L. Kelso, to whom this volume is presented, often said, commenting on the geography of the Holy Land, "Where there is water, there is life!" The jacket strikingly portrays this geographical fact and when taken as a visual metaphor of Christ as "living water" (John 4:7-15), points to an even more central key of exitence for James Kelso and for all men. No student of Dr. Kelso could forget the verses and the truth imparted in them which is the "motto" of his life. To each succeeding student generation from 1923-1963, to his audiences in lectures, even in his later books, Paul's words to the Philippian and Galatian churches were James Kelso's "key to existence"—"for me to live is Christ . . . It is no longer I who live, but Christ who lives in me" (Philippians 1:21; Galatians 2:20b). Thus, the volume in his honor receives its title.

The essays of this book are diverse, both in content and in style. Considering the multi-faceted competence and influence of Dr. Kelso, they could hardly be otherwise. Careful exegesis, attention to archaeological, literary and historical details, a Christ and Spirit-centered theology, a passion for honesty, a forthright pastoral attitude, a deep commitment to world evangelism—all are part and parcel of one man's contribution to generations of students and consequently to the life of his church and to the Kingdom of God. Often *Festschriften* take the form of essays centered about a single theme, usually the honored professor's most prominent field of professional work by scholars in his area of specialization. This volume, in accord with the man it honors, attempts to disclose something of the breadth and depth of James Kelso's life work and influence through original essays by his students each writing in his own field of competence.

A brief history of the book is in order. A dozen years ago, in 1960, at Beitin, Jordan, William H. Brownlee, Theophilus M. Taylor, a number of others, and I, were on the staff of the Bethel evacavation undertaken jointly by Pittsburgh Theological Seminary and the American School of Oriental Research in Jerusalem. In the conversation there, a more or less unanimous agreement seemed to be that the contributions of

James Leon Kelso to archaeology were substantial but not widely enough known. As the years passed I became increasingly aware of how very many of my ministerial colleagues, many of them former students of James Kelso, quoted from, alluded to, and in general, acknowledged the deep debt they owed to his love of Scripture and to the emphases of his teaching. In 1970, after a decade of study and teaching, my own experience deepened the conviction that a *Festschrift* would be a proper vehicle with which to honor our beloved professor. Brief discussion at that time with Addison Leitch and Robert L. Kelley, Jr. and Jack B. Rogers confirmed the decision to seek wider support for the idea of a published volume of essays. In the summer of 1971, I wrote to thirty men and women who had been students of Kelso, proposing the plan and sketching briefly the format. The overwhelming response of this group spurred our efforts. In April of 1972 when the project seemed in peril, Bruce W. Thielemann suggested and subsequently wrote a letter to Kelso's friends and former students, enlisting their aid. That the volume is now being read by you is a witness to their devotion and to their gifts; a witness that the work of the man has been imprinted on the lives of many.

I would like to thank all who have contributed to this volume, the essayists, the hundreds of friends of James Kelso, Dr. D. D. Dillon, the publisher, who himself is a former student of Kelso. Special thanks are due to William H. Brownlee for his courtesy in supplying some of the photographs and for constant support and advice; to Esther Flowerday of Hope College who helped with the typescript; to Bruce Thielemann and his staff at Glendale Presbyterian Church, Glendale, California, for their handling of correspondence and the publication contributions; to John W. Stewart, a former student of Kelso and Associate Dean of Hope College, whose general encouragement and patient ear were readily available.

We are pleased and honored to present these essays to James Leon Kelso on the occasion of his eightieth birthday, October 21, 1972.

R. A. C.

Hope College
Holland, Michigan
July 3, 1972

Contents

PART I.
BIBLICAL STUDIES
AND BIBLICAL ARCHAEOLOGY

PART II.
THEOLOGY AND ETHICS

PART III.
CHURCH AND MINISTRY

Abbreviations

BASOR	*Bulletin of the American School of Oriental Research*
HTR	*Harvard Theological Review*
IDB	*Interpreter's Dictionary of the Bible*
JB	Jerusalem Bible
JBL	*Journal of Biblical Literature*
JPOS	*Journal of the Palestine Oriental Society*
LXX	Septuagint
MT	Masoretic Text
NEB	New English Bible
RSV	Revised Standard Version
TDNT	*Theological Dictionary of the New Testament*
ZNW	*Zeitschrift für die Neuentestamentliche Wissenschaft*

James Leon Kelso

*Professor of Old Testament in Xenia, Pittsburgh-Xenia and
Pittsburgh Theological Seminaries 1923-1963*

By Theophilus M. Taylor

*T*HIS BOOK is dedicated to one of the most unusual men in
American theological education of the mid-twentieth century,
Professor James Leon Kelso of Pittsburgh Theological Seminary, by his former students and colleagues. Known to his wife
as "Jimmy," to a few close friends and colleagues as "James"
or "Jim," and to his students simply as "Kelso," he won the
hearts and devotion of all with whom he worked.

Like the Semites of ancient and modern times who were
the subject of so much of his study, Dr. Kelso tended to see
things in black or white, with very little room for in-between
grays. When students first came into contact with him he
appeared to them as an enigma: at once a hard taskmaster
and a vendor of mercy. But the longer they sat in his classes
and lived under his tutelage, the clearer it became that he
had his own brand of consistency. The longer one knows him
the more new, unexpected, fascinating facets of his life turn
up.

Several characteristics endeared him to his students. He had
the uninhibited honesty of a child and would tell you in no
uncertain terms whether he thought something was right or
wrong. Even if you didn't ask the question, it is likely that
if he knew about the situation he would volunteer his opinion.

1

He had a deep and personal concern for every one of his students, above all for slow learners and those with an inbred phobia for *foreign*, and especially *dead* languages.

His purpose as a teacher was well summed up in the brief catalogue description of his course in Old Testament Theology: "The aim is to acquaint the student thoroughly with his Bible and to get him started on his own treasure-hunt through the Hebrew Scriptures." The exciting quest for scriptural treasure-trove he tried to inspire in every student. In most cases he was successful. While his classroom methods were unconventional they were indelibly effective in producing constructive results. Anyone who learned Hebrew under him cannot help but recall his agile antics descriptive of the various verbs.

All students who had difficulty with the Hebrew language, variously estimated by themselves at 85% to 95%, found that, although he demanded an earned passing grade in the course, he was more than willing to give an unlimited amount of private, or semi-private, tutoring to get them "over the hump,"—to the place where they could begin to appreciate the language if not enjoy it.

His lectures are remembered for the wealth of homiletical fodder he was always able to conjure up out of any Old Testament passage, and for the picturesque Semitic gesticulations with which its presentation was accompanied. His language was as volatile as his gestures. Who can forget his use of the word, *phenomenal,* not employed in any prosy or philosophical sense, but rather in an earthy "Hollywoodesque" idiom, like the terms gigantic, colossal, and extravaganza, descriptive of a Cecil B. de Mille spectacular? "Phenomenal" was used liberally to describe anything that was good, right, or proper.

And who can forget the typical Kelsonian final examination with its hundred questions on the most minute details of Old Testament history, linguistics, and theology, each of which was to be answered accurately and succinctly—with one word, if possible. Then there was always a final 101st "question," reading something like this, "Write everything else you know about this subject." This he usually explained as an offer of special grace so that the crestfallen and exhausted student might make some attempt at redeeming himself for all the blank spots left in the examination by supplying supposedly relevant information on questions that had not been asked.

As a Semitist and Old Testament scholar, Dr. Kelso had two pet antipathies: (1) "pagan Greek logic," which he rightly opined is scarce, if not missing, in the Bible, and (2) "systematic theology," which was its Third or Fourth Century step-child, and hence also largely foreign to the Bible. These antipathies he sought diligently to instill into his students.

Dr. Kelso had two mentors who stood out above all others. One was President Melvin Grove Kyle of Xenia Theological Seminary, under whose personal supervision he was initiated into the mysteries of biblical archaeology. The other was Professor William Foxwell Albright, renowned archaeologist and Orientalist of Johns Hopkins University, who was Director of the American School of Oriental Research at Jerusalem when Professor Kelso accompanied Dr. Kyle on the first season's excavations at Tell Beit Mirsim in 1926. The influence of these two great men was clearly perceived in the instruction meted out to his students by Dr. Kelso. Few students escaped reading Kyle's *Mooring Masts of Revelation,* or Albright's *From the Stone Age to Christianity,* and *Archaeology and the Religion of Israel;* once they were published.

James Leon Kelso, the son of Evan Edward and Bertha Walle Kelso, was born in Duluth, Minnesota, on October 21, 1892. His parents, who were humble folk, early moved westward, and James was brought up and had his early schooling in the Snake River country of southwestern Idaho and later in bustling Portland, Oregon. From the time he started high school he worked, contributing to the meager family income and laying some aside for his further education. He worked in his spare time during the day and studied pharmacy at night. This stood

3

him in good stead and provided a means of further livelihood through college and seminary. It was at a picnic at Oswego Lake sponsored by the Portland High School Adelphi Debating Society, of which he was President, that James met Adolphina Pearson in 1911, who nine years later was to become his wife.

Having graduated from Portland High School in 1912, James travelled back across the country that fall to Monmouth College, Monmouth, Illinois, where he enrolled. In June 1916 he received his Bachelor of Arts degree from Monmouth and entered Xenia Theological Seminary, then at Xenia, Ohio, in the fall of that year. Two years later he received the Th.M. degree from the seminary and was ordained to the gospel ministry by his home Presbytery of Puget Sound, returning to the United Presbyterian Church, Bloomington, Indiana, which he served as pastor until 1923. In 1920 he persuaded his childhood sweetheart, Adolphina Pearson, to become his bride and mistress of the manse at Bloomington. This was a congregation on the edge of the Indiana University campus ministering to townspeople, faculty and students, not to mention Dr. William Lowe Bryan, President of the University, who taught a men's class on Sunday mornings. Dr. Bryan was recognized as one of the outstanding educators and administrators in American higher education. While at Bloomington, James found time to complete an A.M. degree at Indiana University and begin work on a doctorate.

It was from the then second largest congregation in Indiana Presbytery that James Kelso was called back to his own seminary alma mater in 1923 as Professor of Old Testament. In the meantime the seminary had moved from Xenia, Ohio, to more commodious quarters in the university section of St. Louis, Missouri. A year earlier Dr. Melvin Grove Kyle had become President of Xenia Theological Seminary. In 1924 Dr. Kyle began work as a field archaeologist in Palestine, leading an exploratory expedition in search of the biblical Sodom and Gomorrah. Returning to Palestine in 1926, he took Professor and Mrs. Kelso along with him on the first expedition to Tell Beit Mirsim, most likely site of the biblical Kirjath Sepher.

It was this experience which clinched Kelso's interest in archaeology. The young professor and his wife had gotten sailings on a small freighter of the Faber Line. When the captain of the little vessel saw all the flowers, fruit, candy and messages that had been sent to the boat by friends in St. Louis, he quite naturally assumed that the young couple were newlyweds, even though they had been married six years. Perhaps it was indicative of the burgeoning "Semitism" of the would-be archaeologist that, either figuring he might as well make the most of a good thing, or that what the captain didn't know wouldn't hurt him, James neglected to set him straight on the matter. The delectable result of the whole affair was that the young couple was feted on the entire voyage; and they enjoyed a second honeymoon, with daily surprises, parties, and banquets.

Upon arriving in Jerusalem considerable time was consumed in the inevitable bartering involved in gathering equipment and completing the necessary formalities with government authorities. At last things were in readiness, and because of the summer heat, the party finally set off at night, under a moonlit sky. Since southern Palestine in the 20's had little that could masquerade as a motor road, and the excavation site was considerably off the beaten path, the expedition transported its staff, workers, and equipment aboard camels.

The particular brute which served as the young professor's mount was first loaded with tents for the expedition. When these had been piled high, a mattress was superimposed, and upon this precarious perch he was ordered to scramble. Well along on the journey, while making their way down one of the narrow defiles that break the rugged Judaean countryside, the mattress scraped both walls of the ravine, and the novice archaeologist, holding for dear life, had visions of toppling off and being trampled by the rest of the caravan. While this and numerous other disconcerting experiences might have dampened the ardor of a less persistent young American, it only served to whet the appetite of James Kelso. He took to all the novel experiences like a duck to water.

Dr. Kyle returned to Tell Beit Mirsim every other year—in 1928, 1930, and 1932; and Dr. Kelso accompanied him as a staff member the last two seasons. Dr. Kyle died on May 25, 1933; and the following year, this time as President, Dr. Kelso led a memorial expedition to Beitin (Old Testament Bethel) in Dr. Kyle's honor.

The results of the four seasons' work (1926-32) at Kirjath Sepher are presented in three volumes of *The Annual of the American Schools of Oriental Research*, under the subtitle: *The Excavation of Tell Beit Mirsim*, the last volume of which appeared in 1943. In this volume Professor Kelso and Professor J. Palin Thorley, then of the University of Pittsburgh faculty, coauthored chapter IV, "The Potter's Technique at Tell Beit Mirsim," which comprises about a third of the book. Professor W. F. Albright of John Hopkins University, author of the remainder of the volume, wrote in the preface that the Kelso-Thorley chapter was "the first detailed technical analysis and evaluation of any pottery excavated in the Near East. Nothing comparable can be found in archaeological literature." It was the first time that a field archaeologist and a ceramic scientist had collaborated in a study of ancient pottery. It was in 1890 in Egypt that Sir Flinders Petrie pioneered the dating of the strata in an archaeological excavation by observing the changing styles, evolution, and sophistication reflected in the development of the potter's art. Kelso and Thorley not only added much to our knowledge of Iron Age pottery in Palestine, but, what was of greater significance, they helped narrow the margin of error in Palestinian stratigraphical chronology.

The pottery found at Tell Beit Mirsim ranges from the XIII through the VII centuries, B.C. Referring to some of the museum pieces that were salvaged, the authors wrote:

On the whole, we do not produce any better shapes today. The best workmen were already close to "Greek" perfection, and their work actually had more life and vitality to it than much of the more mathematically perfect Greek shapes. Indeed these Israelitic potters, if they had been employed in Greek pottery establishments at the period of the latter's best skill, could have quickly adjusted themselves to Greek refinements and their work would have been quite equal to that of the Greeks. Thus the old view that the Israelites had no artistic skill must certainly be revised in the field of ceramics (p. 100).

Kelso and Thorley followed up their report of the pottery from Tell Beit Mirsim with brief studies of a more general nature. In an article in the *Bulletin of the American Schools of Oriental Research* (No. 104, December, 1946) they made a ceramic analysis and comparison of Late Mycenaean and Late Bronze Age (XIV—XIII centuries, B.C.) vases found at Djett, a Moslem village on the edge of the Plain of Sharon. In *The Smithsonian Report for 1946* (1947) they had an article on "Palestinian Pottery in Bible Times," in which they outlined the pottery chronology of Palestine from the Neolithic Age (c.6000-4500 B.C.) to the Roman Period (63 B.C.-A.D. 325), and demonstrated that the various strata of an excavation in Palestine could at that time be dated with accuracy to within about 50 years. The margin of error tends to be reduced by the new corroborative data that comes to light with the work of every responsible archaeological expedition. Then, in 1948, Dr. Kelso produced "The Ceramic Vocabulary of the Old Testament," which was printed as *Supplementary Studies*, Nos. 5-6, of the *Bulletin of the American Schools of Oriental Research*, in which more than a hundred technical ceramic terms appearing in the Hebrew Old Testament are described and their biblical references given.

Due to the uncertainties and impracticalities for archaeology caused by World War II, it was not until 1949-50 that Dr.

Kelso, during a year's sabbatical leave from Pittsburgh-Xenia Theological Seminary, was able to return to Palestine again. During that year, besides his exploits in field archaeology, he served as Director of the American School of Oriental Research in Jerusalem and as President of the Board of Trustees of the Palestine Archaeological Museum.

It was during this period in Jerusalem that he conducted the famous winter and spring excavations at Tulul Abu el 'Alayiq (New Testament Jericho), where "the winter capital of Herod the Great and a resort site for the rich" came to light. This magnificent complex of buildings, built probably in the reign of Caesar Augustus (18 B.C.—A.D. 6), reflects the opulence of Rome and Pompei. It was obvious to the archaeologists that "only experienced Roman architects and master builders could have erected them." It was as if "a section of Augustan Rome [had] been miraculously transferred . . . from the banks of the Tiber to the banks of the Wadi Qelt."

> A royal reception hall or a pleasure pavilion crowned Tell 1 and was connected with the lower gardens and buildings by a grand staircase. At the bottom of the stairway was a large building with a light, airy pergola in front of it. To the west stretched a great sunken garden. A retaining wall, consisting of a long series of niches with an exedra or hemicycle in the center, constituted the main feature and southern boundary of the sunken garden. There were 25 niches on each side of the exedra, and in front of the niches and exedra was a water reflecting basin. Beyond the garden another large building, somewhat similar to the one at the eastern end, gave balance to the pattern. Across the wadi to the north two other large buildings completed the *opus reticulatum* group (*Excavations at New Testament Jericho and Khirbet en-Nitla—Annual of the American Schools of Oriental Research*, Vols. XXIX-XXX, 1955, p. 10).

Both *The New York Times* and *The Times* of London, as

well as many other papers around the world, gave the excavation of New Testament Jericho wide coverage, recognizing the great significance of these finds.

It was in the summer of 1954 that Dr. Kelso was again able to return to Palestine for archaeological work. This time he determined to go back to Beitin (Old Testament Bethel) where he had conducted the Kyle Memorial Expedition twenty years earlier. He first explored the site of the earlier excavation and then moved to an area just east of the local mosque. Recognizing that for centuries since the time of Abraham it has been customary in the Near East, even when major cultural and religious changes have occurred, for the same sacred sites to be respected and frequented by successive regimes, Dr. Kelso hoped that the mosque which was known to have been built over the remains of an earlier church, might also prove to be the location of Jeroboam's temple, where Amos had preached. Abraham, when he came into the land of Canaan, built his altars and worshipped at sites such as Shechem and Bethel, already sacred to Canaanite worship. This is in a built-up section of the modern village so that the areas available for excavation without damage to existing buildings were very limited, and the hope went unrealized.

Two other summer campaigns were conducted at Beitin, one in 1957, and the last one in 1960. These proved more rewarding, with additional portions of the Canaanite city wall dating from about 1700 B.C. turning up, averaging 12 feet in thickness wherever it appeared. City houses adjoined it on the inside, and artifacts ranging from Chalcolithic down to the Iron Age were found.

Following that season's excavation, which had been extended some ten days longer than had been originally planned, Dr. Kelso was laid low by an infarction. Hospitalized in the Lutheran Augusta Victoria Hospital on the Mount of Olives for several weeks, he was delayed getting back to his classes at the seminary. Mrs. Kelso, who has stood by him in all kinds of situations, served as his constant secretary and companion on all his "digs," and whom he described in the dedication of one of his later books as "an archaeologist in her own right," wrote somewhat philosophically of the experience in a way that characterizes the Calvinism of them both.

> I remember flying home in 1957 and looking down at the ocean below. Now and then we saw a ship which looked very small ploughing its way through the water leaving its long white wake trailing after it. The boat seemed to be working hard in order to move ahead while our plane seemed to fly so easily in spite of terrific head winds. I remember thinking that you could see the water against which the ship was struggling, but I couldn't see the wind or even feel it in the plane. Travelling is like that. We set our dates and work very hard to be ready to leave at the appointed time, but something that we can't see comes along and changes our course." (Letter from Jerusalem, Sept. 5, 1960)

The Kelsos did return from Jordan later that fall, and he was able to resume his teaching responsibilities the following year.

Dr. Kelso's formal retirement from Pittsburgh Theological Seminary faculty came in 1963 after forty years of teaching. In that academic year, having attained the age of seventy, the mandatory retirement required by the Seminary board caught up with him, and he became Emeritus Professor of Old Testament History and Biblical Archaeology. But this did not mean retiring into a life of ease which both he and Mrs. Kelso richly deserved. James Kelso has always been a disciplined man and one whose evangelical fervor has never cooled. Continuing to be in demand for lectures, Bible studies, and preaching, and as a consultant in his chosen field, he has generously given of his time, energy, and wisdom to colleagues, students, and friends.

Since 1963 he has continued to share his vast knowledge

of the ancient Near East with a wider audience than the scholarly one to which the technical reports of his excavations were addressed. Dr. Kelso has carried throughout life a concern for the biblical education of the layman in the Church. It was for them in particular, and for ministers struggling to interpret the Word of God in the Scriptures to today's people, that Dr. Kelso produced his later books: *Archaeology and Our Old Testament Contemporaries, Archaeology and the Ancient Testament, An Archaeologist Looks at the Gospels,* and *An Archaeologist Follows the Apostle Paul.*

One of the most familiar sights at Pittsburgh Seminary, both before and after his retirement, was that of Dr. Kelso, wrapped loosely in a faded blue smock, poring over broken pottery fragments in the work room or in the Bible Lands Museum. This museum, now housed in dust-proof, well-lighted display cases, is one of the most extensive seminary museums in this country. It contains the archaeologist's share of the more important artifacts unearthed in the long series of expeditions in which Xenia, Pittsburgh-Xenia, and more recently Pittsburgh Theological Seminary has been co-sponsors with the American School of Oriental Research in Jerusalem. These antiquities range from before the time of Abraham to the second and third centuries, A.D. Dr. Kelso must be looked upon as the father of the Bible Lands Museum. Nearly all the exhibits come from expeditions he has led, and it is his technical skill as a field archaeologist that has enabled them to be identified and dated, and it was under his guidance that the physical arrangements for the museum were designed.

Two years after he returned from his triumphant excavation of New Testament Jericho, which as we have shown was heralded world-wide, the United Presbyterian Church of North America gave James Leon Kelso its highest honor, when he was elected Moderator of its General Assembly at Albany, Oregon, on May 29, 1952. It was appropriate that he should be elected Moderator in Albany, for the prophet and his wife had returned to their own country, less than a hundred miles from their childhood homes in Portland. They have had a long and a good life together, and all whose lives have been touched by theirs, including all of us who have had a small hand in the preparation of this volume in Dr. Kelso's honor, are the richer for it. We bless the God and Father of our Lord Jesus Christ who has blessed us in them.

PART ONE

Biblical Studies
and Biblical Archaeology

Introduction

By ROBERT A. COUGHENOUR

JAMES LEON KELSO is a many-talented, many-faceted person. In an address given on May 3, 1963, the occasion of Dr. Kelso's retirement from Pittsburgh Theological Seminary, William Foxwell Albright characterized him as a man of

> genuine humility and unassumed modesty . . . a graduate pharmacist who put his knowledge of chemistry to use in the study of ancient pottery. . . . [One who has written with J. Palin Thorley] an unequalled monograph . . . by far the best study of the technology and craftsmanship involved in ancient pottery. . . . A man who believed that the aim of theological training is to make us better Christians, more honest, more honorable, and more productive, each in his own field.

Whether his training of hundreds of men and women over forty years of teaching has fulfilled the aim Albright said was Kelso's, none of us can assess. What can be assessed is Kelso's own productivity in his profession. The annotated bibliography of James Kelso's published writings appended to this volume witnesses to his contributions in this area.

Dr. Kelso was a field archaeologist, an expert in ancient pottery, a professor of Old Testament, and perhaps above all these matters of professional competence, he was a teacher of wit and charm.

As is frequently the case, the unpublished materials, includ-

15

ing the verbal cajolings from an active teacher in the classroom, make as much if not more of an impression on the student. Presumably to help a struggling young teacher get good source materials for his own homework, Dr. Kelso sent to me, nearly a decade ago, a large stack of old notes, clippings, musings, illustrations and jottings. Careful scrutiny of these have provided further illustration of his basic positions, his passion for Biblical studies, his continuing desire to render Biblical scholarship understandable for all churchmen.

Take for an example Dr. Kelso's notes on learning Hebrew grammar and Hebrew vocabulary. Long before the "inductive method" of teaching Hebrew was common, as opposed to the "descriptive method" of learning large segments of grammar and vocabulary never again to be seen by the average student, Dr. Kelso sought those passages which would teach the largest number of grammatical points with the simplest vocabulary. His way of going about the teaching of Hebrew was later to be refined and carefully analyzed by others, but for him it was the natural thing to do.

Consistent with his understanding of the ancient Hebrew mentality, he "acted out" as many verbs as possible. No student who ever sat under Kelso can forget the antics associated with verbs like "go up"—when he ascended the chair in his classroom, or "go down"—when he stepped with agility off the chair, and on one unfortunate day got his foot caught in the wastebasket!

Another unpublished bit of material that his students will remember is his method of teaching Hebrew nouns. Most often nouns are learned by frequency of occurrence. Kelso taught them that way too, but he added his own classifications of nouns by natural groupings. When one learned the word "man," he also learned the body parts, e.g. "arms," "legs," "hair," "kidneys," "heart" etc. When one learned the geographical word "hill," one also learned "valley," "grass," "rock," and the like.

Dr. Kelso's remarkable knowledge of Biblical geography was always impressive. His study notes reveal a careful treatment of each geographical area of Palestine, listing all the Bible passages connected with each place name, each road, each event in Israel's history. Much of this research filtered into his lectures, but always in a way that could be easily grasped. For example, in his "Expanded Notes on Detailed Geography and City References in the Old Testament," I found the following outline for presentation which, at a glance, shows his concern for clarity:

> Geography is a pre-requisite for Bible Study.
> Many mistakes [are found] even in the best commentaries
>   when geography is forgotten.
> How to study geography of Palestine?
>   (1) Its location on the globe
>   (2) Its location on the Mediterranean
>   (3) Its relation to Africa and Asia
>   (4) Its relation to distant countries according to the
>   direction peoples came to it:
>   a. via Egypt—Ethiopia/Libya
>   b. via sea—Philistines
>   c. via desert—maurauding tribes
>   d. via North—Scythians/Hittites/Arameans/
>   Assyrians/Babylonians/Persians/
>   Greeks/others
>   (5) In relation to contiguous nations
>   a. Amalekites—Edomites—Idumaeans
>   b. Canaanites
>   c. Amorites
>   d. Phoenicians
>   e. Midianites
>   (6) In relation to itself:
>   a. main geographical divisions
>   b. tribal units
>   c. roads and cities
>   d. climate
>   e. vegetation
>   f. customs and manners

Typical of Dr. Kelso's epigrammatic style of instruction are his notes on "Major Mistake Types in Misinterpreting Bible History." On a single page for each type, Dr. Kelso wrote the following:

Mistakes regarding the *nature* of Scripture

Bible is the history of revelation (God is the hero) not a history of the Jews, nor a textbook of science, or ethics.

Bible is of unique authorship—H.S. *and* men.

Bible is uniquely trustworthy: Remember, God can do even the supernatural naturally.

Bible has a unique totality.

Bible has a unique continuity—Each episode must be studied both in light of its context and in light of all scripture.

Bible is epitelesmatic (to a definite future but immediate application must never be lost sight of).

Bible has a finish (closed canon).

Other examples include the mistakes regarding qualified interpreters; in evaluating Bible Saints and Sinners; Biblical Chronology; Common factors in Biblical and secular history. A brief listing of famous Kelsonian "one-liners" illustrates his maxim-like style:

God teaches by history as much as by theology. What He does is as important as what He says.

The Holy Spirit must be the interpreter of His book. We need Spirit-filled students.

The interpreter must always keep in mind his own ignorance, prejudices, and sins.

God can work through both saints and sinners: Judas Iscariot *and* Paul.

Beware of drawing universal conclusions from unique data.

Don't read the *unexpressed* mind of God. Don't conjecture what He thought. Look at what He did!

Discrepancies are seldom discrepancies if studied. Nevertheless, some remain (copyist).
How's come we think we're so smart? Don't underestimate
the brilliance of ancient peoples.
Keep your feet on the ground and your heart in heaven
when studying the Bible.

For a final example of Kelso's pedagogical simplification,
take these words found, characteristically, on the back of an
envelope:

Right attitude = major factor in use of Bible
  (1) How to get this?—My meat and drink is to do the
    will of Christ.
  (2) How to grow in it?—Practice it!
  (3) How to master it?—Obey it!

Suggestions for Bible Devotions:
  (1) Study in the Bible the great problems of life before
    meeting them
    a. Death
    b. Loss of power and influence
  (2) Study in the Bible great joys you read about, but
    don't experience
    a. Prayer
    b. Personal work in evangelism
  (3) Master the Bible by books
    a. read at one sitting
    b. study it over and over (25 times)
    c. practice what it teaches.

Dr. Kelso taught many courses in his long teaching career.
In all of his teaching, whether in textual criticism, Old Tes-
tament-New Testament relations, Hebrew language and exegesis, or in Biblical Archaeology, James Kelso taught "the
whole man"—information and ideas for intellectual stimu-
lation, spiritual food for his "heart."
James Kelso was acclaimed by W. F. Albright as an expert

in ancient pottery; Kelso's own writings show his competence as a field archaeologist; and perhaps these brief examples will excite memories of his popular pedagogy—his wit—his eccentricities. For all these facets of James Kelso his students are most grateful.

The essays of Part I were chosen to illustrate the influence Dr. Kelso exerted in the matters of painstakingly careful exegesis of Scripture (the exegesis of Ezekiel 24:1-14 by William H. Brownlee); his devotion to the science of Biblical Archaeology and its use in understanding Scripture (John A. Thompson's essay on "The god Molech"); his concern to show the instruction of the inter-testamental period in relation to the New Testament (Kenneth E. Bailey's contribution on "Women in Ben Sirach and in the New Testament"); and finally, to demonstrate the controlling emphasis of his life—discipleship to Jesus Christ—Richard S. McConnell's essay on "The Lordship of Jesus and Our Discipleship".

Ezekiel's Copper Caldron And Blood On The Rock (Chapter 24:1-14)

By William H. Brownlee

THE COOKING SONG

On January 15, 588 B.C., Nebuchadnezzar arrived with his army to suppress the revolt of his erstwhile vassal, King Zedekiah of Judah. Prior to the arrival of the army, the prophet Ezekiel had described the flight of the people into Jerusalem from the unwalled villages of the countryside, depicting it as a gathering of impure metals into a refining furnace. Instead of providing protection for the refugees, Ezekiel said the city would rather be like a blazing furnace for refining of metal of its slag. Only after such an ordeal would the people be restored to their true spiritual mettle. Now that Nebuchadnezzar has arrived, the prophet introduces a variation upon the same theme. This time Jerusalem is compared to a rusty caldron, filled with pieces of a sheep or goat that are being cooked. Then pure copper will be extracted from the rusty pot by melting it down as scrap metal.

Only has James L. Kelso raised the question as to what this cookingpot looked like and the exact material of which it was made.[1] It would be a very large kettle (or caldron) similar

21

to some Iron II ceramic vessels; but since it was made of
n°ḥṓšeth, it was a vessel for cooking sacrificial feasts in the
temple. The Hebrew designation of the metal is ambiguous,
meaning either bronze or copper; but Dr. Kelso has built a
strong case for its consisting of copper, since copper has a
higher melting point than bronze: "Copper withstands heat
better than bronze, and the altar of burnt offerings on windy
days must have had a very high temperature." [2] The future
temple described in later chapters of Ezekiel was to be provided with special kitchens for cooking sacrificial meals
(46:19-24); and it is entirely possible that this is in imitation
of a traditional feature found also in the temple of Solomon.[3]
Although there would be less need for the vessel to consist
of copper for use in the subsidiary kitchens than for use upon
the altar, even here copper would be better; for the passage
implies that, in any case, the fire would be built hot enough
to smelt the copper after the broth has been drained off.

The text concerning the caldron may be translated as follows:

I

2   Son of man,
3   portray it to the house of rebellion;
      portray it and say to them,[4]
      "Yahweh [5] has spoken thus:
      'Put on the pot, put it on;
      yea pour some water into it.
4   Gather its meat-cuts into it:
          every good cut,
          thigh and shoulder,
          the choicest of pieces! [6]

II

5   'The choicest of the flock do take—
      a stack of wood beneath it.
      Boil its meat-cuts, boil them,[7]
      yea seethe its pieces within it—

6c	in a pot whose rust is internal,
d	whose rust cannot come from it,
f	for which no lot has been cast.

III

e	'Remove now meat-cut by meat-cut,
11	and set it empty upon the coals,

          that it may glow,
            its copper be scorched,
its corrosion be smelted within it,
            its rust consumed—

12	for never comes from it

          such severe rust! [8]

IV

9	"Therefore, has Yahweh spoken:

  'Woe to the bloody city!
I too do pile on the fuel,

10	do heap up the wood,

    do kindle the fire,
      do seethe the flesh
      and pour off the broth,[9]
      that its bones be charred!

V

12c-13	'In each is your rust; [10] in your corrosion is lust!

  Since I cleansed you, but you were not clean,
from your corrosion you can never be clean,
till I vent my fury upon you.

14	I, Yahweh,

  have spoken [10a] and will act.
I will not relinquish,
will not spare,
will not repent!
According to your ways and your deeds
  I judge you, says Yahweh."

The long list of imperatives concerning how to cook the sacrificial meal are not addressed to the people; for this was work for a priest, in this case, Ezekiel.[11] Yet this is what "Yahweh has spoken." It is not simply that Yahweh has given these orders to Ezekiel, though indirectly it is so; but that here we have a cooking song placed in the mouth of Yahweh himself. While performing a task, one sings in the imperative each of the duties to be performed. Yahweh, Himself, is cooking and these are the words of His song.[12] The acts prescribed by the song are not entirely in logical sequence; but I have resisted the temptation to rearrange the text, remembering a familiar caution of Dr. Kelso: "Semitic logic was not the same as western logic." As a matter of fact, it is quite probable that such a cooking song would consist of a series of ejaculary imperatives organized along other than chronological considerations. Surely, the choice of the animal to be butchered would come first; but this detail is delayed until 5*a*. This prescription is followed by "a stack of wood beneath it," which is not constructed with any appropriate verb. Rather than tamper with the text, I leave these irregularities and look for some other organizing principle. As I have divided the strophes, the first one sets forth the essential facts of the cooking song. It portrays a pot put on to cook some choice pieces of meat. The second strophe is linked to the first by word association, by the repetition of the word "choicest." This strophe adds further details concerning the cooking. It specifies the quality of the animal, the use of fuel, the actual boiling, and the nature of the pot. The third strophe declares what is to be done after the cooking is over. The fourth strophe is in part interpretive and in part consequence of the implied deep corrosion of Jerusalem; but this last is not made explicit until the fifth strophe which presents the reason for Yahweh's action.

Omitted from the above restoration are portions which concern another theme, *Jerusalem "the bloody city."* Actually,

Verse 6, which stands presently as introductory to Verses 7-8, may consist entirely of language authentic to the cooking song itself:

a   Therefore, has Yahweh spoken:
b   "Woe to the bloody city,
c   a pot whose rust is internal
d   whose rust cannot come from it.
e   Remove now meat-cut by meatcut
f   for which no lot has been cast.

Clauses *a* and *b* appear in identical form in Verse 9, where they introduce appropriately the interpretation of the cooking song; but here they are followed by lines in the imperative which continue the cooking song. Clauses *e* and *f* require a reversed order, since the prepositional phrase "for which" calls for a feminine antecedent. In Hebrew the "pot" is feminine, but "meat-cut" is masculine. Still, editorially, the present order was intended; for it forces one to contemplate the "meat-cuts" as removed from the "bloody city," thereby intimating that we are to interpret the "meat-cuts" as exiles. The casting of lots was a priestly practice. No lot would be cast for a rusty kettle, because no priest would want to use it, for it would be ceremonially unclean. The present text, on the other hand, teaches that the meat-cuts are likewise undesirable, for who would want meat which was cooked in an impure caldron? Since this is Yahweh's cooking song, it teaches that Yahweh has rejected the inhabitants of Jerusalem. The amplified references to blood in Verses 7-8 may well imply that the city's "rust" (or "corrosion") is the "blood" of her murderous acts. For an iron caldron, this would be a congruous figure of speech, for it would have red rust; but we are here concerned with a copper vessel, whose rust would be green. Consequently, not only does the interpretation appear to be introduced here prematurely, it may even imply an incorrect understanding of the rust.

25

Dr. Kelso, through his profound knowledge of metallurgy, has explained the nature of the problem of the rusty pot. The reason that the rust could not be cleaned out is that it was not all on the surface. In case the pot was made of hammered copper, one would need to think of a deep scratch which could not be cleansed by surface scouring. In the case of a molten vessel, its casting may have enclosed tiny air bubbles, by means of which the rust had penetrated into the interior. Interestingly, Kelso points out, the Hebrew word for "rust" means also "disease" and "Modern metallurgy likewise calls a peculiar type of corrosion 'copper disease.' " [13] This explanation of the rust leads us to paraphrase slightly the words "a pot whose rust is *in it*," as "a pot whose rust is *internal*," for the context makes clear that Ezekiel does not mean the inner surface of the vessel, but the inside of the metal.[14] Since the pot cannot be cleansed in any other way, it must be melted down as scrap copper for reuse in another vessel. Ezekiel's own knowledge of the smelting of metals is shown also by 22:17-22.[15]

The imperatives of the cooking song are continued, I believe, in Verses 11-12. Their reference to the smelting completes the requisite action concerning the caldron. These verses, I believe, were placed editorially between strophes IV and V by way of making explicit the fact that "the bloody city" like the pot suffers from internal corrosion and must be re-smelted if it is to be of any future use. In the order presented above, these verses depict the climax of the activities prescribed by the song and they reiterate for the sake of emphasis the fact that the caldron's corrosion (literally, "impurity") is internal and that it cannot be removed by ordinary scouring.

If Verse 10 is correctly identified as belonging to the divine judgment upon Jerusalem, then its ambiguous verb forms should be interpreted as a series of infinitive absolutes, and not as imperatives of the cooking song (as in the Revised Standard Version). Yet, the reason for the choice of such a series of verb forms was not merely for emphasis, but by way of adapting the pronouncement of doom to verbal forms which are ambiguously reminiscent of the cooking song. There is actually a minor inconsistency which shows that not all details of the cooking song are to be given any special interpretation. Nothing is made of the removal of the "meat-cuts" or "pieces" (*'a ṣāmîm*) in Strophe IV. Instead, after the broth, including the meat, has been emptied out, the "bones" (*'a sāmôth*) are to be charred. In the cooking song the "pieces" to be removed include both bones and flesh as Verse 4 makes clear.[16]

The reduction of the ingredients in the pot to charred bones finds an astonishing parallel in the vivid, poetic portrayal of Lamentations 4:8:

Now their visage is blacker than soot,
they are not recognized in the streets;
their skin has shriveled upon their bones,
it has become as dry as wood.

Here is the flesh of Jerusalem from which all the broth has been drained, leaving only bones, but thinly covered with the shriveled and blackened skin of starvation and suffering. It is too much to suggest that Ezekiel had intended such a literal application of his imagery of the charred bones. It is either literary coincidence or reflection upon the text of Ezekiel which explains the poetic depiction of Lamentations. In any case, the imagery of the two poets is remarkably similar.

An important aspect of the cooking is the permeation of the rust with all of its impurity into every piece: "In each is your rust." Here also is the nature of the defilement interpreted: "In your corrosion is lust!" The word rendered "lust" (*zimmah*) is used elsewhere in Ezekiel for adulterous behavior of Yahweh's wives (16:27; 23:29, 44, 48) and of actual sexual immorality (22:11). Allegorically, it stands for infidelity to Yahweh: the service of other gods and the consequent corruption of life. The thought seems to be that those who take refuge in Jerusalem will become steeped with the infidelity of this unholy city.

Curiously, nothing is said regarding the resmelted copper in the interpretation. The possible notion that out of the old rusty pot may yet emerge a new Jerusalem is at best only implicit. Elsewhere the prophet stressed the survival of a righteous remnant; but he seems to have been content here with depicting an inexorable doom. Neither Strophes IV nor V contain any hint as to significance for the smelting of the pot. In fact this feature in the cooking song could have been intended mainly to emphasize the gravity of Jerusalem's corruption. Strophe V stresses this idea, referring in Verse 13 to an earlier attempt by Yahweh to cleanse the city, an effort which had failed. This may allude to the earlier siege of Jerusalem in 597 B.C.; or, even more appropriately, it may refer to the reforms of King Josiah.[17] These reforms were ineffective, since the corrosion of society was so deeply engrained that these external reforms were ineffective. After Josiah died, the counter reformation under his successors brought about a recrudescence of all. the old manifestations of inner depravity.

The lack of detailed correspondence between the interpretations of Strophes IV and V and the prescriptions of Strophes I to III shows that what we really have is not allegory in any technically accurate sense of the term, but a cooking song placed in the mouth of Yahweh, which was then applied in a general sense to Jerusalem. The occasion was probably a sacrificial feast on the eve of the siege, for sacrifices before battle were common.[18] Other priests waited in line to get the copper vessels assigned them by lot; but Ezekiel took a discarded pot for which no lot was cast by way of presenting symbolically his message. I believe he was in Jerusalem and that he actually cooked as prescribed; for cooking songs were normally sung only while cooking, and Ezekiel was noted for his symbolic actions.[19] One therefore agrees with Eichrodt that "there is no occasion for any doubt that the prophet performed the actions there described." [20]

According to 24:1 f., Ezekiel recorded the very day of the events. This has led to a dispute over whether the date is genuine and whether through divine inspiration Ezekiel knew from remote Babylonia the date of the Babylonian siege.[21] To me, the question is not one of presuppositions as to what is or is not possible; but it is a matter of the internal evidence of the book itself. It is this which repeatedly suggests that the prophet is actually in Palestine, most often in Jerusalem itself.[22] In the present case, if Ezekiel acted out the cooking, where would he find a situation in the Exile in which a feast would be observed on the eve of the siege of Jerusalem, with the Jewish priests casting lots for use of the sacred cooking pots? This strongly implies the prophet's presence in Jerusalem, where naturally he knew the dating of the events. However, it seems probable from form-critical considerations that the bare date of Verse 1 alone is original, which is an expansion of the formula "The word of Yahweh came to me" through the addition of the date. That 24:2 with its command to record the date is also original creates no problem from general considerations, since it seems to have been characteristic of the prophet to record as a divine command his most significant actions.[23] Since 24:1 marked the fulfillment of his earlier prophecies, he would naturally record the date. However, when we come to the establishment of the poetic beginning of the following passage, we find difficulty with Verse 3 until we see that it should fit the pattern of other oracles, such as 34:2:

Son of man,
prophesy against the shepherds of Israel,
prophesy and say to them:
O shepherds,[24] Thus spoke Yahweh: . . .

Using this literary pattern as a key, we now look at 24:2 f.:
2 SON OF MAN, write down the date of today (the king

29

of Babylon laid siege to Jerusalem this very day) and
3   PORTRAY IT TO THE HOUSE OF REBELLION,
      PORTRAY IT AND SAY TO THEM,
      THUS HAS YAHWEH SPOKEN:

The address to the Son of Man has been separated from its
poetic completion by the insertion of an amplified reference
to the date. This looks like an editorial effort to inform the
reader of the significance of the date which Ezekiel had originally presented without commentary. The verb *mašal*, which
I here translate "portray," has generally been rendered "allegorize" (or "utter an allegory"). The second time one meets
this word in the traditional Hebrew text, it is vocalized as
a noun, the cognate object of the verb: "*Allegorize* to the house
of rebellion *an allegory* and say to them." This, however, is
not in the style of Ezekiel. No emendation of the original
consonantal text is required to arrive at the new punctuation;
but the implication is clear as to the secondary character of
most of the contents of Vs. 2. Moreover, other dates in the
book are not elaborated in this fashion. The exact meaning
of the verb is no serious matter; for if one wishes to translate
it both times as "allegorize," the verb will still be somewhat
appropriate; but one must not understand the cooking song
as fully allegorical; for it was not interpreted with precision
as to all its details. If one takes into account that action
accompanied the words, "portray" seems to be quite an appropriate rendering, embracing as it may both words and acts.

Ezekiel's dramatic portrayal made a deep impression. His
comparison of the "bloody city" to a rusty copper caldron
became proverbial. Hence as the rigors of the siege continued
and increased, the very leaders of the city took up the cry:
"This is the caldron and we are the flesh" (11:3).[25] As on
other occasions, no doubt, Ezekiel's beautiful voice and skillful
rendition of this work song won admirers, who listened to him
as to a "crooner of love songs" but who failed to heed his
message as the word of God.[26]

BLOOD ON THE ROCK

Embedded within the foregoing passage is another, briefer
poem, which I restore as follows:
6a   Therefore, has Yahweh spoken:
 b   "Woe to the bloody city,
7   for blood in her midst she has shed.[27]
      On exposed bedrock she put it;
      she did not spill it upon the ground
      to cover it with dust!
8   "To arouse fury,
          to invoke vengeance,
          you put your blood
          on exposed bedrock
          that it be not covered."

The "Therefore," may or may not be original to this passage;
for it may have originally begun simply: "Thus has Yahweh
spoken." In any case the passage like many another may begin
with a pronouncement of "Woe"—this being a complete ora-
cle, despite its brevity. Another passage devoted to the theme
of the "bloody city" is 22:1-16. The only textual problem is
the central clause of verse 8, which in the Masoretic Hebrew
text reads, "I put her blood," However, as the Dead Sea Isaiah
Scroll abundantly proves, "I put" might also be read as "you
put." [28] This seems more agreeable to the context, so we
surmise that misunderstanding led to an erroneous "her blood"
for "your blood." For surely the Lord would not take credit
for the murderous acts of Jerusalem. The context is one of
the gravity of Jerusalem's sins.

According to the prescriptions of the Torah, the blood of
animals needed to be covered with dust, except when poured
out upon the altar.[29] Men might try to cover with dust the
blood of murdered men, but this would be ineffective, as the
blood of righteous Abel shows, for it "cried out from the dust."
Here we find Jerusalem charged as deliberately displaying

blood upon exposed bedrock. What does this mean? It is not likely that ordinary murderers of the city made a deliberate point of carrying the blood of their victims to some rare point of exposed bedrock. All that we have to guide us as to the purpose of this exhibit of blood is the words, "To arouse fury, to invoke vengeance." To Ezekiel this meant to invoke God's wrath *upon Jerusalem;* but it may have meant something else to those putting it there, to invoke divine vengeance *upon the enemy.* This possibility is illustrated by II Kings 3:27, in which it is stated that when the king of Moab sacrificed his eldest son upon the wall, "there came forth great wrath upon Israel." We do know that child sacrifice was practiced in Ezekiel's day, and that he condemned it with rigor.[30] It is this sin which made Jerusalem more wicked than Sodom and Samaria.[31] Since, ordinarily, even animal blood was either covered with dust or poured out upon the altar, one may suppose that there could have been also some pagan cult act of displaying animal blood upon bare rock in connection with invoking the curses of God upon the foe.

The unusual performance demands an explanation, and to answer it we have only the powers of speculation joined with very scanty information. One curious datum, which may or may not be relevant, is the discovery of blood upon bedrock beneath the north gateway of ancient Bethel, where Dr. Kelso conducted his fourth campaign in the summer of 1960.[32] This was in a sector which Dr. Theophilus M. Taylor was excavating. First of all they noticed that the exposed rock was unusually white, showing that the natural limestone had been subjected to intense heat. Therefore, they asked the workmen to sweep it clean, and even wash it, in order to display the exceeding whiteness of the stone. This done, they noticed another feature. There were dark stains which damp looked red. Since one was here dealing with stone that had been covered since the Middle Bronze Age, it is astounding that Dr. Taylor had the audacity to suggest that it might be sacrificial blood. This, however, he did; and a Palestinian medical student who was working there offered to bring the necessary chemicals the next day to determine whether the stains were blood. The chemical test was positive, not only on the bedrock inside the gateway, but at several other places on bedrock outside this gateway. How so much blood could have been preserved so many thousands of years, despite all explanations, is a mystery. Naturally, part of the answer must be that it was covered over soon after being shed. Another part of the answer must be that it must have been shed very copiously for such numerous vestiges to be still visible and also identifiable chemically. Unfortunately, it is believed, that the kind of the blood is beyond detection, so that we do not know whether all the blood is animal, or of what kind of animal. Perhaps someday, however, this mystery too may be resolved.[33]

Such a vast bloodletting "on exposed bedrock" at Bethel surely indicates some cultic purpose. That purpose was not necessarily one of calling down divine wrath upon the enemy; but it may nevertheless be connected in some way with the security or sanctity of the gateway which was built over it. Just inside the gateway was a well-built palace or temple, where the inhabitants feasted upon the bones of cattle, sheep, and goats. The corner of one of the Middle-Bronze-Age buildings of that area has been exposed, showing beautifully cut and carefully laid masonry which Dr. Kelso has described as like that of a church edifice.[34] Between that point and the gateway proper, no excavation has yet been carried out. One important part of the area (that next to the gateway) is still one massive pile of field stones collected there by the gardeners of the town. The gateway itself, in fact, was also once covered with more of this same rockpile. Dr. Kelso correctly surmised that these stones may mask an important structure. Through much effort and expense he removed the imposing mass which covered the gateway proper; but for lack of funds he never exposed more of the area. Someday, if and when the conditions are right, more of this area may be exposed and the precise nature of the buildings inside the gateway may be more nearly determined.[35] In any case, the very fact that there was some sort of sacrificial rite in which large masses of blood were shed upon exposed bare rock at Bethel (for whatever purpose, even if this was simply incidental to the performance of sacrifice) encourages us to speculate as to a cultic background for Ezekiel 24:6-8, as well. Those who are heirs to Dr. Kelso's archaeological questing for solutions to problems in the Bible should not abandon the search to know what the meaning of blood "on exposed bedrock" means.

HERMENEUTICS

Ezekiel received God's word for "the house of Israel" in particular circumstances of history. Is there a word of God in this for us today? It cannot be emphasized enough that the nature of God is disclosed in all His acts, so that if we understand the meaning of His action in one event, it may yet apply to many more. The God of Israel is also "the God of the whole earth." [36]

Although Ezekiel spent far more time preaching doom to the people of Judah than in haranguing the foreign nations; yet he did at least point the moral of divine judgment upon Judah's nearest neighbors; also in his indictment of Jerusalem as an unfaithful wife of Yahweh, he emphasizes that this is to be done "in the sight of many women," apparently as a lesson to them.[37] Yahweh's wife is more than the city; for the city is chosen as a special embodiment of the nation. The other "women" who are to learn the lesson are not simply other cities of the land of Israel, they are personified nations.[38] Now that meanwhile all nations have come to know of Yahweh's action toward Israel through the monotheistic religions of mankind, those nations who appropriate the Hebraic revelation of God into their faith should be among all those "women" who have the sensitivity to take warning.

This does not mean that every passage of the Old Testament will find an exact analogy in our day in the United States of America; but it does mean that if we take the prophets of Israel seriously, we are justified in looking to see if any of their oracles contain God's word in a form applicable to us in our circumstances. Dr. John R. McNaugher used to argue that all one-hundred fifty Psalms should be available for singing in the *Psalter,* saying, "This psalm may not speak to us now; but the time may come when we shall need it." The question, then, concerning Ezekiel 24:1-14 is whether its oracles contain God's word for us today.

In any effort to apply the message of Ezekiel's cooking song, we need to interpret the parabolic significance of the basic elements: the pot, the rust, the meat-cuts, and the kindled fuel. The pot is Jerusalem into which has been gathered, not simply its ordinary inhabitants, but refugees from the countryside. These latter would appear to be the meat-cuts which Yahweh has gathered into His pot. The rust is the corrosive immorality of Jerusalem itself. The fuel and fire beneath the pot represent divine judgment which is visibly present in the siege of Jerusalem by the Chaldeans. The meat that is cooked in such a filthy pot will become impure like the pot, and so it will be burnt to a crisp in thorough-going judgment.

An intriguing question arises from these circumstances as to whether "the choicest of the flock" and "the choicest of its pieces" represent a higher esteem for the rural population over those of the city. General considerations would suggest that it is not necessarily so, since this may be traditional language of cooking songs. Elsewhere, Ezekiel was concerned for straying at highplaces where an impure cult was practiced; so at most there would be only a relative superiority of the people from the small country villages.[39] Yet there may be something in this, for "the bloody city" was a place of crime, oppression, official corruption, idolatrous profanation of the temple, and popular disdain for the holy things of Yahweh's worship. Ezekiel accused Jerusalem of building a "vaulted chamber" (an idolatrous cult center and brothel) "in every square (16:25)." Thus Jerusalem would seem to be far worse than the rural villages as a place of seduction to sin. Hence specific considerations would lead us not to reject the notion that the relatively better people of the countryside and outlying villages are "the choicest of the flock." The crowding in of these refugees into Jerusalem does not mean safety for them, Ezekiel declares, but the rigors of siege, in which through a crushing density of population they are all thrown into contact with the corruption of the unholy city. This total process causes the whole people to "stew in their own juice" of moral and spiritual corrosion.

If one can follow this exegesis, then he can see what has been taking place in the United States during the twentieth century. Rural people have been crowding into the cities, not as refugees from a foreign invader, but they have been drawn there for other reasons. Yet it is inside these cities where crime, prostitution, gambling, alcoholism and dope addiction are rife that "the choicest of the flock" have too often become a part of the corruption which fills the city. The older generation of city settlers may hold onto their moral and spiritual ideals, only to witness to their sorrow the lessening of moral and spiritual ardor of their descendants. They are like Lot whose sons-in-law were not ready to follow him and his daughters as fugitives from the imminent doom of Sodom and Gomorrah. The sophistication and pleasures of the city commanded greater devotion than the urgent plea of Lot that they join him and his daughters in seeking salvation elsewhere.

As we have developed the application, it might seem that the story of Sodom and Gomorrah is more suitable for the message we wish to convey than Ezekiel 24:1-14; for it would appear to be ordinary economic processes that have brought people in increasing numbers to the cities. The industrialization of the economy, the mechanization of farms, and rapid transportation (so that even the rural people do their trading and seek their pleasures in the cities) are all factors which have built up the cities and have continuously reduced the rural population both on the farms and in the small towns. Yet a major factor in this urbanization of our country has been our absorption into war-time economy. There have been two World Wars, a Korean War, and the wars of Southeast Asia. The corrosive effects of war, even when wholly just, are inevitable. Surely, all will agree whatever their judgment of particular wars, that we have been too much involved; and that, especially in Vietnam, we have not been wholly in the right. All these wars have involved most of our economy and have drawn our people into the cities to work in our factories. More than this, the wars themselves have brought our youths into the theaters of war as well—thrusting them into situations where they are confronted with the enticements of liquor, narcotics, and prostitution. The "choicest of the flock" are thereby seethed in an unholy environment which corrodes with the lust of impure living the very fabric of our society. Thus, it is not just the economic processes and modern communications which have served to corrupt American life; but it is war in all its ramifications. We have spilled blood unjustly around the world; [40] and within our own society the rapid rise of crime involves ever increasing murder. The blood shed in our midst has included that of one president and two candidates for president of our nation. Unless we can find a way to stop all this killing, the inexorable judgment of God will befall us. We cannot hide our sins with claims of good intention; they stand exposed before the holy gaze of our Lord and Judge!

Already stewing in our impure juice, we would seem to be without hope. The rust of materialism, militarism, hedonism, and agnosticism have eaten their way beneath the surface; so that the corruption of America is an *internal corrosion* which cannot be purged by superficial reforms. It is the whole spirit of our society which must be regenerated if the United States

37

of America is not to end up on the scrap heap of discarded civilizations. What we need is a disinvolvement from military engagements and the launching of new war that is wholly spiritual, directed at the corrosive power of sin. We must not abandon our inner cities to material and spiritual decay but seek to transform them into wholesome places to live.

Kelso had observed that the Hebrew noun "rust" (*hel'ah*) can also mean disease; but G. R. Driver thought that it was particularly used of gangrene.[41] The one thing that copper rust and gangrene have in common is the green color of decay and death. (Interestingly, in the Greek text of Rev. 6:8, the "pale horse" of death is really green.) Gangrene is commonly fatal, being as ineradicable as the deeply engrained filth of Ezekiel's caldron. So fatal is sin also in its unchecked corrosive power that it leads to the moral and spiritual death of every man and every society. "With men" our salvation "is impossible; but with God all things are possible." Even if we should require resmelting through the flames of relentless judgment, we know that God is able to bring out the pure copper for His reuse and to employ it as a vessel inscribed with the words: "Holy to the Lord."

NOTES

1. "Ezekiel's Parable of the Corroded Copper Caldron," *JBL*, lxiv, 1945, pp. 391-3.
2. *Ibid.*, p. 393.
3. See my discussion in *The Interpreter's One-Volume Commentary on the Bible*, (hereafter cited as *IOVCOB*), Nashville: Abingdon, 1971. pp. 431*b*-433. A few details of the description of Ezekiel's temple (together with the drawing on p. 435) will be revised in the second printing.
4. Introductory formulae in Ezekiel are normally poetic, cf. 34:2, to be discussed below.
5. The Masoretic text reads "The Lord GOD,"—everywhere in Ezekiel this is a surrogate for the original "Yahweh" which stood alone.

6. Or "bones," but as the context shows this means pieces containing large bones, like the thigh and shoulder.
7. The Masoretic Text reads "Boil its boilings." Two manuscripts read "Boil its meat-cuts." The conjectured restoration here is partly metri causa and partly in imitation of vs. 3d: "Put on the pot, put it on," followed by "yea" (*gam*).
8. The first clause of vs. 12 is omitted with the Septuagint.
9. This clause is read according to the suggestion of Julius A. Bewer, *The Prophets* (N.Y.; Harper & Bros., 1949), p. 394.
10. The MT reads: "In the fire is its rust." Instead of *'ēš* ("fire"), we should read *'iš* ("each"). The same mistake was made in Ezekiel 8:2, as the LXX shows. "Its rust" is corrected to "your rust" in view of the fact that this clause is needed to complete the first line of Strophe V. The 2/2 rhythm is transitional from ˙Strophe IV to Strophe V. At the same time, it can be accommodated to the following four-beat stichs.
10ₐ I omit *bā'ah* ("it comes") as grammatically obtrusive.
11. In Ezek. 46:19-24, it is prescribed that priests cook for themselves and that the Levites cook for the people. However, in pre-exilic times (as shown by repeated references to "the priests, the Levites" in Deuteronomy) no distinction was made between priests and Levites. In II Chron. 35:10-14, where anachronistically there is a distinction, the Levites do all the cooking.
12. In Joel 3:13 (4:13 in Hebrew), we seem to have citations from harvest and vintage songs placed in Yahweh's mouth. On work songs, see Otto Eissfeldt, *Einleitung in das Alte Testament* (Tübingen: J. C. B. Mohr), pp. 118f.
13. Kelso, "Ezekiel's Parable," p. 392.
14. Ancient Hebrew lacked such an adjective, so the ambiguous "in it" required explanation from context ("whose rust cannot come from it").
15. So also Kelso, "Ezekiel's Parable," p. 391.
16. See above, at note 6.
17. Ezekiel was an ardent supporter of the Deuteronomic reform which had fallen into abeyance in his own day. See *IOVCOB*, pp. 412a, 417a, 430a: "Ezekiel's Poetic Indictment of the Shepherds," *HTR*, 1i, 1958, pp. 191-203.
18. Cf. I Sam. 13:8-12; Ps. 20.
19. Ezek. 4; 5:1-3; 12:1-6; 37:15-17. Even his behavior at the death of his wife was given a symbolic meaning (24:15-17).
20. Walther Eichrodt, *Ezekiel, a Commentary* (Philadelphia: The Westminster Press, 1970), p. 338.

21. Cf. the discussion of Eichrodt, *Ezekiel*, pp. 335-7; Walther Zimmerli, *Ezechiel* (Neukirchen: Neukirchener Verlag, 1969), I. 561-3; I. G. Matthews, *Ezekiel, An American Commentary on the Old Testament* (Philadelphia: The American Baptist Publication Society, 1939), p. 91.

22. According to C. C. Torrey, *Pseudo-Ezekiel and the Original Prophecy* (New Haven: Yale University Press, 1930), the original book dealt with a fictive prophet during the reign of Manasseh. George R. Berry, "Was Ezekiel in the Exile?" *JBL*, 49 (1930), 87-93, eliminated false features in Torrey's view, arguing that Ezekiel was historical and that he carried out his ministry in Jerusalem at the dates assigned him in the book. Volkmar Herntrich, *Ezechielprobleme* (Giessen: Alfred Töpelmann, 1924), pursued the path of Berry. My fullest treatment of the prophet's original locale is to be found in *Major Critical Problems in the Book of Ezekiel* (a thesis prepared while in residence at Duke University, but in order to obtain the Master of Theology at Pittsburgh-Xenia Theological Seminary in 1946). In 1947, I produced a Ph.D. thesis at Duke University, *The Book of Ezekiel—the Original Prophet and the Editors*. My maturist criticism of the book is to be found in *IOVCOB:* and, although this last is much briefer, it supercedes in many respects my unpublished theses. On the locale, see esp. pp. 411a—412a. The most dramatic proof that Ezekiel was in Jerusalem is his sermon at the east gate of the temple, during which one auditor died (11:1-13).

23. It is not just instructions for symbolic actions (for which see above at note 19), but, also for what appear to be involuntary actions (as in 12:17-20; 21:6-7). The experience of 33:22 is described in 24:25-27 in the form of a divine word to the prophet at the time of its happening. 33:21 in contrast, is simple narrative recording of the fulfilment of the premonition of the evening before.

24. The Hebrew might also be translated "to the shepherds"; but this redundancy would be otiose, even as a gloss. In Ugaritic, *L* served as a vocative; and this usage is preserved in what W. F. Albright has called: "An Aramaean Magical Text in Hebrew from the Seventh Century B. C.," *BASOR*, 76 (Dec. 1939), 5-11, esp. n. 7, p. 7. This interpretation of Ezekiel was proposed by G. R. Driver in *Biblica*, 35 (1954), 302.

25. 11:1-13 represents a different trip to the temple from that of Chap. 8. It is an undated account, but it probably was a visit to the east gate of the temple from inside the city during its

siege. See Eichrodt, *Ezekiel*, pp. 118 f., 134 f., also *IOVCOB*, 418*b*.

26. 33:30-33.

27. More literally, the text states: "for her blood in her midst has been [i. e., has taken place]." Here "her blood" means "blood shed by her." Since the Hebrew does not yield an idiomatic sentence in English, paraphrase is justified.

28. It had long been known that when a pronominal suffix follows a verb of the second feminine singular in the perfect, its pronominal afformative takes the long *î* which is characteristic also of the verb in the first person singular. As previously ascertained, this vowel preserves the original pronunciation of the verb even without the suffix. The text of IQ Isa ᵃ now illustrates this spelling (e.g., Isa. 47:6 f., 10, 12, 15; 48:8).

29. Cf. Gen. 4:10; Deut. 12:24; Lev. 17:13. See also Ezekiel's condemnation of living by murder in 33:23-29, "The Aftermath of the Fall of Judah according to Ezekiel," *JBL*, 89 (1970), 393-404, esp. 401-404.

30. See 16:20 f.; 20:26, 31;23:37-39.

31. 16:44-52. The original text of vs. 45 read: "As your mother's daughter, you spurn your children—your mother (was) a Hittite, and your father an Amorite!" This indictment refers both to the practice of exposing unwanted infants (16:2-5) and to the sacrifice of children (16:20).

32. James L. Kelso, "The Fourth Campaign at Bethel," *BASOR*, No. 164 (Dec., 1961), 5-19, esp. p. 12; *The Excavation of Bethel* (1934-1960). The Annual of the American Schools of Oriental Research, 1968, pp. 20 f.

33. Dr. Kelso believed the vestiges of blood to be too disintegrated to make possible the identification of the kind of blood. Yet future developments of science may yet clarify the matter. By intention, Kelso left unexcavated a large section of the west half of the corridor of the gate. It is entirely probable that, when it is uncovered, more of the blood stains will appear, for probing to bedrock outside the gateway to the northwest also brought to light more bloodstains, as confirmed by the chemical tests. The unexcavated area inside the gateway appears at the west end of the rock ledge (at the right edge of the photograph) in the *BASOR*, No. 164, p. 13, figure 6; *Excavation of Bethel*, Plates 106*b* and 108*b*. In the area below (east of) the rock ledge, individual stones also showed blood stains. It was the intention of Plate 107*c* to display blood spots on these rocks; but the

plate is too unclear to demonstrate this. In further excavation, one should try to clean the rock without using water. This made the reddish color of the blood more apparent, but it doubtless also removed the blood from areas which otherwise would have appeared covered. Since no one was looking for blood at first, this result could not have been anticipated. See the pictures of Blood on the Rock at Bethel and Testing for Blood on Bedrock.

34. *Excavation of Bethel,* § 113, p. 26; Plate 109; "Béthel, la ville aux faux sanctuaires," *Bible et Terre Sainte,* 47 (May, 1962) 8-15, with attention here to p. 10 and the photograph at the lower left of p. 14. The excavation of this spot was one of my responsibilities. Only one corner of this structure has been unearthed.

35. The U-shaped gate was never fully uncovered; but since the stairs as exposed were ascending eastward from the west end of the loop-back of the gateway as they disappeared beneath the remaining heap of field stones, any traces of the upper level of the stairs would be at a higher elevation than the preserved ground level to the south. This led Dr. Kelso to conclude that the removal of any more of the overlying rockpile would not be worth the expenditure. However, the stairs may have opened into the upper level of a structure whose lower storey remains to be excavated. Alternatively, the original bedrock with all its bloodstains may have stood related to some unknown structures beneath the stairs; and these, in turn, may have been related to the "church edifice." With his limited funds, Dr. Kelso has done an important job of locating the excellent features of ancient Bethel, while leaving to future generations of scholars clear plans as to where to dig in clarifying further its history. No place was ever more vexatious for an archaeologist than Beitin, whose houses, gardens, and orchards blanket the ancient city of Bethel; but Kelso always displayed patience and sympathy with these people, being content to spot-dig wherever he could. The lives of the present inhabitants, he believed, should not be scorned for the sake of the scholar's quest for learning.

36. Isa. 54:5; and also 52:12 in IQ Isaᵃ.

37. Ezek. 16:41.

38. So interprets the ancient Targum of Jonathan at 16:41 and 23:48. This latter reference would be the clearest of all if it were not that it seems to be a part of a post-exilic supplement (23:36-49),

in which the punishers of Oholah and Oholibah are no longer the Chaldeans, but "righteous men" (vs. 45). This seems to prescribe punishment of the cities of Samaria and Jerusalem by righteous Jews in accordance with Deut. 13:6-18—at a time when these cities headed only small districts in Palestine, so that the meaning of 23:48 might be similar to that of Deut. 13:11, a warning to other Judean cities. Yet see Eichrodt, *Ezekiel*, p. 333. See also the *IOVCOB*, 421*a*, and 425*b*.

39. See especially, 6:1-7; 7:16; 18:6, 11, 15; 20:23-28; 34:6. On this last verse, see *HTR*, 1*i*, pp. 192, 199. *The Jerusalem Bible* follows me in its interpretation of 34:6: "Probably alluding to worship on the "high places.' " One thing to keep in mind is that these cult shrines were Yahwistic and to varying degrees syncretistic. Yet, no matter how Yahwistic such a religious center would be, it was under the Deuteronomic ban which restricted sacrifice to the one center at Jerusalem.

40. This is true, not simply in wars in which we have engaged directly (for which there is usually partial justification), but also in wars between small nations in which we have provided the arms with which they attacked each other. Our arming of Israel, while at the same time allowing her to expand with impunity and to dispossess the native Palestinians is the grossest case of American injustice.

41. "Ancient Lore and Modern Knowledge," in A. Caquot and M. Philonenko, *Hommages a André Dupont-Sommer*, Paris: Librairie d'Amerique et d'Orient, Adrien-Maisonneuve, 1971, pp. 277-286: with attention here to pp. 283 f. Driver distinguished between the two similar roots *ḥālāh* ("be sick, or weak") and *ḥālā'* ("be infected with gangrene"). The word for copper rust is derived from the latter. The New English Bible reflects his views in II Chronicles 16:12-14 ("Asa became gravely affected with gangrene in his feet") and Ezekiel 24:6 ("O pot green with corrosion").

The God Molech In The Light Of Archaeology

By John A. Thompson

D<small>R.</small> J. L. K<small>ELSO</small> often said in class that archaeology is shedding new light on the Bible. It is certainly true that in the past few decades archaeological discoveries have clarified the text of the Bible, its language, its history, its geography, its customs, and its religious beliefs and practices. Sometimes archaeological evidence has been used to support widely differing conclusions regarding biblical material. For example, the Hebrew word *molekh* (Lev. 18:21; 20:2,3,4,5; I Kings 11:7; II Kings 23:10; Jer. 32:25) has been interpreted in the light of some archaeological evidence as "votive offering" but in the light of other evidence as Molekh, a Canaanite god of the underworld.

INTERPRETATIONS OF THE NAME MOLECH

The oldest recorded interpretation, and probably the best, is that of the LXX in Leviticus. These ancient translators evidently considered the form a participle and rendered the word by Greek *archōn*, "ruler," in Lev. 18:21; 20:2,3,4,5. The Hebrew vocalization (with a short *e* in the second syllable) is probably that of the Canaanite rather than that of the Hebrew participle (which has a long *e*).[1] A similar LXX Greek interpretation is *basileus,* "king," in I Kings 11:7 (LXX, III Kingdoms 11:5). The LXX translaters also found this word in Hebrew *malk͕ k̄hem,* "your king," (Am. 5:26) and transliterated as *Moloch,* which is followed by the quotation of this verse in Acts 7:42. The second *o* in this Greek form of the name may result from assimilation to the first *o.* Some have suggested that the LXX translators were influenced by the divine name Muluk, which occurs in the Mari tablets.[2] These Mesopotamian cuneiform tablets, however, precede the LXX translation by about 1,500 years, and a closer example of Muluk in time must be found to establish a connection with Moloch in the LXX.

The word *molekh* always appears in the Bible with an article. This fact indicates that Molech is really a title, "the ruler." Since this title was suitable for many gods, it is not surprising that Molech is identified with several other deities.

Many have followed the suggestion by Abraham Geiger in 1857 that Hebrew Molech consists of the consonants of *melekh,* "king," pronounced with the vowels of *bōsheth,* "shame," to show contempt for an idol.[3] A supposed analogy was the name of the Canaanite goddess Ashtoreth, purportedly substituted for a hypothetical Ashtarath. N. Schneider, however, has called attention to a pagan Palmyrene form of this goddess's name, '*shtwrt,* where the *w* indicating a long *o* cannot have a contemptuous meaning.[4] Therefore considerable doubt is cast on the *bōsheth* explanation of the vocalization of Ashtoreth and of Molech.

In 1935 Otto Eissfeldt proposed that *molekh* in the Bible was not a divine epithet, but simply a sacrificial term meaning "votive offering."[5] The basis for Eissfeldt's theory is a doubtful word, *molc(ho)mor,* presumably Punic, in an otherwise Latin inscription of the second century after Christ from Ngaus in Algeria.[6] Because Syriac *mulkānā* means "promise," Eissfeldt followed J. B. Chabot in interpreting *molc(ho)mor* as "promise of a lamb."[7] Then Eissfeldt went on to interpret the consonants *mlk,* which he vocalized *molk,* in some Punic inscriptions as "votive offering," and he applied the same meaning to the biblical *molekh.* Many have accepted this explanation of Punic *mlk.*[8] R. Charlier, however, has returned to the translation of Punic *mlk* as "king," [9] which is certainly the most common meaning in the Semitic languages. Some have also followed Eissfeldt in applying the meaning "votive offering" to the biblical *molekh.*[10] Other scholars have rejected his explanation of biblical *molekh* and have maintained that the biblical word refers to a pagan god.[11] Regarding *molekh* some have proposed mediating explanations, e.g., that its interpretation is uncertain in Lev. 18:21; 20:3-5; II Kings 23:10; Jer. 32:35 and that it refers to a god in I Kings 11:7,[12] or that it was adopted by the Israelites with the meaning of sacrifice but that it was soon understood as a king god.[13]

OCCURRENCES IN HEBREW BIBLE

The name Molech occurs eight times in the Hebrew Bible. Four times in Leviticus (18:21; 20:2,3,4) in contexts condemning practices of the Canaanites devoting children by fire to Molech. Usually the phrase *he'ebhīr l',* "devote to," used in these verses is followed by some pagan god to whom children were offered, as in Ezek. 16:21; 23:27. Lev. 20:5 warns of God's judgment on any one who "plays the harlot after Molech." This expression of spiritual adultery is elsewhere used of relations with pagan gods (Ex. 34:15,16) or with mediums and wizards (Lev. 20:6). In I Kings 11:7 Solomon is condemned for building a shrine for Molech, "the abomination of the Ammonites," together with other altars to pagan gods for the sake of his foreign wives. In II Kings 23:10 the cult place of Molech is listed among the shrines of foreign gods which King Josiah destroyed. Finally in Jer. 32:25 God condemns the worship of Molech by child-sacrifice together with other idolatries of the Judeans. In these passages Molech, according to analogy, refers to a god; and Eissfeldt's proposed meaning, "votive offering," does not easily agree with the context.

Some think that "king" (Heb. *melekh*) in Isa. 57:9 KJV refers to the god Molech (so RSV), who is here associated with the underworld, Sheol. The context speaks of idolatries including child sacrifice (vs. 5). Perhaps Isa. 30:33 contains an allusion to Molech and his shrine at Topheth (so RSV mg.) in the description of the "burning place" (*tophteh*) of the "king" (*melekh*), presumably the king of Assyria.

From these references it appears that Molech was a Canaanite and Ammonite god, that he was connected with the underworld, and that to him children were sacrificed with fire by the Canaanites and also by some idolatrous Israelites.

THE WORSHIP OF MOLECH

The distinctive feature of Molech worship was the devotion of children by fire (Lev. 18:21). Some have interpreted this ritual as a mere purification,[14] or a dedication,[15] or as either a dedication or a sacrifice,[16] or as sexual relation with a heathen woman.[17] The common understanding of the phrase "devote by fire" is indicated by the fact that while this phrase is used in II Kings 16:3, the Chronicler in the parallel passage (II Chron. 28:3) clearly states that Ahaz burned his sons as an offering. Other passages (e.g. Gen. 22:9,10; Deut. 12:31; Ps. 106:37,38; Isa. 57:5,9) make it clear that the children were first slaughtered and then burned, like animal sacrifices. The medieval Talmudic dictionary called *Arukh* says that the children were placed alive on the hot arms of the image of Molech and roasted to death, while people beat drums so that the father might not hear his son's cries.[18] These details seem to be derived from the classical accounts of the worship of the Carthagian Baal Hammon.[19] Most of the infants buried in jars in Canaanite levels at Gezer, Megiddo, Taanach, Shechem,

Bethel, Dothan, Gibeon, and elsewhere in Palestine presumably died naturally. Some of them buried near sanctuaries, as at Gezer and Taanach, may have been sacrificed, possibly to Molech.

THE IMAGE OF MOLECH

The idols to whom children were sacrificed are described as being in human male form (Ezek. 16:17,21). To them children were offered to be devoured, presumably by fire burning before or within the idols (Ezek. 23:37). No specific description of Molech is given in the Bible. According to the LXX of II Sam. 12:30, the image of the related Milcom in Rabbah, the capital of Ammon, had a gold crown in which was a precious stone. The medieval *Arukh*, as cited above, describes the image of Molech as having a bull's head, seven compartments in its body, and the outstretched arms of a man, on which children were roasted to death after the image had been heated by fire within. Perhaps this picture of Molech is influenced by the classical descriptions cited above of the brazen image of the Carthaginian Baal Hammon (identified with the Greek Kronos and Roman Saturnus) with outstretched arms on which children were laid to roll down into a fire-pit. In North Africa there are representations of Baal Hammon with a bearded head and horns.[20]

THE PLACE OF MOLECH WORSHIP

The valley of the son (or sons) of Hinnom was the scene of child-sacrifice near Jerusalem (II Chron. 28:3; 33:6; Jer. 7:31; 19:2-5) and of the worship of Molech in particular (II Kings 23:10: Jer. 32:35). This valley is probably in particular (II Kings 23:10; Jer. 32:35). This valley is probably the Wadi er-Rebabeh, which begins west of the city wall and then turns south-east to the south of Jerusalem and joins the Kidron Valley. Jeremiah declares that because of the child-sacrifices in the valley of the son of Hinnom it will be strewn with dead Judeans, and he calls it the Valley of Slaughter and the Valley of Dead Bodies and Ashes (7:32; 19:6). The place of eternal fiery torment of rebels against God seems to be in this valley (Isa. 66:24). Gehinnom ("Valley of Hinnom") became a later Jewish name for hell (Enoch 26:1-27:3; 90:26; Sibylline oracles IV. 185), and the derived *geenna* is used for fiery hell in the Greek New Testament (e.g. Mt. 5:22).

The specific place of Molech's shrine in the valley of the son of Hinnom was called Topheth (II Kings 23:10; RSV of Jer. 7:31,32 and 19:6,13,14) or Tophet (KJV of the Jer. references.). This place was probably in the lower part of the Wadi er-Rebabeh near its junction with the Kidron Valley. The name Topheth may bean "burning-place," like the related *tophteh* in Isa. 30:33 (see II above). Tophet, like Gehinnom, later became a name for hot and fiery hell. The biblical associations of the place of Molech's worship link him with the underworld.

RELATION OF MOLECH TO OTHER DIVINE BEINGS

Molech is related to some other gods by similarities in name or worship. That Molech is probably originally a title, "ruler," helps to explain why he is identified with some of these gods.

Milcom. This god of the Ammonites [21] is mentioned together with Molech in I Kings 11:5,33: II Kings 23:13. The Masoretic Hebrew of I Kings 11:7 calls Molech "the abomination of the Ammonites," practically identifying these two gods. Milcom is from the same root as Molech, *mlk*, with the ending *m*, which makes the noun definite,[22] just as Molech in the Bible is preceded by the Hebrew article.

Some of the ancient versions also find Milcom in other

passages dealing with the Ammonites, where the Masoretic Hebrew reads *malkam*, "their king." In II Sam. 12:30 and the parallel I Chron. 20.2, Milcom (RSV mg.) suits the context better, because the great weight of the gold crown, at least sixty pounds, is more likely for an idol than for a person. In Jer. 49:1,3 Milcom (RSV) suits the context better because of the following "his people" in verse 1 and "his priests" in verse 3. In Am. 1:15, which also speaks of the exile of the Ammonites, either translation is possible. In Zeph. 1:15, because of "swear by" and the parallel with Yahweh preceding, RSV's Milcom is more likely. Here KJV takes the Hebrew as a proper name, Malcham.

Chemosh. He was the god of the Moabites and is named in the same context as Molech and Milcom in I Kings 11:7,33; II Kings 23:13. Jephthah calls Chemosh the god of the Ammonites, thus practically equating him with Milcom (Judg. 11:24). Mesha, king of Moab, sacrificed his son as a burnt-offering, doubtless to the national god, Chemosh (II Kings 3:27). The Moabite Stone (line 17) identifies Chemosh with Ashtar, the god of the planet Venus, to whom pagan Arabs offered human sacrifice.[23] A Babylonian text [24] identifies the god Kammush (the Babylonian form of Chemosh) with Nergal, the god of the underworld.

Baal. Jeremiah speaks of child-sacrifice by fire to Baal at Topheth, the site of Molech's shrine (19:5,6). In 32:25 the prophet condemns the people for building high places of Baal in the valley of the son of Hinnom in order to sacrifice children to Molech. In other words, these two gods were worshiped in the same way and at the same shrine. A possible explanation is that Molech, "ruler," was regarded as an aspect of Baal, "master," who was the most widely-worshiped Canaanite deity.

Baal was worshiped by the Carthaginians with the epithet

Hammon, probably meaning "hot." Perhaps this epithet refers to the fire within his image into which children were cast. He was identified with the Greek Kronos and the Roman Saturnus. To Baal the Carthaginians annually offered a child by fire,[25] and they once offered 500 children after they were defeated.[26] This literary evidence of child-sacrifice to Baal Hammon is confirmed by the cemetery of Tanit and her consort Saturnus, or Baal Hammon, at Salammbo, south of Carthage.[27] Here the charred bones are limited to those of sacrificial animals and especially of young children, and above the burials are dedicatory steles.[28]

Phoenician El. El was the chief god of the Phoenician pantheon, and he was identified with the Greek Kronos, like Baal Hammon. According to the Ugaritic epics (I AB1:8; II AB 4:24,38,48), El is called *mlk*, "king." The Phoenician history of Sanchuniathon [29] states that in the event of great calamity the Phoenicians would allot one of their children to be sacrificed to Kronos, i.e., El. Thus the Phoenician El shares with Molech the epithet *mlk* and child-sacrifice.

Adrammelech and Anammelech. These were gods of the Sepharvites, whom the Assyrians brought into Samaria in place of the exiled Israelites (II Kings 17:31). The city of Sepharvaim may be identical with Sibraim (Ezek. 47:16), a city in Syria which was captured by the Assyrians. To these gods children were sacrificed by burning. Furthermore, the second element in each name, *mlk*, is probably the title ("king") of a god or the name of a god (Melech), in either case with the same consonants as Molech.

Nergal. The name of the Mesopotamian god Nergal means "lord of the great city," that is, of the underworld, as becomes clear from such Sumerian epithets for him as Lugal-kesh-da, "king of the underworld," and Lugal-uru-sha-ga, "king of the inner (or lower) city." He is identified with the god of fire, Girra.[30] In Assyrian lists of gods Nergal is often equated with the god Malik, "ruler" or "king," [31] the Accadian participle equivalent to the Canaanite participle, Molech, "ruler."

Melqart. Melqart was the Phoenician god of Tyre, and his name means "king of the city," i.e., of the underworld.[32] The first element in the name, originally *mlk*, has the same consonants as Molech. To Melqart also human sacrifices were offered. He was identified with the Greek Herakles.

Demons. Idolatrous Israelites are said to have sacrificed their children to "demons" (Ps. 106:37). Like Molech, these demons, Hebrew *shēdīm*, were associated with the underworld.

The Angel Malik. According to the Qur'an (43:77), the angel Malik rules over the damned in hell. There was an Arabian deity, Malik, and P. Jensen has suggested that the Qur'anic angel may carry on this deity's name and function.[33]

Yahweh. Some (e.g., W. R. Smith,[34] E. Meyer,[35] and G. F. Moore [36]) have tried to identify Molech with a primitive or paganized Yahweh. It is true that Yahweh is called *melekh*, "king," (e.g. I Sam. 12.12; Ps. 10:16; Is. 6:5) a title which is similar to Molech, "ruler," but the contrasts between them are basic and many. Yahweh is ruler over all things, while Molech's domain seems to be the underworld in Canaanite mythology. Yahweh demands exclusive worship, but Molech was worshiped together with other deities such as Baal, Milcom, and Chemosh. Yahweh forbids and condemns child-sacrifice (e.g. Deut. 12:31; Jer. 7:31; Ps. 106:37-40), while this is the characteristic form of the worship of Molech. Finally, while Yahweh's Temple was on Mount Zion (e.g. Ps. 74:2), the shrine of Molech was at Topheth in the valley of the sons of Hinnom (II Kings 23:10). Yahweh, the good God of heaven, is very different in character from Molech, the Canaanite "ruler" of hell who demanded the sacrifice of children.

NOTES

1. H. Bauer, P. Leander, *Historische Grammatik der Hebräischen Sprache des Alten Testamentes* (Halle: Max Niemeyer, 1922), pp. 195, 232.
2. G. Dossin, "Signaux lumineux au pays de Mari," *Revue d'Assyriologie*, 35 (1938), pp. 174-186.
3. A. Geiger, *Urschrift und Üebersetzungen in ihrer Abhängigkeit von der innern Entwicklung des Judentums* (Breslau: Hainauer, 1857), pp. 299-308.
4. N. Schneider, "Melcom, das Scheusal der Ammoniter," *Biblica*, 18 (1937), pp. 337-343.
5. O. Eissfeldt, *Molk als Opferbegriff in Punischen und Hebräischen und das Ende des Gottes Molech* (Halle: Max Niemeyer, 1935).
6. J. and P. Alquier, "Stèles votives à Saturne découvertes près de N'gaous (Algérie)", *Comptes rendus de l'Academie des Inscriptions et Belles-Lettres*, 1931, pp. 21-26.
7. J. B. Chabot, "Note complementaire de M. J.-B. Chabot," *Comptes rendus de l'Academie des Inscriptions et Belles-Lettres*, 1931, pp. 26-27.
8. W. F. Albright, "Molk als Opferbegriff in Punischen und Hebräischen und das Ende des Gottes Moloch, von O. Eissfeldt," *Journal of the Palestine Oriental Society*, 15 (1935), p. 344. R. Dussaud, "Précisions épigraphiques touchant les sacrifices puniques d'enfants," *Comptes rendus de l'Academie des Inscriptions et Belles-Lettres*, 1946, pp. 371-387. J. G. Février, "Molchomor," *Revue de l'histoire des religions*, 143 (1953), pp. 8-18. H. Cazelles, "Molok," *Supplément au dictionnaire de la Bible*, ed. L. Pirot et al., V (Paris: Letouzey et Ané, 1957), cols. 1337-1346. R. de Vaux, *Studies in Old Testament Sacrifice* (Cardiff: University of Wales Press, 1964), pp. 75-84.
9. R. Charlier, "La nouvelle série de stèles puniques de Constantine," *Karthago*, 4 (1953), pp. 3-48.
10. R. Dussaud, "Précisions épigraphiques"; W. J. Harrelson, "Molech, Moloch," *Dictionary of the Bible*, ed. J. Hastings, revised edition ed. F. C. Grant, H. H. Rowley (New York: Scribner's, 1963), p. 669 ("more probable"). W. Röllig, "Moloch," *Wörter-*

buch der Mythologie, ed. H. W. Haussig, I (Stuttgart: Ernst Klett, 1965), pp. 299-300. W. F. Albright, *Yahweh and the Gods of Canaan* (London: Athlone Press, 1968), pp. 205-206.

11. E. Dhorme, "Otto Eissfeldt, *Molk als Opferbegriff im Punischen und Hebräischen und das Ende des Gottes Moloch,"* *Revue d'histoire des religions,* 113 (1936), pp. 276-278. A. Bea, "Kinder für Moloch oder für Jahwe? Exegetische Anmerkingen zu O. Eissfeldt, *Molk als Opferbegriff,"* *Biblica,* 18 (1937), pp. 95-107. N. Schneider, "Melcom, das Scheusal der Ammoniter," *Biblica,* 18 (1937), pp. 337-343. J. A. Thompson, *Human Sacrifice among the Semites and the God Molech,* Baltimore: Johns Hopkins University, unpublished dissertation, 1943. W. Kornfeld, "Der Molech. Eine Untersuchung zur Theorie O. Eissfeldt," *Wiener Zeitschrift für die Kunde des Morgenlandes,* 51 (1952), pp. 287-313. W. F. Albright, *Archaeology and the Religion of Israel,* 3rd ed. (Baltimore: Johns Hopkins Press, 1953), (cf. his view cited in preceding footnote). K. Dronkert, *De Molechdienst in het Oude Testament* (Leiden: Luctor et Emergo, 1953). E. Dhorme, "Le dieu Baal et le dieu Moloch dan la tradition biblique," *Anatolian Studies,* 6 (1956), pp. 57-62. R. de Vaux, *O. T. Sacrifice,* pp. 87-90.

12. J. Gray, "Molech, Moloch," *Interpreter's Dictionary of the Bible,* ed. G. A. Buttrick *et al.,* IV (New York: Abingdon, 1962), pp. 422-423.

13. H. Cazelles, "Molok."

14. LXX and Vulgate of Deut. 18:10.

15. Vulgate of Lev. 18:21; Mishnah, Sanhedrin 7.7.

16. Maimonides, *Guide of the Perplexed,* III.37,47.

17. Syriac Peshitta of Lev. 18:21; 20:2,3,4,5; Mishnah, Megillah 4.9 (where his interpretation is rejected).

18. Nathan ben Jehiel, *Sepher 'Arukh ha-shalem,* ed. A. Kohut, S. Krauss (Jerusalem: Shiloh, 1969 or 1970).

19. Diodorus, XX.14; Plutarch, *De superstitione,* 12.

20. W. Rölling, "Baal-Hammon," *Wörterbuch der Mythologie,* ed. H. W. Haussig, I (Stuttgart: Ernst Klett, 1965), pp. 271-272.

21. N. Schneider, "Melcom."

22. C. Brockelmann, *Grundriss der Vergleichenden Grammatik der Semitischen Sprachen,* 2 vols. (Berlin: Reuther & Reichard, 1908-1913), I, pp. 472-474.

23. J. Henninger, "Menschenopfer bei den Arabern," *Anthropos,* 53 (1958), pp. 721-805.

24. L. W. King, *Cuneiform Texts, Part XXIV* (London: British Museum, 1908), Plate 36, line 66.
25. Diodorus, XX.14.
26. *Ibid.*, XIII.86.3.
27. L. Poinssot, R. Lantier, "Un sanctuaire de Tanit a Carthage," *Revue de l'histoire des religions*, 87 (1923), pp. 32-68.
28. R. de Vaux, *O. T. Sacrifices*, pp. 81-84.
29. Quoted by Porphyry, *De absinentia*, II.56.
30. S. M. Langdon, *Semitic Mythology*, Boston: Jones, 1931, pp. 135, 136.
31. P. Jensen, "Die Götter *Kemosh* und *Melekh* und die Erscheinungsformen Kammush und Malik des Assyrisch-Babylonischen Gottes Nergal," *Zeitschrift für Assyriologie*, 42 (1934), pp. 235-237.
32. W. F. Albright, *Yahweh and the Gods of Canaan*, pp. 126,211-212.
33. Jensen, "Die Götter *Kemosh* ," pp. 235-237.
34. W. R. Smith, *Lectures on the Religion of the Semites*, 3rd ed. with introduction and additional notes by S. A. Cook (New York: Macmillan, 1927) p. 372.
35. E. Meyer, "Molech (Moloch)," *Ausführliches Lexicon der Griechischen und Römischen Mythologie*, ed. W. H. Roscher, II.2 (Leipzig: Teubner, 1894-1897), cols. 2650-2652.
36. G. F. Moore, "Molech, Moloch," *Encyclopaedia Biblica*, ed. T. K. Cheyne *et al.*, III (New York: Macmillan, 1902), cols. 3183-3191.

Women In Ben Sirach
And In The New Testament

By Kenneth E. Bailey

BEN SIRACH'S ATTITUDE TOWARD WOMEN

WOMEN IDENTIFIED BY THEIR RELATIONSHIPS TO MEN

Ben Sirach, the reputed author of the apocryphal book commonly called *Ecclesiasticus*, discusses women at some length, but always in the context of their relationships toward men. From this perspective his understanding of the nature of women and their place in the community is investigated. Examined here are the categories of mother, wife, daughter, women in general, married women, virgins, servant girls, widows, and harlots.

Mother. The major section on the "Mother" is in 3:1-6.[1] The passage is constructed of fourteen parallelistic couplets. Eight of them mention only the father. Six include father and mother. Thus the father dominates twenty-two lines and the mother six lines. The weight is obviously given to the father. Nevertheless, the mother is given her place in the family. The following points are made:

1) The mother has rights over her sons (3:26).
2) To honor her is like amassing a fortune and should be done "with the whole heart" (3:36; 7:27).

3) To take care of her is a duty to God (3:66).
4) Her anger is potentially damaging and is a curse from God (3:16b).
5) To dishonor her is an ignoble act (3:11b).
6) Her sense of shame is to be a controlling factor in ethics (41:17).

Thus, the fifth commandment is very much a force for Ben Sirach. The mother is inferior to the father, yet, at least partially, "because of her birthpangs" (7:27) has an important, secure place in the family. There is no criticism of any type of mother.

Wife. Ben Sirach heartily approves of marriage and has many good things to say about a good wife.

1) He delights in a happy marriage which is reserved for those who fear the Lord (25:1, 9; 25:13—26:18).
2) A good wife needs to have beauty, a kind and gentle tongue. If suitable to her husband, she is a "pillar to lean on." She should be silent, modest, chaste and a good housekeeper (36:21-25; 26:13-18).
3) A good wife is better than wealth (40:19).
4) Rich or poor, a good wife is always glad of heart (26:1-4).

Positively, Ben Sirach advises:

1) Do not be jealous of her. Do not teach her evil (9:1).
2) She is sometimes the victim of slander (28:17).
3) If she is wise, good and charming, do not turn against her (7:19; 7:26a).

Negatively, he cautions:

1) If you don't like her, don't trust her (7:26b).
2) If she interferes (in money matters) lock everything up and keep careful records of supplies issued to her (42:6,7).

3) Deed her no property while you are alive (33:20).
4) Do not give your soul to her or let her support you.[2]
5) If she is not obedient, get rid of her.[3]
6) Her spite is the most unendurable experience man has to suffer (25:13-26). Thus a good man can be happy with a good woman. He can and does wrong her. She needs to be kept in her place or dismissed. Her spite is unbearable.

Daughter. Ben Sirach's discussion of daughters is totally negative. Their very existence is a family loss.[4] He discusses at some length the fact that daughters are a life long tribulation to the father from their youth on into and through their married life. The father is always under threat of disgrace from the daughter (7:24-29; 22:3-5; 26:9-12; 42:9-11).

Women in General. Perhaps the touch-stone to Ben Sirach's attitude toward women is seen in his remark, "Sin began with a woman, and thanks to her, we all must die" (25:24). He also notes, "No wickedness comes anywhere near the wickedness of a woman, may a sinner's lot be hers" (25:19). His third comment on women in general borders on the vindictive. He writes,

Moth comes out of clothes
and woman's spite out of woman.
A man's spite is preferable to a woman's kindness.
women give rise to shame and reproach.[5]

The wise man will have no social relationship with women (9:1-9).

Married Women. The discussion of married women is in the form of advice to the man—to have nothing to do with her. Do not look at her, do not sit at table with her and drink wine with her. She belongs to someone else and is a constant source of temptation to the man who must beware lest he "succumb to her charms." The assumption apparently is that married women are for the most part temptresses and one should avoid them (9:7-9). The married woman herself is given a long, stiff warning about sexual purity. The results of infidelity are spelled out for her in dramatic and vivid terms (23:22-27).

Classes Briefly Mentioned (virgins, widows, servant girls). There is only a single line for each of the above classes. One is to avoid staring at a virgin (9:5); to be like a husband to widows (4:10); and to avoid carrying on with his servant-girl (41:21-24).

Harlots. The theme of the wiles of the harlot is a favorite theme of the sage in wisdom literature. We do not have here the dramatic or extensive descriptions as found in the book of *Proverbs.* At one point Ben Sirach demonstrates a very practical turn of mind where he writes:

Do not give your soul to whores,
or you will ruin your inheritance (8:3; 19:2).

There is no discussion of the harlot as a person and no breath of a suggestion that she is a person savable or worth saving. She is strictly a "mud puddle" to be avoided.

WOMEN APART FROM THEIR RELATIONSHIPS TO MEN

Here Ben Sirach is silent. In the list of heroes in chapters 44-50 there are no women. At no place is a woman seen as having any function in the cult or in society generally except to provide for the man.

SUMMARY OF BEN SIRACH'S VIEWS ON WOMEN

By way of summary, Ben Sirach sees woman as distinctly

inferior to man. Except for one's wife, women are considered to be a source of evil and thus to be avoided. The positive adjectives Ben Sirach uses to describe women are: wise and good; charming; sensible; obedient; silent; well-trained character; modest; chaste; and beautiful.

"Silent", "obedient" and "modest" indicate women's place in subordination at all times to men. "Charming", "chaste" and "beautiful" characterize their relationships to men. Only "wise" "good and sensible" and "of well-trained character" does the sage apply also to men.

On the negative side, she was responsible for evil coming into the world and is continually responsible for much of the evil that plagues the life of man in every age. The inferiority of her position in all of life is clearly delineated.

NEW TESTAMENT ATTITUDES

DIVERGENCES OF BEN SIRACH AND THE ACTS OF THE APOSTLES

Representative sections of Acts are selected and discussed briefly.

Baptism. The selection of baptism (vs. circumcision) as the initiatory rite for the new community meant that women could fully participate in the rite on an equal basis with men. A significant shift in the attitude toward women from that which prevailed under the old covenant is implied in this change of rite.[6]

The Editing of the Joel Text in the Pentecost Sermon. Peter's sermon of Pentecost in its entirety is a carefully constructed poem. One section of the Joel quotation has been edited by the poet in a manner significant for our subject. This section of the quotation from Joel now stands in Peter's speech with the following structure:

1 (in the last days) I will pour out my spirit upon all
  flesh and they shall prophesy
2 your sons and your daughters shall
    3 and your young men shall see visions
    4 and your old men shall dream dreams
5 yea, and on (my) menservants and (my) maidservants
6 in those days, I will pour out my Spirit (and they
  shall prophesy).[7]

The words and phrases in parentheses are the poet's additions
to the Joel text (both MT and LXX). Clearly the poet is making
additions in order to achieve a chiastic balance to his six lines.
In the top half of the structure we find "*your* sons and *your*
daughters." Balancing prepositions are then added to line five.
However, the poet added "my" and not "your" as we would
expect. (The other additions are identical to the opposite lines
in the structure.) Thus, the poet's own attitudes are evident.
Men *and women* are now in a special way God's servants
who will prophesy. Such an understanding of the place of
women in the community would be quite revolutionary to
Ben Sirach.

Other Evidences in Acts. Obedience is required and judgment
applied equally to Ananias and his wife Sapphira (5:1-11). In
the healing of Dorcas, Peter does not take witnesses with him
into the woman's chamber (as is recorded of Jesus in a similar
situation).[8] Peter thus takes significant social liberty (9:36-43).
Rhoda as a servant girl evidences from her great joy that she
is a part of the Christian fellowship in the house (12:12-17).
(Ordinarily the servant would not be.) The second section of
Acts (marked off by the famous "we" passages) has numerous
references to women in the church.[9] Priscilla and Aquila teach

Apollos (18:24-26). Philip has four unmarried daughters who are mentioned as prophetesses (21:9).

The story of Lydia is of particular significance (16:14,15; 16:40). Lydia believes Paul's proclamation of the Gospel and offers her hospitality to the apostle. Paul, and presumably Luke, accept her offer "to come to my house and stay." When trouble develops in the town, Paul is imprisoned by the authorities. He allows himself to be beaten before revealing the fact that he is a Roman citizen. The authorities are trapped and frightened. They come on Paul's demand, and personally release him from prison. They know that serious repercussions could come of having publically beaten a Roman citizen without a trial. Paul *then* visits Lydia. He thereby says indirectly but clearly to the community and to the magistrates, "Look out for this woman and her friends, or I may have to report my case to the higher authorities!" Thus, Paul demonstrates a very astute understanding of power, a skillful use of his Roman citizenship to protect the infant church, along with a heroic willingness to use his own suffering as a tool to achieve his goal—and all of it for a tiny community led by a woman.

In summary, the record of the Book of Acts shows an emerging Christian community in which women are granted full participation with men and have a distinctive place as individuals aside from their relationships to men. A radical departure from Ben Sirach is thus evidenced.

DIVERGENCES OF BEN SIRACH AND ST. PAUL

At some points, some of the writings attributed to St. Paul seem to share some common ground with Ben Sirach. The points of agreement are outside the problem delineated for this presentation. First examined is what Stendahl calls "a significant breakthrough" in Gal. 3:28 and I Cor. 11-12; and second by the *Haustafel* of Ephesus 5 with its problem of "subordination."

The Breakthrough of Galatians 3:28 and I Cor. 11-2. Stendahl in a recent book points out that Gal. 3:28 has a quotation in it from Genesis 1:27.[10] Three contrasts are set before the Galatians. In Christ "there is neither Jew *nor* Greek, there is neither slave *nor* free, there is no male *and* female." Stendahl argues that this shift from "nor" to "and" is significant, and further, that Paul is quoting Gen. 1:27 in the third pair. The intent is that the basic order of creation (male and female) has been significantly changed in Christ. Of the three pairs (Jew/Greek, slave/free, male/female) which are to achieve a special oneness in Christ, only the first was realized by the Early Church. The second dynamic was achieved only after many centuries of struggle. The third is yet to be achieved.

In I Cor. 11:2-16 Paul gives advice along rather conservative lines regarding women in the Church. Corinth had special problems, and Paul was writing to those problems. Some of what he says might be in harmony with Ben Sirach. Yet, in the middle of the discussion a radical departure gives a glimpse of the same breakthrough of Gal. 3:28. He writes, "Nevertheless, in the Lord woman is not independent of man nor man of woman; for as woman was made from man, so man is now born of woman. And all things are from God." While this is given almost as an aside, it indicates, nevertheless, a much deeper appreciation of the worth of women than the passage would have without it.[11]
Stendahl writes:

> Paul's parenthesis in the argumentation concerning sub-ordination in I Cor. 11 is best understood as an incidental reference to the insight expressed more fully in Galatians 3:28. First Corinthians 11 provides a glimpse of that insight, but one that is not able to transcend the inherited fundamental view, which needed special emphasis in the circumstances at Corinth.[12]

The Haustafel *in Ephesians 5:22-33.* By way of introduction,

Romans 5 must be noted. There Paul diverges significantly from Ben Sirach. Ben Sirach asserted that sin came into the world through Eve. This view was perpetuated through the first century.[13] For Paul, we die in *Adam,* not Eve.

For our subject, the most significant theological theme in Ephesians 5:21-33 is its Christological context. Women are to be "subject" to their husbands as "head" but only "as Christ is head of the church." Paul then reminds husbands that Christ loved the Church and gave himself for it. Ben Sirach advised that if the women was disobedient to get rid of her. Paul's Christological framework and imagery for the relationship makes this alternative unthinkable.

Markus Barth, in a recent statement, asserts that the word "subordinate" is used strictly for the context of marriage and should not be generalized into a statement about women and men as such. Only in marriage is the woman's place subordinate to the man, not in society at large.[14] Whatever "subordinate" means, it cannot be derogatory. In the same passage men are told, "Be subject to one another out of reverence for Christ," and "the Church is subject to Christ." Later in I Cor. 15:28 Paul speaks of Christ being subject to God the Father. Clearly there can be no "order of being" implied, but rather a delineation of functions.

Fritz Zerbst argues convincingly that when Paul uses the word "head" to describe man's position over the woman in marriage that this is distinctly different from "powers". Nowhere does Paul say that man has "power" over the woman in marriage. Zerbst writes:

> The New Testament contains no command directed to woman that she should obey the man. The women is merely told that she has been subordinated to men, that man is her "head" and that she should willingly accept this divine arrangement. In these contexts the New Testament always addresses the woman. It never tells man to subject woman to himself. It never speaks of the

"power" of man. It never draws the deduction from woman's subjection that she should obey her husband in the manner in which children and servants are to obey their parents and masters.[15]

Schlier in an article on "head" discusses the creatureliness of man and woman. He indicates that the "determination of their being" as creatures is for the man directly and the woman indirectly through man to God.[16]

Zerbst summarizes Paul's attitudes toward women where he writes:

> Paul is able to place woman next to man in a manner totally unheard of in the Judaism of his time. He in no wise contests woman's position in the congregation, her participation in prayer, worship, and learning, or her share in redemption. No where does he invalidate Gal. 3:28. On the basis of religious and historical parallels, one must say that Paul's attitude and position with regard to the woman question is as far removed from Judaism as it is from Greek emancipation endeavors.[17]

DIVERGENCES OF BEN SIRACH AND THE SYNOPTICS GOSPELS

Without opening the synoptic problem it is perhaps most appropriate to examine the synoptic materials using the generally accepted synoptic categories. We examine "Q" Triple Tradition, Matt.—Mark, "M" and "L".

The "Q" Source and Women. A relatively small percentage of the passages dealing with women in the synoptic gospels are found in the "Q" source. There is the reference to "the queen of the south" (Mt. 12:42, Lk. 11:31), the brief parable of the women with her bread making (Mt. 13:33; Lk. 13:20), and the women grinding on the last day (Mt. 24:41; Lk. 17:35). The new beginning is there but it is faint. Women are to be saved and judged along with men, and a peasant woman can be used in an illustration. Maertens' judgment is too sweeping, but worth noting. "There are few women in the oldest Gospel narratives and very little concern is shown for them." [18]

The Triple Tradition Pericopae and Women. The material appearing in all three synoptics and relating to women falls into three categories: First, stories of Jesus healing women.[19] The second category is the women at the cross, the burial and the resurrection. (Lk. 23:49, 24:11 and parallels). The women are mentioned as followers of Jesus and are given unusual prominence in the resurrection accounts (even though this is not reflected in I Cor. 15:3-5). Third, the remarkable divergence from prevailing attitudes in Jesus' assertion that in the resurrection there will be no sexual distinctions. As Oepke remarks:

> In holding out the prospect of sexless being like that of the of the angels in the consummated kingdom of God . . . He indirectly lifts from women the curse of her sex and sets her at the side of man as equally a child of God.[20]

The Matthew-Mark Pericopae. Four pieces of tradition fall into this category. One is negative—Herodias and her daughter; (Mk. 6:14-29 and parallels). One grants women more protection in divorce (Mk. 10:2-9 and parallels). One has some harsh features—the healing of the Syrophenician woman's daughter (Mk. 7:24-30), and the last is a very touching story of the anointing at Bethany (Mk. 14:3-9). A developing story of Jesus who demonstrates a concern for and a fellowship with women becomes clear. Jesus' relationship with women breaks through the kind of world represented by Ben Sirach and his antagonistic view of women.

Matthew's Special Source. The story of the wise and foolish virgins, Rachel weeping over her children, and the women in the genealogy are unique to Matthew. Little can be gleaned from the parable since the women are apparently only a part of the dramatic framework of the story and not there to indicate any specific attitude regarding women. The same may be said of Rachel's grief in the Genesis account quoted by Matthew. But in the case of the genealogy, both the presence and the types of women is startling. Ben Sirach's list of heroes has no women. In contrast, Matthew's mentions range from Ruth the noble, to Rehab the harlot. Thus, indirectly, all women are given a new status in the Christian scheme of things. The harlot is not a source of evil to be avoided, who destroys the inheritance of men, but rather a woman who can be redeemed, and as in the case of Rahab, is worthy to be named in the ancestry of the Messiah.

Luke's Special Source. The Gospel according to Luke displays the greatest concern for women, evidenced in any writing of the New Testament. Vincent Taylor has a convenient list of the women that appear only in Luke:

1) The widow of Nain (8:11 ff).
2) The woman in the city (7:36ff).
3) Joanna and Susanna (8:3).
4) Martha who was distracted with much serving (10:38ff).
5) The woman with the spirit of infirmity (13:10).
6) The women who lamented Jesus on His way to the cross (23:27ff).
7) The woman and the lost coin (15:8ff).
8) The widow and the unjust judge (18:1).
9) The birth stories of Mary, Elisabeth, and Anna (1,2).

In addition to the materials unique to Luke, Luke's interest in women shows through in slight editorial changes in two units of Q material which we prefer to list here. The changes make them uniquely Lucan. First is the story of the servants at the feast (Lk. 12:35). Luke adds the fact that there were women servants. Secondly, the account of divorce recorded in Luke 16:18, the author shifted the emphasis to an accusation of the man involved rather than of the woman (Lk. 16:18).

The material of the travel narrative (Luke 9:51-19:27) has blocks of material arranged in a chiastic structure with Jerusalem at the center and at the outsides. The material falls into the following pattern: [21]

1 Jerusalem
  2 Follow me
   Mission of the 70
    3 What shall I do to inherit
     Love your neighbor—the good Samaritan
     Love the Lord—Mary and Martha
      4 Teach us to pray—friend at midnight
        5 Healing
         Kingdom of God
         Son of Man
         6 Pharisees and money
          the rich fool
           7 eschatological warnings
             8 the rejection of Israel—the fig tree
               9 healing of the woman
                 10 Jerusalem
                 10 Jerusalem
               9 Healing of the man with dropsy
             8 Acceptance of the outcasts
           7 Eschatological warnings
         6 Pharisees and money
         Dives and Lazarus
        5 Healing of ten Lepers
        The Kingdom of God
        The Son of Man
      4 Prayer—the woman and the judge

    3 What shall I do to inherit?
  2 Follow me—the blind man
    Mission—Zacchaeus
1 Jerusalem

Some of the material does not fit into the over-all pattern. The majority of the material which does fall into a structure is included in the outline. In a number of rather striking cases, a man appears on one side of the structure and a woman on the other. This can be seen especially in number three where Mary and Martha illustrate the Deuteronomic answer to the question on the upper half while on the lower side it is the rich young ruler. In number five the queen of the south appears in the story of the healing of the dumb man, while at the bottom, women are a part of the Son of Man saying. In number eight the woman and her coin balance the fig tree. In number nine, the healing of a woman balances the healing of a man.

The presence and dominance of women is unmistakable in the birth narrative in Luke. Two people receive the child in the temple at his presentation. One of them is a woman. At the end of the gospel, the two men on the way to Emmaus remember the witness of the women to the resurrection (Lk. 24:22), even if the church of Luke's day had apparently overlooked it (I Cor. 15:3-5). Luke mentions women in a significant way a total of twenty four times in his gospel.

In summary it can be said with Margaret Ermarth,

> Jesus did not say much about women. His views were expressed primarily in his actions, and these actions constituted a dramatic breakthrough within that society whose dismal views on the female and on sex have been pointed out.[22]

Clearly, in all levels of the Church's tradition, and most clearly in the edition of the tradition compiled and edited by Luke, the total attitude toward woman stands in sharp contrast to that of Ben Sirach. Luke presents a picture of Jesus as a Saviour concerned for all of God's children, ready to seek both harlots and tax collectors and to welcome them into full fellowship with himself and with God's people. The woman bent double is a "daughter of Abraham" even as Zacchaeus is a "son of Abraham."

CONCLUSION

Ben Sirach describes women as inferior to man, useful only in the service of man. Her birth is a loss. She is ultimately responsible for the fact of sin in the world. She is to be treated kindly but never fully trusted. The only woman any man is to associate with for any reason is his own wife.

In contrast to this, the synoptic picture of Jesus is that of a Saviour who cares for all of God's children and treats even the harlot with concern and compassion. Women associate openly and meaningfully in the band of his first followers.

Paul was obliged to walk the razor's edge between a degradation of women evidenced in attitudes like those of Ben Sirach on the one hand and the immorality of Corinth on the other hand. Paul granted an equality to women unheard of in the oriental world of which he was partially a part. Yet he did not guide the church in the direction of an unstructured, standardless community such as he opposed in Corinth. Thus, the Church's picture of Jesus and the writings of Paul do indeed evidence significant divergence from the attitudes toward women seen in Ben Sirach.

In a day when Women's Liberation movements of varying shades and hues bid fair to color the Biblical witness on women, these data from the Synoptics, Acts, and Paul, aid in clarifying the powerful change of direction the Christian faith released to the civilized world.

NOTES

1. All passages referenced in the body are from the book indicated in the heading of the section in which the passage appears, unless otherwise noted. All English quotations of Ben Sirach are from the *Jerusalem Bible* (N.Y.: Doubleday, 1966).
2. 25:22-26; 9:1b. This last reference may be to the harlot which follows in 9:2. There is no apparent overall structure which might help us. The theme of "wife" seems to be repeated in the second half of the verse and so we have tentatively understood it in this way.
3. The LXX reads:

   Ἐι μὴ πορεύεται κατὰ χεῖράς σου
   ἀπὸ τῶν σαρκῶν σου ἀπότεμε αὐτήν

   (If she does not walk according to your hand from your flesh— amputate her)
   This gives us very strong imagery indicating the penalty of disobedience.
4. 22:3-5; Cf. especially 22:3b, "The birth of a daughter is a loss." Middle-eastern customs still require one to offer condolences when a girl is born.
5. 42:12-14. It must be noted that Ben Sirach is at this point demonstrating attitudes that are an accurate description of contemporary village attitudes held almost universally on the peasant level of society in the Middle East. Ben Sirach is not thereby a bitter old man with some unfortunate personal experience, but rather, he mirrors attitudes we can reasonably assume to have been almost universal.
6. The origin of the rite of curcumcision is beyond the scope of this essay. However, it can be noted that the ancient Egyptians had a circumcision for women (as do the modern Egyptians). This rite is depicted on the walls of the tomb of the doctor of Sakkara (Old Kingdom) as seen by the author. Israel's circumcision was, by contrast, only for men. Cf. Clarence J. Vos, *Women in the Old Testament Worship* (Delft: N. V. Verenigde Drukkerijen Judeis and Brinkman, 1968), pp. 53f.
7. Acts 2:17-18; Joel 2:28-32. There are numerous early examples of this type of poetic structure in the Old Testament. cf. Norbert Lohfink. *Das Hauptgebot. Eine Untersuchung literarischer Einleitungsträgen zu Dtn 5-11* (Romae: E Pontificio Instituto Biblico, 1963), pp. 67, 183, 195, 214, 233.

8. Luke 8:51. Cf. Albrecht Oepke, " γ ο ν η ", *Theological Dictionary of the New Testament*, Vol. I, ed. Gerhard Kittel, Tr., G. W. Bromiley (Grand Rapids: Wm. B. Eerdmans, 1964), p. 784.

9. Leading women are mentioned in the church in Thessalonica (Acts 17:4). Beroea (Acts 17:12) and at Athens (17:34; 18:2).

10. Krister Stendahl. *The Bible and the Role of Women* (Philadelphia: Fortress Press, 1966), pp. 32-37.

11. I Cor. 11:11-12; Stendahl, *The Bible and the Role of Women*, p. 35.

12. *Ibid.* p. 35. In this connection Stendahl writes profoundly of the tendency to try to "outdo the Amish" (p. 28) and of the "archaising deep freeze" (p. 35) that is always a temptation for the church. The church always faces the problem of the old and the new, of creation and redemption, of the continuity and discontinuity with the past. In regard to this dynamic tension Stendahl writes:
   "When Paul fought those who defended the old, as in Galatia—his bold vision of the new expressed itself most strongly, as in Galatians 3:28. When he discerned the overstatement of the new he spoke up for the old, as in I Corinthians. Our problem is not to harmonize the two tendencies into a perfect system. It is—as always in truly Christian theology—to discern where the accent should lie now, the accent in the eschatological drama which we call the history of the church and the world" (p. 37).

13. A fragment from *The Gospel of the Egyptians* says, "The Saviour himself said, "I am come to undo the works of the family" Cf. E. Hennecke, W. Schneemelcher, eds. *New Testament Apocrypha*, Vol. I, tr. by R. McL. Wilson (Philadelphia: Westminster Press, 1963), pp. 166-167.

14. Markus Barth, *Thesis Theological Cassettes*, Vol. II No. 9 (Pittsburgh: Thesis, Inc., 1971).

15. Fritz Zerbst. *The Office of Women in the Church*, tr by A. G. Merkens (St. Louis: Concordia Publishing House, 1955), p. 77.

16. Heinrich Schlier. " Κ Σ φ α λ η ", *TDNT*, III, 679.

17. Zerbst, *The Office of Women*, p. 60.

18. Thierry Maertens. *The Advancing Dignity of Women in the Bible*, tr. Sandra Dibbs (De Pere, Wisconsin: St. Norbert Abbey Press. 1969), pp. 133f.

19. The healing of Peter's mother-in-law (Lk. 4:38-39 and parallels);

the healing of Jairus' daughter and the woman with the issue of blood (Lk. 8:40-56 and parallels).

20. Oepke, *TDNT*, I, 78S.
21. Some of the material in the travel narrative does not fit this pattern. We have omitted this material in order to show the relationships of the structure more clearly. The chiastic structure of the material was first noticed by M. D. Goulder, "The Chiastic Structure of the Lucan Journey," *Studia Evangelica*, II, ed. F. L. Cross (Berlin: Akademie-Verlag, 1964), p. 195-202. The structure given above is the author's rather extensive reworking of Goulder's proposal.
22. Margret Sittler Ermarth. *Adam's Fractured Rib* (Philadelphia: Fortress Press, 1970), p. 16.

The Lordship Of Jesus And Our Discipleship

By Richard S. McConnell

THE OUTSTANDING POINT I remember from the teaching of Professor James Kelso is his emphasis that Jesus Christ is our Lord. Many people want Jesus to be their Savior, Professor Kelso declared again and again, but not many want him as Lord; yet, if we do not want him as our Lord, then he cannot be our Savior either. His was a simple, clear-cut position; yet it was a penetrating insight into life in the parish and in the world of scholarship.

The major problem in the parish today is that many want the comfort and supposed security or "insurance" of belonging to a church, but not many are interested in thorough-going commitment and faithfulness to a personal Lord who asks of a disciple much more than most want to consider giving. Similarly, a major problem in the world of scholarship is the urgent need of so many to prove their brilliance as scholars, to exalt their own ideas, and to criticize sharply those of a different school of thought. There is constant competition, even warfare, in the world of theological scholarship. Often one is left with the question: To whom or to what is the scholar committed? Does the lordship of Jesus Christ play any role in scholarship? Can faith be divorced from theological scholarship?

Many scholars seem to believe that those who wrote the gospels ingeniously invented most of what is there or felt free to create whatever suited their need, as if the writers had no clear idea of what it meant to be faithful to the teaching of their Lord. It is apparent that the Gospel Writers editorialized the traditions and used some of their own language, but the implication or assertion that much of their material is unreliable is a very serious matter. To understand rightly the biblical text takes more than the tools of scholarship. It takes personal encounter with the Lord behind the text. Professor Kelso did not miss the major themes in Scripture, and he did not let his students miss them either. Moreover, he believed these themes were the instruction of God to us. With him there was no basic lack of harmony between faith and scholarship, though faith did not blind him to the problems of texts written by human beings with fallible and limited knowledge.

One idea in particular which Professor Kelso emphasized as central in the Old Testament, the lordship of God over all of life, is especially relevant to the study of Matthew's Gospel. This essay studies some of the passages concerning the lordship of Jesus and our discipleship. When Jesus' views are referred to, it is with the understanding that this is Matthew's portrayal of Jesus.

Matthew portrays Jesus as the man of authority. He is presented as the authoritative interpreter of the old Torah and as the God-sent proclaimer of a more advanced revelation of God's will. That Jesus is Savior is important in this Gospel. Matthew explains that Jesus' name means "he saves" (1:21). But the greater weight is given to the fact that Jesus has the right to command obedience and faithfulness because he expresses the will of God. Thus, the Sermon on the Mount ends with the exhortation that the wise man who builds his life on a solid foundation is precisely he who *hears* the words of Jesus and *does* them (Mt. 7:24-27). Also Jesus says, "Not every one who says to me 'Lord, Lord,' shall enter the kingdom of heaven, but he who does the will of my Father who is in heaven" (7:21). Matthew makes clear that the will of the Father is known through Jesus, not through the rabbis or in any other way. "All things have been delivered to me by my Father; and no one knows the Son except the Father; and no one knows the Father except the Son and any one to whom the Son chooses to reveal him" (11:25).

The key passage in Matthew in which the authority of Jesus is related to the authority of the old Torah and the rabbinic interpretation of the Torah is 5:17-48. Jesus presents himself as the one who has the true understanding of God's revelation. "You have heard that it was said to the men of old. . . . *But I say to you.* . . ." (5:21-22; 27-30; 31-32; 33-37; 38-42; 43-48). This repetition is designed to make clear that Jesus has the knowledge and authority to reveal the will of God. That knowledge and authority is determinative for discipleship. The warning is, "Unless your righteousness exceeds that of the Scribes and Pharisees, you will never enter the kingdom of heaven" (5:20). This verse introduces the following section, vv. 21-48, which illustrates that "better righteousness."

In this section we find six antithetical statements beginning with the formula, "You have heard that it was said. . . . But I say to you. . . ." Either Jesus is setting his teaching over against the Old Testament Law or over against the rabbinic understanding of the Law. Evidence points to the latter. As the heading (v. 20) suggests, Jesus is giving instruction in a righteousness that exceeds that of the Scribes and Pharisees. W. G. Kümmel states:

> In these statements (5:21-48) Jesus places his teaching against a statement of the Torah, but he quotes these statements of the Torah expressly as a component of the tradition of the fathers. . . . *Šămă'* [hear] and *'ămăr* [say] are frequently used terms of the belief in tradition and in its traditional understanding.[1]

The meaning of the formula can best be rendered :You have received as tradition what was first proclaimed to the men at Sinai. It was rabbinic belief that God gave orally to Moses other laws besides the written Law. These were handed down orally. The written or oral laws, plus rabbinic deductions from them over the years, made up the tradition with Moses being the authority behind the whole. The chain of tradition established the authority of the rabbis. The rabbis did not believe that they had a law book,

> but rather, that God had made known his will through his once-for-all revelation to the fathers, and that this revelation was passed on and will be. In place of the prophets now appear the scribes; they also stand in the chain of tradition and therefore proclaim God's will with authority in the present.[2]

The rabbinic tradition became all important, for it was the authoritative interpreter of Scripture. Startling his hearers, Jesus attacks this tradition with a simple, straight-forward, "But I say to you." There is no appeal to Scripture, no citing of other great teachers as was rabbinic custom. He found no need to prove his teaching was in harmony with that of Moses and did not even set forth a logical argument. Rather he proclaimed the will of God as one who had his authority directly from God. No wonder the people were amazed and felt he taught with authority and not as the scribes. And no wonder the Scribes and Pharisees regarded him as a radical upstart whose teaching was invalidated by its lack of support in the legal decisions of great teachers of previous generations. Jesus found his authority in his relationship to the Father and his knowledge of the Father's will, a claim which most scribes and Pharisees found too staggering to accept.

Jesus' bold claim was that he, and not the honored tradition, was the authoritative interpreter of Scripture and the will of God for the present time. According to Matthew, Jesus claimed to have come not to abolish the law but to fulfill it (5:17) which can be interpreted to mean that Jesus came "to realize completely the commanding and essential content of Scripture by means of acting and teaching." [3] The section 5:21-48 illustrates how Jesus interpreted the essential content of Scripture and thus gives concrete expression to the kind of behavior ("the better righteousness") expected of disciples. Here we see several things going on: (1) Jesus is not concerned with laws as written or handed down but with the will of God which seeks expression through the law; (2) He uses as the ultimate norm the command to love God and one's neighbor; thus all laws must be seen in light of this norm; (3) He radicalizes and intensifies the demands of some laws and in this way completes or perfects the old Torah.

This section begins with an interpretation of the sixth commandment, "You shall not kill." Jesus internalizes the command to include showing anger and hurling insults at another person. Like killing, such behavior expresses an attitude of lovelessness and hatred toward one's fellow man. Jesus gives enormously more scope to this old law and thereby makes clear the attitude toward others that God has always wanted. This understanding is reinforced by the following saying, 5:23-26, in which Jesus instructs one not to worship God with an offering if a brother has an accusation against him. Rather, first he must become reconciled to his brother.

The meaning of the second antithesis is that the one who commits adultery, or would like to, abuses a woman to satisfy his own desire, violating the commandment of loving concern. Internalizing this old commandment illuminates God's intention behind the written law and at the same time shows how much more demanding God's will is than the written law reveals. In the fifth antitthesis Jesus rejects the "eye-for-an-eye" principle. Some held the returning of injury for injury was a just exercising of one's own rights, but for Jesus such demand for private rights was inconsistent with loving concern for others.

Surely it is significant that the last antithesis concerns loving one's neighbors and hating one's enemies. There was no command in the Old Testament or in other Jewish literature which advocated hating enemies, but in practice "neighbors" meant only Israelites and full proselytes. Despite Leviticus 19:34 which broadened the meaning to include "strangers," Gentiles and Samaritans were looked down on and even hated. The radical view of Jesus is that these too should be shown loving concern.

The love commandment is obviously right at the heart of Jesus' interpretation of the Law. This gives us the clue to "the righteousness that exceeds that of the Scribes and Pharisees." If a disciple can grasp some of the far-reaching dimensions of the love commandment, he perceives God's will. Just here the Scribes and Pharisees failed, for they kept the details of the law but "neglected the weightier matters of the law, justice, mercy and faith." (23:23). Jesus' concept of righteousness could not involve the idea of earning favor with God in order to gain entrance into the kingdom, an idea that was a major element of rabbinic faith. Jesus' concept of love excludes such a view. Rather, acts of loving concern demonstrated the reality of one's faith and the vitality of one's discipleship. The tremendous seriousness of the better righteousness is underlined in Matthew's Gospel. Without a manner of life which fulfills or tries to fulfill the double commandment of love, there is no entrance into the kingdom (5:20).

The section 5:21-48 also portrays the authoritative teacher annuling certain Old Testament laws and practices. In the matter of divorce Jesus regards the letter of divorce given to a wife as a concession of Moses because of the hardness of men's hearts. Jesus declared that the real intention of the will of God in respect to marriage is a lasting, indissoluble union. In abolishing divorce Jesus was not setting out to abolish the old Law arbitrarily. Rather he was setting forth the radical nature of God's will and at the same time abolishing the abuses which had arisen because of Moses' concession (divorces were allowed for very trivial reasons). The letter of divorce was originally given as a protection for the wife. Now the circumstances required Jesus to take the stand he did.

Similarly, in regard to the practice of making oaths Jesus seems primarily concerned with its abuse. God's name was used lightheartedly in connection with all kinds of trivial activities. In respect to this practice Jesus proclaims God's will for disciples; that they be so truthful they will never need to confirm their statements by an oath.

The principle of "an eye for an eye" was not originally intended to be cruel but as a check on vengeance. Jesus abolished the whole principle and put in its place the higher ethic of non-retaliation. When you are sued for your inner garment, give your outer garment as well (a poor person only had one)! How far Jesus intended true disciples to go! By this radical ethic Jesus pictured the extraordinary life the disciples were expected to live.

By his own authority Jesus set aside certain Old Testament laws and practices, but never arbitrarily. Rather, he proclaims God's will for the present time which is far more demanding than the leaders then realized and more demanding than the laws of the Old Covenant. The revolutionary content of his words, which at that time made many reject him, were fitting to one who had the authority to determine how the Law should be understood. Jesus setting aside what he regarded as no longer expressing God's will demonstrates he was not bound to the Old Testament Law but rather was free from it and had authority over it. To him belonged the right to decide what in the old Law was valid and what was not. Though Jesus' instruction advances beyond the revelation of God's will in the Old Testament, at the same time he affirmed and reinforced commands basic in the Old Testament (the love commandments and the Decalogue). Mainly it was the rabbinic interpretation of the old Law and its tremendous expansion by many casuistic laws that Jesus opposed. Jesus rather simplifies the understanding of God's will by reducing the Law to a few basic commands or principles.

An instructive example of how Jesus interpreted the Law is found in his handling of the grain-field episode. The Pharisees accused his disciples of breaking the Sabbath because they plucked a little grain. According to their legal practice, the rabbis had specified many kinds of work that broke the Sabbath law. One such law held that plucking ears of grain was regarded as reaping and therefore forbidden on the Sabbath. While the Scribes and Pharisees were terribly concerned lest the Sabbath law be broken, Jesus' concern was to assert God's scheme of priorities in which human need takes precedence over keeping laws. He put this squarely to the Pharisees, stating that if they understood Hosea 6:6, "I desire mercy and not sacrifice," they would not have condemned the accused. Clearly in Jesus' view their casuistry ran counter to the will of God which requires mercy be shown to persons in need, even if it is only the ordinary need of hunger. Here again we see the favorite emphasis in Matthew on the love commandment. The episode contrasts outward obedience to the Sabbath law and the charge to show mercy and concern for others.

In the subsequent episode, Mt. 12:9-14, Jesus healed a man with a withered hand on the Sabbath. Some asked him, "Is it lawful to heal on the Sabbath?" in order to accuse him before the rabbis, who taught that healing might only be done on the Sabbath if life was endangered. Jesus' position was very different: "It is lawful to do good on the Sabbath." In other words, God's will is that people be helped. Any interpretation of God's laws that involves an overriding of the love commandment is opposed to God's will. Although in these two Sabbath episodes it is rabbinic interpretations that are called into question, Jesus' use of the Hosea citation (Hosea 6:6 is quoted in Acts 12:7) and the categorical nature of his statement, "It is lawful to do good on the Sabbath," demonstrate that he subordinated all Sabbath laws to the love commandment. In Matthew's Gospel the love commandment is elevated to the position of a norm or basis from which all laws are to be interpreted and evaluated. Further, Jesus has the knowledge and authority to determine how the Sabbath is to be kept so that God's will is honored. Moreover, the disciples are bound not to the law—Old Testament or rabbinic—but rather to Jesus, who makes clear the instruction of God in the new age. Jesus is Lord and not the Law.

Another striking point concerning Jesus' lordship arises in the grain-field episode. Jesus cites the work of the priests on the Sabbath which "profanes" the day, but the priests are considered guiltless. Temple service, sacrifices, and rites such as circumcision had priority over work prohibitions. Jesus argued that if these duties are superior to the Sabbath laws so is service to one who is greater than the Temple (12:6). The Temple was regarded by the Jews as the place where God's glory was manifested. In the new era which dawned with Jesus, Jesus is the one in whom God's glory and truth is revealed. There is also an implied comparison of service in the Temple and the service of disciples to Jesus. The service of the disciples as they accompanied Jesus concerned showing mercy to the needy which by implication has greater significance than performing duties in the Temple.

Other passages which add to the picture of Jesus' lordship and corresponding discipleship are the two in which the word *téleios*, "perfect," is found. The concluding verse to the section 5:21-48 is one that has troubled and puzzled readers for a long time: "You, therefore, must be perfect, as your heavenly Father is perfect." The verse summarizes the foregoing section and so, apparently, in the author's mind, describes in a general way the kind of behavior expected of disciples. In the Septuagint the word *téleios* means "wholeness in the sense of entirety and undividedness." [4] In Mt. 5:48 *téleios* could mean being wholly obedient to God or wholly like God. This verse is evidently modeled on the declaration of Lev. 19:2, "You shall be holy; for I the Lord your God am holy." The *imitation of God* was regarded as the highest task of the Jew.[5] The context in Matthew explains how the disciple is to be like God. The verses 5:43-48 assert that to be "sons of the Father" disciples must love their enemies and pray for those who persecute them. As God pours his gifts of sunlight and rain on the unjust as well as the just, so must disciples be generous to enemies as well as to friends. The disciples are required to do more than the Gentiles, who greet only their friends, just as their righteousness must greatly exceed that of the Scribes and Pharisees. That "more" is to be found in this radical kind of love which Jesus taught. Thus, the disciple who seeks to be "perfect" is really one who follows the teaching of Jesus, who makes Jesus his Lord. "Being perfect" does not have to do with good performance of a multitude of laws but with Jesus' interpretation of the Law and will of God.

The second passage which contains this word *téleios*, descriptive of the disciple's manner of life, is the significant one about the rich young man (19:16-22). The rich man asks what good deed he must do to enter life. Jesus answers that if he would "enter life," he must keep the commandments. When asked, "Which ones?", Jesus cites the second half of the Decalogue and adds to them the command to love one's neighbor which is a summary of these commandments. The young man claims to have kept these commandments. Then Jesus replies, "If you would be *perfect*, go, sell what you possess and give to the poor. . . ." Only Matthew's account has this phrase

about being "perfect." Jesus was clearly testing the man to
see if his observance of the Law was only mechanical and
half-hearted, or if he had surrendered himself to God. Furthermore, if he was really concerned about his neighbor he could
show it by giving to the poor. So "being perfect" is again
connected with the love commandment and the fulfillment
of the Law; and most importantly, "being perfect" is connected
with a faithful following of Jesus or obedience to him. Strikingly, in 5:48, "being perfect" involves being like God in God's
radical kind of love, and in 19:21 "being perfect" has to do
with faithfully following Jesus and showing a self-sacrificing
concern for the poor. The point is noteworthy. Obedience to
God and obedience to Jesus are one and the same.

Perhaps the most important passage for our subject is the
concluding one in Matthew, 28:18-20:

> All Authority in heaven and on earth has been given
> to me. Go therefore and make disciples of all nations,
> baptizing them in the name of the Father and of the
> Son and of the Holy Spirit, teaching them to observe
> all that I have commanded you; and lo, I am with you
> always, to the close of the age.

Otto Michel had said of this passage:

> Only under the theological presupposition of Mt. 28:18-20
> has the whole Gospel been written. . . . Indeed, the
> conclusion returns in a certain way to the beginning and
> teaches that the whole Gospel, the history of Jesus, is
> to be understood "from the back forwards." Mt. 28:18-20
> is the key to the understanding of the whole book.[6]

These concluding words summarize the outstanding themes
of the Gospel: Jesus exercises authority over all men; his teaching determines the life of disciples, the people of God; his
promise is to be their helping Lord at all times.

What precisely is meant by the remarkable statement: "All

authority in heaven and on earth has been given to me"? In the use of the word "authority" (*exousía*), there does not appear to be a particular Matthean usage and emphasis in comparison with Mark and Luke. Of course, in all the Synoptics there is an emphasis on the "authority" of Jesus. Mark speaks of the authority of Jesus in respect to his teaching, his power over the demons, and his ability to forgive sins. There is no special nuance to the concept in Matthew's usage. This common Synoptic background makes the use of *exousía* in 28:18 all the more striking, for it is without parallel and bears much theological weight.[7] W. Foerster explains that where the subject is God's power, *exousía* is a fitting expression for the "unlimited sovereignty of God," since he possesses the power and freedom to exercise it.

> Accordingly, *exousía* designates in the first place the absolute possibility to act, which belongs to God, concerning which every question about the relation of the power and the right of this authority is superfluous since he is the source of both.[8]

Mt. 28:18 has the word "all" before "authority" which indicates the unlimited character of Jesus' sovereignty. The few occurrences of the expression, "Lord of heaven and earth" in the Old Testament and Apocrypha deal with the sovereign lordship of God and not merely with God as Creator.[9] The joining of "all authority" with the phrase "heaven and earth" further clarifies the unlimited nature of Jesus' lordship emphasized in this passage. It is noteworthy that in 11:25, a passage similar to 28:18, Jesus addresses God as "Father, Lord of heaven and earth." The lordship he there assigns to the Father, in 28:18 he applies to himself. Whereas the Old Testament spoke of Yahweh as Lord and Creator of the whole world, now in Matthew's Gospel the same is said of Jesus.

Mt. 28:18-20 should be seen in connection with the Old

Testament in three main points: (1) Jesus having authority over the whole world; (2) Jesus instructing his disciples to observe all he has commanded; and (3) Jesus' promise to be with his disciples always. In particular, the Son-of-Man saying, (Dan. 7:13,14) has some relationship to this passage. Daniel's passage speaks of the Son of Man receiving from the Ancient of Days "dominion and glory and kingdom, that all peoples, nations, and languages should serve him; his dominion is an everlasting dominion, which shall not pass away, and his kingdom one that shall not be destroyed." Similarly, in Matthew's text the Father has delivered power and dominion to the Son. There are noticeable differences between the passages.[10] But significantly, Mt. 28:18 proclaims that the fullfillment of the promise in Dan. 7:13,14 has now taken place. The Son's rule over people has begun, and his salvation and his teaching is becoming available through his disciples' mission to all people.

"All authority" is given to Jesus, but Matthew emphasizes the authority given to him as teacher. The fact that the Gospel is organized around five major teaching sections which conclude with a certain formula indicates this, and of course, the passages relating to the Law bear this out. Moreover, the disciples are commanded to teach everything Jesus has taught them. Mt. 11:25-27 proclaims Jesus' authority to teach: "All things have been delivered to me by my father" (the wording is reminiscent of Mt. 28:18) "and no one knows the Son except the Father, and no one knows the Father except the Son and anyone to whom the Son chooses to reveal him." Jesus is the revealer of the Father and of the Father's will, hence the ultimate ground of his authority. Jesus has the authority to heal and the power to cast out demons, but these features do not play the prominent role they do in Mark.

Jesus also exercises authority as the judge of men. Mt. 7:21-27 portrays Jesus as the divine world judge who "on that day," the day of judgment, turns away from the kingdom those who boast in their own works. Jesus warns that not those who cry

"Lord, Lord," but those who do "the will of my Father" enter the kingdom. But this will of the Father is to be found in the words of Jesus: "Everyone then who hears these words of mine and does them will be like a wise man who built his house upon the rock" (7:24). So the destiny of men is determined by their obedience to Jesus.

Mt. 24:35 makes a remarkable claim about the permanent authority of Jesus' teaching: "Heaven and earth will pass away but my words will not pass away." The rabbis made a similar claim about the validity of the Pentateuch. There may be an allusion to the rabbinic view here. However, we are also reminded about what Isaiah said of the word of Yahweh: "The grass withers, the flower fades; but the word of our God will stand forever" (40:8). The teaching of Jesus has the same permanence as the word of God.

Jesus' charge to his disciples to teach others "to observe all that I have commanded you" (28:20) reinforces his teaching authority. The phrase "all that I have commanded you" (*pánta hósa eneteilámēn*) makes the reader recall the same phrase often used in the Pentateuch.[11] In Deuteronomy usually Moses is the subject of "I have commanded" but elsewhere it is Yahweh, and in any case, Yahweh is the ultimate Law-giver. Now Jesus is the one whose words are Yahweh's. In Deuteronomy the well-being of the chosen people and their "health" under the Covenant was related to their keeping the commandments. In Matthew's Gospel, discipleship and belonging to the kingdom rest upon keeping Jesus' teaching. O. Michel puts it well:

> The commanding Christ stands in the center of the first Gospel; the command of Jesus contains something of the brilliance of the divine glory as do the commands of the old covenant, indeed more than they."[12]

The work and mission of the disciple is both to do and

to teach what he has received from his Lord. A disciple has a personal relationship to Jesus. In the pericope Mt. 12:46-50 Jesus pointed to his disciples and said, "Here are my mother and my brothers" (in Mark 3:31-35, Jesus pointed to the crowd). The true relative of Jesus is he who "does the will of my Father in heaven" (12:50). In a striking way Matthew defines a disciple as a brother or sister of Jesus, but this relationship is always described as "doing what I command you."

Jesus is the Teacher of the Church, indeed the only Teacher. Mt. 23:8-10 makes this emphasis: "But you are not to be called rabbi by men, for you have one teacher, and you are all brethren. . . . Neither be called masters for you have one master, the Christ." The work of the disciple is to proclaim the full teaching of his one Teacher. He is the new kind of scribe whose teacher is the greatest rabbi of all. This appears to be what is meant by the interesting statement which concludes the seven parables about the kingdom of God in Mt. 13: "Therefore every scribe who has been trained for the kingdom of heaven is like a householder who brings out of his treasure what is new and what is old" (13:52).

The disciple does not work by himself but has Christ constantly present with him to give help. This is the fulfillment of the promise made often in the Old Testament that Yahweh is present to protect, to deliver, and to aid.

> "Fear not, for I have redeemed you; I have called you by name, you are mine. When you pass through the waters I will be with you. . . . when you walk through fire you shall not be burned, . . . For I am the Lord your God, the Holy One of Israel, your Savior" (Isa. 43:1-3).

To individuals and to the whole people, Yahweh often made this promise. Now Jesus, the Risen Christ, makes it to the new disciples of the kingdom. Their future is bound up with their relationship to him.

To some extent, of course, Matthew's hand is evident in

the fashioning and wording of these passages. Comparison with Mark and Luke makes this clear. But to what extent must always remain uncertain. In any case, we err if we try to escape the centrality of the lordship of Christ witnessed to in Matthew, in the other Gospels, and the rest of the New Testament. It is unfortunate just to talk about the editorial or redactoral work of Matthew or to regard his material as the preaching of the early Church, though this is in part true, for thereby the force of the witness is lost.

Professor Kelso's teaching agrees with the witness of Matthew's Gospel that we need Christ, not only as Savior, but also as Lord; and if we do not want him as Lord, then we do not have him at all.

NOTES

1. W. G. Kümmel, "Jesus und der Jüdische Traditionsgedanke," *Zeitschrift für die Neutestamentliche Wissenschaft* 33 (1934), p. 125.
2. *Ibid.*, p. 117.
3. Richard S. McConnell, *Law and Prophecy in Matthew's Gospel* (Basel: Friedrich Reinhardt Verlag, 1969), pp. 25-30.
4. Gerhard Barth, "Das Gesetzverständnis des Evangelisten Matthäus," *Überlieferung und Auslegung in Matthäusevangelium*, eds. G. Bornkamm, G. Barth, und H. J. Held (Neukirchen Kreis Moers: Neukirchen Verlag, 1960), p. 91, Note 2.
5. Hans Joachim Schoeps, "Von der *Imitatio Dei* zur Nachfolge Christi," *Aus Frühchristlicher Zeit* (Tübingen, J.C.B. Mohr, 1950), pp. 288-290.
6. Otto Michel, "Der Abschluss des Matthäusevangelium," *Evangelische Theologie* 10, (1950-51), p. 21.
7. Wolfgang Trilling, *Das Wahre Israel* (Leipzig: St. Benno-Verlag, 1959), p. 8.
8. W. Foerster, *Theologisches Wörterbuch zum Neuen Testament*, II, pp. 561-563.
9. Gen 24:3 says that Abraham's servant is made to swear by "the Lord, the God of heaven." This implies God's omniscience. Judith 9:12 names God as "Lord of heaven and earth, creator of the

water, King of your whole creation." Creation is connected with kingship. Tobit 7:17 concerns God's giving of joy.

10. Trilling, *Israel,* pp. 6ff.
11. Note Ex. 7:2; 23:22; 29:35; 31:11; 34:11; Dt. 1:3,41; 4:2,40; 6:1,3; 12:11,14; 13:18; 27:1.
12. Otto Michel, "Menschensohn und Völkerwelt," *Evangelische Mission Zeitschrift* II (1941), p. 265.

PART TWO

Theology and Ethics

Introduction

By Robert A. Coughenour

James Leon Kelso's attitude toward theology reminds one,
analogously, of the prophet Amos' words, "I am no prophet,
nor a prophet's son . . ." (Amos 7:14). Professor Kelso vigorously
denied being a theologian. And just as Amos prophecied to
Bethel anyway, so James Kelso did theology despite his denial.
To extend the likeness one step further, his antipathy toward
systematic theology was nearly as "doom-like" and unrelenting
as Amos' prophecy. It allowed for a "glimmer of grace" only
conditionally. If the theologian would "obey," he might be
a Christian theologian. The good professor's attitude must have
disconcerted his colleagues just as much as it baffled his students. Nevertheless, Kelso's "broadsides" were rarely, if ever,
personal attacks and were always accompanied by an indomi-
table sense of humor that seemed to soften the otherwise harsh
commentary on "systematics" in which he engaged.

Turning to Dr. Kelso's more positive and practical theological instruction, I rely once more on his unpublished notes.

James Kelso prefers to use Biblical categories of description
for the beliefs he holds. The Spirit-interpreted Bible is his
norm. The following gleanings from his "annual senior address"
in 1959 clearly demonstrate the point. He chose the title
"Semitic Semantics" more, I think, for its alliteration than
for the sermon's theological content, which is far more Christian than "Semitic."

Dr. Kelso began with a charge familiar to his students. "Read nothing but the Bible the year following your graduation. This is the only way to learn God's religious vocabulary (which, by the way, is not yours, judging from the sermons I've heard from you since you came to seminary)." Next, he discussed the Westminster Confession's Shorter Catechism definition of God, phrase by phrase.

> God is a spirit, infinite, eternal, unchangeable in his being, power, holiness, justice, goodness and truth.

"This," he said, "is the language of the world, not the language of the Bible." Then, as if to justify the catechism definition before continuing, he allowed, "You must know *both* the language of your people and of your God." His commentary on the phrases followed:

(1) God is a spirit says the definition, but the Bible says God is Father, Son *and* Holy Spirit. The Bible language says there is a spirit of God, a spirit of man, a spirit of animals, and even evil spirits. John was using good "Semitic Semantics" in the Greek of John 4 where he says the Spirit is God, i.e., God is the actor.

(2) The definition says God is infinite, but the Bible says God is both finite and infinite. Under the same category, Christ is God and Christ is Man, and he remains so.

Infinite is a rare word in the Bible. It's used only three times in the King James Version. (Do you realize how rare some of our own theological terms are in the Bible? Omniscient and omnipotent are never used in the Bible. Omnipresent and infallible are used only once each, and then only in the King James Version.)

(3) The definition says God is eternal, but the King James Version uses it of Israel too, so again the term is not unique of God. It's used of God only three or four times. The most common usage is in the phrase "eternal life", and that usage is for humans.

94

(4) Unchangeable looks like a safe term for God, but it is used only once and then in the phrase telling that Christ has an unchangeable priesthood.

(5) Being is *never* used of God and only three times of men. One of them in a quote by the Greek poet Epimenides.

(6) Wisdom and (7) power come closest in the language of men and of God, but man's vocabulary "short changes" both words as Paul clearly shows in I Corinthians.

(8) Holiness in a categorical sense rarely appears in the New Testament, but in a major sense in the whole Bible as the totality of all God is and all God does—*If the Bible has any definition of God, this is it!*

(9) Justice in the Bible includes mercy, but our religious vocabulary differentiates between the two, making them antithetical.

(10) The Biblical use of goodness, like wisdon and power, has points in common with our religious usage, but again we miss the Biblical concept by failing to recognize the two-sided meaning of goodness as being both goodness as a personal quality and good deeds.

(11) Truth. In our religious vocabulary we wander all over the lot looking for its meaning. The vocabulary of the Bible is clear. Jesus Christ says, "I am the Truth." Jesus Christ is the incarnation of truth.

At the heart of James Kelso's theology is obedience to Jesus Christ. His comment on John 1:43 where Jesus calls Philip to be his disciple is typical of Kelso's emphasis.

> Jesus said to Philip, "Follow me." Theologians couldn't do better. If you want to learn *real* theology take your red pen and ink out the passages in the gospels you've obeyed.

Illustrating the same point is a comment on Jesus' words in 4:34, "My meat is to do the will of him that sent me, and to accomplish his work." Kelso laid that text alongside Paul's words in Philippians 1:21, "For me to live is Christ . . ."

That means to live as Christ lived. To help with the
sick—help the poor—help the sorrowing—help Christians—help the lost. The point is that's the Bible's theology, imitate Christ. Do what he did.

Following Calvin, James Kelso never failed to emphasize
the Sovereignty of God, but even then his own stresses crept
into the theological proclamation. An example may be taken
from an Easter sermon in the 1940's.

Easter's message is a message of the Risen Lord, but notice
"risen" is an adjective. Emphasize the noun.

On Palm Sunday he was Lord of his Church.
On Good Friday he was Lord of the Redeemed
On Easter Sunday he was Lord of Creation.

When you look backward from Easter you can see *what*
a *Lord* he was!
He is *Super-Sovereign*—that's what Calvin emphasized.

Just as Dr. Kelso simplified his Biblical pedagogy to make
himself clearly understood, he also attempted to simplify his
theology and encouraged his students to do the same. The
following list under the title "Simplify your Christianity"
demonstrates:

(1) Physician Heal Thyself!—This is good advice even
    on the lips of an enemy of Jesus. Be moderate with
    food; rest; exercise your body and your faith in God;
    and get a yearly check-up!
(2) Read your Bible!
        read commentaries; read other's sermons; lastly,
    and
        least significantly, read some theology. Whatever
    you
        do, fall in love with the Bible.
(3) Sing your theology! Presbyterians argue, Methodists
    sing.

(4) Confess your sins-cut them out!

(5) Walk around with God! Take your graduate degree with the Trinity. Do what Christ did. Obey God!

(6) Appreciate silence! "Be still and know that I am God."

(7) Talk with your hands! Get your whole body into your theology.

As a professor of Old Testament theology, Dr. Kelso could not avoid dealing with matters of ethics. Just as his theology was "baptized" in the notions of the Bible as normative, obedience as demanded, God's sovereignty as paramount, and simplification as pedagogically necessary, so were his ethics.

Dr. Kelso outlined his treatment of ethics to include such knotty problems as the Canaanite extermination by Joshua's troops, the hardening of Pharaoh's heart, God's use of "sinners as well as saints," and the standard ethical questions of duties of the family, marriage and divorce, political theory, economics, war, and government. In all these, Jesus' two-fold summary of the law, "Love God, and love your neighbor as yourself", comes into play quickly followed by exhortation, "obey" in imitating Jesus Christ.

The theological and ethical determinants of Professor Kelso's life are his zeal for Biblical truth, for Biblical categories, for obedience to the commands of Christ, and obedience to a call as a faithful witness to a Biblical faith. The Christian church today might well profit from these emphases in James Kelso's practical Calvinism.

The essays of Part II reflect the influence Dr. Kelso had on students and colleagues who themselves work in the fields of theology and ethics. These are offered to demonstrate that whether one could agree with Professor Kelso or not, his powerful proclamations had their effect. Jack B. Rogers' essay takes a "second look" at Kelso's pet phrase for theology, "pagan Greek logic." W. Fred Graham's popularly written approach to theological methodology analyzes his own observations on how theologians do their work. Addison H. Leitch's essay assesses James Kelso's theological stance against the background of some contemporary theology. The fourth essay, by Wayne H. Christy, demonstrates one teacher's approach to the moral dilemma of "telling the truth."

Pagan Greek Logic Revisited:

Or, How To Do Theology Without Being Too Systematic.

By Jack B. Rogers

A NY FORMER STUDENT of James Leon Kelso will immediately recognize one of his favorite phrases—"pagan Greek logic"— usually uttered in disgust and followed by a giggle. Kelso hated systematic theology. His own approach to teaching was anything but systematic. He delighted in Hebrew hyperbole and punctuated even the dullest exposition of Hebrew grammar with pungent aphorisms. He rarely quoted from someone else. His statements were uniquely his own and revealed his own, may I say, theology? Alas, I did not appreciate those pearls of wisdom when I sat in his classroom. I was in the thrall of that symmetrical and all encompassing logical theology which he despised. But my orderliness had at least one virtue, While not understanding nor properly valuing Kelso's gems, I at least wrote them down. Now, sixteen years later, I have returned to those faded notes from "Beginning Hebrew" and read again those interjections that kept us awake and entertained. I know something more about theology now and something more about life. Those Kelsonian comments now burst with vitality and wisdom and sanity. Perhaps I assimilated more of those seeds of sanity than I knew, and they grew when the soil was prepared. Perhaps I discovered the same truths in other places and with other persons. In any case,

Kelso makes sense now, and good sense. So with apologies to the old master teacher, I have analyzed and ordered his thoughts into a theology. My research is not exhaustive and is very unscientific. The sources included none of Kelso's early or recent published works. The data comes from those spontaneous outbursts of the man's heart as I copied them down in my class notes. Thus, I introduce here, in print, data hitherto stored only in the souls and proclaimed in the sermons of thousands of Kelso's former students.

KELSO'S CRITIQUE OF SYSTEMATIC THEOLOGY

A compilation of Kelso's statements offers what we may term the ACP's of what is wrong with systematic theology. Theology is characterized negatively as analytical and abstract. It is cultural, causal, compromising and supposedly complete. Furthermore, theology is based on principles, propositions, and philosophy. Let us hear Kelso speak to these categories.

"The Bible uses picture language and the theology books don't have any pictures." So much for abstractions! Analysis fares little better. "Systematic theology moves step by step, and God moves by earthquakes."

Kelso understood very clearly that theology is expressed in terms of culture and what is worse, of western, not mid-eastern culture. Because of our bias, "nothing in the Bible makes sense." Worse yet, "Things mean what people want them to mean." "Ninety percent of what we call Christianity is just decent paganism." Probably his greatest dislike was the easy assumption of theologians that God's ways can be described in our categories of cause and effect. "Hebrew doesn't bother with secondary causes, it goes from one extreme to the other." "There are no universals in the Bible: 999.9 times out of a 1,000, e.g., sin causes suffering, but when you use that as a universal rule you're in trouble." "Statements in the Bible are statistical universals, not really absolutes." Kelso was deeply sensitive to the personal and gracious character of God's dealing with us. He would say: "Beware of Greek logic: David sang about his sin; therefore I say its good for me to sing about mine. The Holy Spirit, however, says it's good for one man and not another." Perhaps his most penetrating statement on this point also reveals the centrality of Christ in his thought. "Theology makes God a mechanist. He has to treat everyone like he treats me. He didn't treat His Son that way." Theology for Kelso was a very human and fallible enterprise. But it had a functional purpose. That purpose was to effect necessary human compromise. "Theology is a peace treaty signed after every big theological battle. Any treaty is only an approximation. After a good fight you get a compromise, never a solution." Kelso also hated the supposed completeness of every systematic theology. "You know why I'm not a theologian?" he would say, "I'll tell you. Because you have to pass for omniscient. And I'm a little short on information in some areas." "The trouble with theology is that it never takes into account all the facts of the Bible and all the facts of life."

Kelso disdained appeals to principle which ignored real problems. "The average preacher doesn't do enough work in Greek and Hebrew to realize the problems in the text, so he gets a doctrine of inspiration." Personality could never be captured in propositions for Kelso. "God is a person, and a person is more than the sum total of the parts of his personality." The thrust of Kelso's critique is summarized in two terse sentences. "I hate apologetics. All you have to do is witness." For Kelso, witness was what the Bible supremely did. "The Bible isn't systematic theology. It is homiletics and pastoral theology."

THE WORTH OF PERSONS

Kelso's theology was not all negative critique. James Kelso

made a very positive affirmation of the worth of persons. "Everyone is made in the image of God. That is why folks are worth saving." That "everyone" was all-inclusive for Kelso. "They (the Pharisees) could never forgive Jesus because he did good to bad people." For Kelso the worth of persons was correlated with the grace of God. "The value of a human life is that Christ died for people." "God is always grace first, then damnation." The witnessing character of the Bible appears again in this context. "If it's a Living Word, then it saves." Far ahead of his time, in his own way, Kelso even anticipated Women's Liberation. "The Bible says, 'Honor your Father and Mother'—they are on an equal plane."

A THEOLOGY OF OBEDIENCE TO CHRIST

It would perhaps not be unjust to characterize James Kelso's theology as a theology of obedience to Jesus Christ. For Kelso, as for Calvin, true wisdom consisted of two parts. "You need to know what the Bible is and how to live it. The first is simple. The last is tragically difficult." Put even more simply, "Works (obedience) is the test that students always flunk." Again the nature of the Bible is clarified and contrasted with our conception of it. "The Bible isn't good advice—it's commandment." "All Christians are heretics. They don't believe that the word of the Lord is the command of the Lord. For them it's just the grandpa advice of the Lord." Christ acted very differently than we do. "The thing that made Jesus unique is that he was the only one who had sense enough to do what the Lord told him." Obedience is what should make Christians different than other persons. "It's not what you preach. It's who preaches it." Kelso always shifted the focus of concern from the theoretical to the practical. "When you obey, you don't need an intellectual answer." With Kelso's concentration on Christ, that practical focus was compelling. "Here is Theology in a sentence: 'It is no longer that I live but Christ lives in me.' "

A SCIENTIFIC, BUT NOT SYSTEMATIC THEOLOGY

Whether we want to be or not, we are all theologians. We all reflect about God and His relationship to the world. As Christians we make generalizations from Biblical data both consciously and unconsciously. The choice therefore is not between having theology or doing away with it, but between having a theology that is true to as much of the Biblical data as possible and true to the facts of life or having a theology that is built on fragments of data and perhaps of biases and prejudices from life.[1] According to my notes, even Kelso one day admitted: "Everybody's got a theology. I do, too. But we all ignore Christ." Ignoring Christ in the Bible and in life distorts our theology as Kelso so strenuously reminded us. Let us then make a preliminary examination of how to do theology (which we will surely do anyway) without forgetting Christ and without falling into the trap of "pagan Greek logic." Such a theology should have a foundation which is not pagan, but Christian. Such a theology should put its faith not in Greek propositions, but in Christ's person. Such a theology should have as its final goal not a logical system, but obedient living. Since the task of a theologian is to serve the church by pointing out false and unfruitful directions of thought and by opening new channels of use for the Biblical data in relationship to life, let me try to think with Kelso on theology.

We may call this a scientific [2], although not a systematic, theology.[3] "Science" is far broader than just work with test tubes and rockets to the moon. My *Webster's New Collegiate Dictionary* defines science as "knowledge obtained by study and practice." An orderly careful study of the Biblical data and a sensitive application of it to life is then the job of the scientific theologian. This does not imply that theology is the Queen of the Sciences as was claimed in the Middle Ages. Every science is on a par. A science comes into being as a special discipline when two things happen. First a body of data is delimited. Secondly an appropriate method for studying that data is developed. Physics came into being when Galileo determined to study the basic nature of matter in motion by the method of observation and experiment. He therefore dropped objects off the tower of Pisa and measured the speed of their fall. He did not speculate on why moss grows on the north side of trees nor observe frogs jumping in a pond. A scientific theologian, therefore, is one who works with a certain body of data (the Biblical witness as Christians understand it and put it into practice) and who must then develop a method for organizing and understanding that data which is appropriate to it. Being careful to heed Kelso's warnings, we will begin to sketch a scientific theology not based on "pagan Greek logic."

THEOLOGY'S FOUNDATION IS NOT PAGAN BUT CHRISTIAN

Every scientific enterprise is based on presuppositions. The "scientific method" always begins with an hypothesis, an educated guess. From the hypothesis we go on to gather data relative to that hypothesis and then to test it and draw conclusions. The words "presupposition" and "hypothesis" used by some sciences have their rough but real equivalent in scientific theology in the word *faith*. Faith is what you start from, your commitment to your data, its reality and validity. Then comes knowledge. You must examine the data, learn about it, test it in real life situations. In theology, historically four general methodological approaches have been used to understand the Biblical data and the data of Christian experience. On the one extreme has been Rationalism. Its method has been to accept only that which makes sense to the autonomous human reason. Descartes was probably the most rigorous exponent of this view. He has had followers both among extreme liberals and post-Reformation scholastic conservatives. Reason for them has been the ultimate criterion of truth. On the opposite extreme are existentialists and fundamentalists. Both, for different reasons, deny the validity of reason and make some kind of blind faith a virtue and the only criterion for action. Most Christians have chosen for an option in the middle, which makes some combination of reason and faith. The two most widely used options can be identified with the historical personages of Thomas Aquinas and Augustine. Both correlate reason and faith. The issue between them is do you begin with reason or with faith? The choice has profound practical consequences.

Thomas Aquinas suggested that we begin on neutral ground with our pagan adversaries. The human reason is capable of looking unbiasedly at the facts and of arriving at valid conclusions. In the religious realm, for example, we may examine existing things; and by using Aristotle's laws of cause and effect we may reason back to a first cause, an unmoved mover and thus logically conclude that God exists. Thomas Aquinas concedes that there is much that reason alone will not tell us that the Christian needs to know. That information is received by faith from Scripture. But according to Thomism, having begun well with reason, faith is an easy and logical next step to take when the logical arguments leading to it seem so sound. Aquinas' theology was the "science" of the Middle Ages when theology was Queen of the Sciences.

All of the above approaches are "pagan" in their methodology. They assume that all men can agree on some neutral, obviously acceptable starting point and will only disagree because of differences in data or method. Augustine is more in accord with contemporary science and is distinctively Christian in recognizing the profound importance of our presuppositions. According to Augustine, all thinkers begin their investigations from some assumed starting point. This starting point is their faith. The faith with which one begins radically determines the interpretation that will be given the data examined. Reason and experience are not excluded, but it is our faith framework which enables us to make sense of the data we encounter. Contemporary scientists in most fields would agree in substance with the philosopher Immanuel Kant, who contended that we make nature! [4] (Nature means not the things external to us but the ordered system of relationships by which we describe them.) [5]

Professor G. C. Berkouwer of the Free University in The Netherlands has offered a suggestive outline for a scientific Christian theology rooted in the Augustinian tradition. Berkouwer suggests that "Theology is scientific reflection on the normativity of revelation for faith." [6] The sentence can be expanded schematically in this way:

Knowledge { scientific—done carefully, orderly, experimentally reflection—everyone does to some extent

Faith { on the normativity—valid—standard for us of revelation—content—the Biblical data for faith
—we are involved
—presuppositions
—all science begins here

In this statement, theological science is similar in method to the most basic outline of the method used in any scientific enterprise. All science begins from some kind of faith. A Christian scientific theology must begin self-consciously and unashamedly from the presuppositions of the Christian faith.

The other distinctive of a Christian scientific theology will be the object to be studied, revelation. At the critical point of the data to be studied, Christian theology recognizes that the Gospel, the Biblical witness to Christ and His salvation, is the object of our investigation. The methodology that we must use must take into account the unique character of our given data if we are to avoid distorting it. This leads to our second main consideration in a scientific, but not systematic theology.

THEOLOGY'S FAITH IS NOT IN GREEK PROPOSITIONS, BUT IN CHRIST'S PERSON

Kelso forcibly reminded us that the Bible comes to us in relational, not propositional terms. That is because the Biblical authors are witnessing to their experience of a person, not describing a rational system of abstract ideas.[7] The object of theology therefore is not a *datum,* a fixed, static object which we can manipulate, but a *dandum,* a living, dynamic person.[8] Professor T. F. Torrance of Edinburgh has written extensively on theology as a science.[9] He makes very clear that the radical difference between theological science and other sciences lies in the object of our study—who is really a living subject—"God himself in his speaking and acting." [10] The God revealed in Jesus Christ can never be the mere object of our inquiries, but is a subject who lays claim on us and asks for our commitment to him.[11]

The enormous practical value of understanding theology as a science is to differentiate clearly between what God says and what we say about Him. The great curse of every propositional theology has been the implicit or explicit identification of the theologian's propositional statements with God's words. Such identification is unscientific at best and idolatrous at worst. Science knows that its method is to build models. These models of reality are constructed with the best data available and using the most sophisticated methods. They are, however, only models and not an exact picture of reality itself. These models work and are useful until better models are made. Genuine science involves a profound humility. We must know that our models are imperfect and always subject to change. Theological science is a human and fallible enterprise. It is based on trial and error. Mistakes are made and can be forgiven. When new data or better methodology is discovered, then old models are modified or replaced by new ones. Far too often the passionate cry of theologians that "This is God's Word" is only the crassest form of special pleading for their own formulations uncritically or inadequately examined. As scientific theologians we must do our best to make generalizations which are adequate to the Biblical data and Christian experience. But we must remember that they are always *our* generalizations and never identical with God's *own* words.[12] The inability of theologians to make this basic distinction has resulted in theology being done like a game of cops and robbers rather than like a scientific enterprise. We have too often chosen up sides thinking that the "good guys" (those we agree with) say and do all good things, and the "bad guys" (those we disagree with) say and do all bad things. Polemics take the place of communication in such a case. Scientific theology enables us to learn from anyone engaged in the enterprise. It also enables us to disagree with the scientific formulations of another fellow scientist without calling into question either his morality or his personal Christian faith.[13] Theology is not religion. Theology is open to public scrutiny and criticism. Religion is the deepest personal commitment of our hearts and is known to and judged by God alone.

The characterization of theology as a science may lead some to fear that this makes the Biblical data the exclusive property of a scientifically trained elite. Lay persons would thereby be excluded. Our intent is quite the opposite. If we make proper distinctions between two levels of understanding the Bible, then all believers are made free and responsible, and scientific theologians can serve and enable them. There are inescapably two levels on which the Biblical data is understood. The first level is the central saving message of the gospel of Jesus Christ. That level is open to all who can read or will listen to the simple story of God's good creation, man's sinful fall, and Christ's gracious life, death, and resurrection for our salvation. That central gospel message is not in dispute.

While individuals (including theologians) have sometimes disguised or distorted it, the creeds and confessions of the church throughout its history have borne steady and unanimous witness to this central message.[14] But beyond that center lies a vast body of supporting material that is often complex, difficult to interpret, and subject to a variety of understandings. Even Peter affirmed that our brother Paul often said things that were difficult to interpret.[15] The insistence of individuals and groups on their own private interpretation in these areas has led to untold dispute, disharmony, and division within the Christian community. Here is the area of needed and useful operation by the scientific theologian. He can serve the Christian community by making available historical, cultural, and philosophical backgrounds and concepts that will help us to make sensible and usable models of difficult Biblical data. At the same time we thus recognize that these models are human approximations and not absolute divine interpretations. If they help, we can use them; if they do not help, they can be discarded or redone. But models never need to be canonized as the final truth in difficult or disputed areas. The confessions of the churches have recognized the distinction between these two levels of understanding.[16] And the history of the church evidences that the fresh work of theologians in each new generation has been necessary to clarify the path that the church must follow in being faithful to the gospel in its own time.

At the very practical level we all have no doubt been involved in senseless and unprofitable disputes generated by a failure to distinguish between the central message of Scripture and the nature of its supporting material. How many times in churches people have quarreled over whether there could or could not have been a fish big enough to swallow Jonah. That is not a question of the message of Scripture as a whole nor even of the message of the book of Jonah. It is a scientific question best settled by examining the data concerning the literary genre, the cultural expectations, and the historical setting of that particular Biblical writing. If the original writer did not mean it to be taken literally, it certainly does no service to the Biblical message to force a false literalism upon it. But a far worse consequence of the attention to a scientific detail is that it may divert attention from the central message of the prophetic writing. Jonah tells about a preacher who is unwilling to go with God's gracious message of forgiveness to a people racially and nationally different from himself. How our prejudice thwarts God's evangelism is very close to the center of the Biblical message. Thank God, the book of Jonah testifies that God continues to be gracious in spite of us and will use us even when we resist Him. Scientific theology is no cure for all of our resistances to the Holy Spirit. It can, however, be useful in clarifying honest misunderstandings. Best of all, it can continually point us to the heart of the Scripture—Christ and His salvation—and help us not to become entangled on the periphery.

The central *truth* of Scripture is not contained in any propositional statement, but is revealed in a person, Jesus Christ. Our Lord said: "*I* am the way, the *truth*, and the life." [17] Taking that personification of truth seriously brings us to the final point of our scientific, but not systematic theology.

THEOLOGY'S FINAL GOAL IS NOT A LOGICAL SYSTEM, BUT A LIFE OF OBEDIENCE

The Biblical data continually reminds us that knowledge is not ultimately valuable, but is useful as it leads to a righteous life. Jesus' statement that *He is* the *truth* is asserted in the context of Thomas' desire for knowledge. Jesus admonishes Thomas to trust in Him rather than know more about Him.[18] When the Spirit is called the "Spirit of Truth" it is in the same context as the Spirit's designation as the "Counselor." [19] Truth at the functional, experimental level is what the Spirit will grant us as the Spirit witnesses to Christ. Theoretical certainty is not intended nor granted by the Spirit as the history of disagreement over truth in the church makes evident. The ability to keep Christ's commandments is not related to having a certain method of interpretation nor a perfect system of understanding. The ability to keep Christ's commandments is related to the depth of the disciples' love for Him.[20] Yet the disciples, as we, continually want certain knowledge when Jesus is calling them and us instead to trustful obedience. Perhaps the paradigm case is recorded in Acts, Chapter One, where the disciples are with their Lord for the last time prior to His ascension into heaven. At such a crucial moment the disciples concern is for one last bit of inside information— "Lord, will you at this time restore the kingdom to Israel?" [21] Jesus again must remind them that such knowledge is none of their business. Power will come from the Holy Spirit; and the disciples task is to be "witnesses" of their experience of the living Christ, beginning where they are and extending eventually to the ends of the earth.[22]

As the disciples did witness to their faith in Christ, persons of widely varying backgrounds and theoretical persuasions were converted. Following the Biblical admonition recorded at the end of Matthew's Gospel, new converts were baptized "in the name of the Father, and of the Son, and of the Holy Spirit." [23] This Trinitarian formula quite early became the basis of instruction in the Christian faith and thus formed the foundation of the earliest creed.[24] The word "creed" comes from the Latin "credo" which means "I believe." The affirmation of a creed was in the first instance an acknowledgement of personal trust in God revealed in Christ. The Apostles' Creed, our oldest known formulary begins significantly "I believe in God." It does *not* say "I believe that God exists" but rather indicates an experiential trust in God as creator and redeemer. Later creeds came into being as statements of catholic orthodoxy. They were human attempts to express clearly in the language and thought forms of a particular time the essence of the Biblical message. They said, in effect, "this, but not this" is our understanding of what the Biblical data means. These creeds, such as the Nicene Creed, were called "symbols." A symbol is a sign to point toward and remind us of something. The principal function of creeds has always been to point us back to the Biblical data and its witness to the living God. As such the ancient creeds were endorsed by the Reformers. At the same time, the Reformers made clear that all creeds and confessions (including their own) were imperfect and reformable. The purpose of confessions was not to enshrine certain forms of human words, but to point us back to the original source of data about our Lord and His relationship to us.

The matter of relationship is crucial to a right understanding of theological statements. Helmut Thielicke has most helpfully pointed out that theology is only properly done as dialogue with God.[25] This means that our purpose is not a final statement of "objective" truth. The purpose of theology is rather to listen to what God says and to become involved in formulating a personal reply. Sin entered human experience the first time that God was spoken of in the (objective) third person instead of the (relational) second person. It was the serpent who spoke, not to God, but about Him and raised the insidious question: "Did God say, 'You shall not eat of any tree of the garden'?" [26] Such a way of stating the question objectively very often leads to the distortion of context so that only a half-truth can be uttered in reply.

The formulation of our reply to God's speaking is absolutely necessary if we are to be related to him. When God says, "Who will go for us?" we must each reply "Here am I! Send me." [27] Theology is a record of that kind of dialogue. Thielicke offers an appropriate definition of the history of theology. "The history of theology is the history of Christians and their decisions made in faith presented in the form of reflections which are the consequence of those decisions." [28] Reflection is necessary to record the nature of our decisions and pass them on as witnesses to succeeding generations. Reflection is necessary, but decision is primary. Christian theology originated when Christ asked his disciples, "Who do you say that I am?" Peter's reply, "You are the Christ, the Son of the living God," is the first doctrinal statement uttered in the form of a confession.[29] Peter's doctrinal confessional statement serves as a witness to us directing us to Christ. The particular formulation of any doctrinal statement should never become for us an end in itself. Much less should we entertain the vain hope for a complete logical and systematic arrangement of all the possible doctrinal assertions which could be made. Too often we become involved in having faith in our confessions rather than in confessing our faith. That danger is as real for rigidly orthodox people as it is for the most radical Biblical critics. Indeed, Herman Bavinck, a noted nineteenth-century Dutch theologian of impeccable orthodoxy, noted that the only kind of criticism which was really damaging was criticism from the heart. That personal resistance to God can dwell quite as comfortably in dead orthodoxy as it can in the most extreme liberalism.[30]

The need for intellectual certainty can be the most damaging kind of idolatry. It is present no less in the need to have an inerrant Bible than it is in the desire for an infallible Pope.[31] The Scripture never promises salvation through certain knowledge. Only trusting faith can receive Jesus Christ as Savior. When Christian theologians respond to their critics by trying to prove on the critics' grounds the truth of the Christian faith, the cause is already lost.[32] Christ came, not that we might know, but that we might believe. A deep trust in Jesus Christ and continued reflection on the Biblical witness to Him can lead to expanding knowledge. That knowledge will be of ourselves and of God.[33] It will be relational knowledge best expressed in relational terms. Perhaps in our time the language of the social sciences, especially psychology, sociology, and anthropology, which describe the relationships between persons, could offer useful forms for our theological utterances. Traditionally, we have used the language of "pagan Greek logic." What I failed to learn from Kelso I later learned from the founder of the discipline of the history of dogma, Adolph Harnack. After writing what is still the definitive work in the history of doctrine, Harnack felt that the entire enterprise of doctrinal formulation was basically a dead end. The reason lay in the definition of doctrine with which Harnack began: "Dogma in its conception and development is a work of the Greek spirit on the soil of the Gospel." [34] One does not have to accpet all of Harnack's theological presuppositions to appreciate the warning which his work presents.

We will continue to do theology. We will continue to make doctrinal statements. Even Kelso did. Indeed, we must because it is part of the process of understanding our relationship to God and of transmitting that understanding to others. But let us remember, as we do theology, that our words are not God's words. And let us remember that words are no substitute for obedient life. So when we do theology, as scientifically as we are able, let us do it as servants of the people of God—not as their masters. Theology should not be apologetics aimed at proving our truth. Theology ought to be a joyful witness to our growing relationship with our living Lord.

NOTES

1. For a brief but helpful discussion of this point, see William Hordern, *A Layman's Guide to Protestant Theology*, rev. ed. (New York: Macmillan, 1968), pp. xiii-xvii.
2. At this time in history and especially in this country, the word "science" is usually identified with the natural sciences. In Europe a much broader understanding of the term prevails. The German word "Wissenschaft," which we translate as "science," means "learning, knowledge, scholarship." Our word "science" comes from a Latin root word meaning simply "to know." A

science therefore is the equivalent of what we would call an academic discipline. It is an orderly way of learning about some particular subject.

3. Scientific work is systematic or orderly in its method but does not claim to possess a complete or systematic knowledge of its content. Scientific work must always be open to correction, modification, and expansion. Because of the connotation of the completeness of a finished product which has attached to systematic theology, I suggest that we substitute the term "scientific" for "systematic" when referring to theology's task of drawing generalizations from Biblical data.

4. Kant proposed a "Copernican revolution" in philosophy with the concept that "objects must conform to our knowledge." A most helpful brief exposition of Kant's thought on this point is found in E. L. Allen, *Guide Book to Western Thought* (London: English Universities Press,1957), pp. 157-160.

5. Albert Einstein is quoted as saying "Only theory, that is knowledge of natural laws, enables us to deduce the underlying phenomena from our sense impressions, "in Werner Heisenberg, *Physics and Beyond: Encounters and Conversations* (New York: Harper & Row, 1971), p. 63.

6. G. C. Berkouwer, "Wat Is Theologie?" *Interfaculatire Colleges Aan De Vrije Universiteit Te Amsterdam, Cursus 1949-50* (Kampen: Kok, 1950), p. 11.

7. The preceeding discussion of presuppositions has much in common with the thinking of Cornelius Van Til. It is at this point of the personal, relational nature of Biblical revelation and the consequences of that nature for our thelogy that I differ markedly from Van Til (as well as from B. B. Warfield). See my article "Van Til and Warfield on Scripture in the Westminster Confession," *Jerusalem and Athens: Critical Discussions on the Theology and Apologetics of Cornelius Van Til,* ed. E. R. Geehan (Nutley, N.J.: Presbyterian and Reformed Pub. Co., 1971), pp. 154-165.

8. For further elaboration of this thought, see Daniel T. Jenkins, "Systematic Theology," *The Scope of Theology,* ed. D. T. Jenkins (Cleveland: Meridian Books, 1968), p. 100.

9. Two recent works are: *Theological Science* (London: Oxford University Press, 1969). and *God and Rationality*. London: Oxford University Press, 1971.

10. An excellent summary of Torrance's views on theology as scientific inquiry is found in John Fleming, "Theology as Scientific

Inquiry and as Christian Commitment," *Bulletin of the Department of Theology of the World Alliance of Reformed Churches + The World Presbyterian Alliance*, X, 3 (Spring, 1970), 12-13.

11. The definitions of theological science by Berkouwer and Torrance focus at two different points. Berkouwer emphasizes the *data* of theology which is Biblical revelation. Torrance emphasizes the *object* of theology—the living subject, God. The two definitions are complementary. Christian scientific theology primarily comes to knowledge of God via the data of revelation.

12. Even when we quote from the Bible we are interpreting the Bible and thus doing theology. The verses we select, the order in which we arrange them, and the context in which we apply them usually are determined by our theological point of view.

13. One could say, as a scientific judgement, that a certain theologian began from presuppositions which were not distinctively Christian. One has no right to say that the theologian is not a Christian person.

14. A most readable summary discussion of representative Reformation documents and their relationship to ancient creeds is presented in Erik Routley, *Creeds and Confessions: The Reformation and its Modern Ecumenical Implications* (London: Duckworth, 1962).

15. II Peter 3:15-16.

16. For example, note the distinctions made in the Westminster Confession of Faith, Chapter I, Sections vii and viii. Section vii begins by noting that "all things in Scripture are not alike plain in themselves, nor alike clear unto all." However, those things necessary for salvation (the central message) are so clear in Scripture that anyone willing to listen "may attain unto a sufficient understanding of them." Section viii, on the other hand, deals with "controversies of religion," those difficult areas which form the supporting material around the central message. In these areas, the answers are to be found by scholarship, specifically in this case, by study of the Biblical text in the original Hebrew and Greek.

For a more detailed discussion of this issue in its historical setting see my *Scripture in the Westminster Confession: A Problem of Historical Interpretation for American Presbyterianism* (Grand Rapids: Eerdmans, 1967), pp. 369-403.

17. John 14:6

18. John 14:5
19. John 14:16,17
20. John 14:15
21. Acts 1:6
22. Acts 1:8
23. Matt. 28:19
24. The definitive work in English on Creedal development is J.N.D. Kelly, *Early Christian Creeds* (London: Longmans, 1960). See on this point, Chapter II, "Creeds and Baptism."
25. *A Little Exercise For Young Theologians*, trans. Charles L. Taylor (Grand Rapids: Eerdmans, 1962), p. 34.
26. Genesis 3:1
27. Isaiah 6:8
28. *A Little Exercise For Young Theologians*, p. 35.
29. Matthew 16:16. For further discussion of the relationship between faith and doctrinal statement, see Bernhard Lohse, *A Short History of Christian Doctrine*, trans. F. Ernest Stoeffler (Philadelphia: Fortress Press, 1966), pp. 8-10.
30. *Gereformeerde Dogmatiek* (Kampen: Kok, 1928), 1, 411.
31. Hans Küng offers a most insightful discussion of the Protestant use of Scripture in *Infallible? An Inquiry*. trans. Edward Quinn (Garden City: Doubleday, 1971), pp. 209-221.
32. A most helpful historical summary of this problem is found in Geoffrey W. Bromiley, "The Church Doctrine of Inspiration," *Revelation and the Bible*, ed. Carl F. H. Henry (Grand Rapids: Baker Book House, 1958). pp. 205-217.
33. Calvin begins his *Institutes* with the affirmation: "Nearly all the wisdom we possess, that is to say, true and sound wisdom, consists of two parts: the knowledge of God and of ourselves." In developing our theological method we should be careful to note his second and qualifying sentence: "But, while joined by many bonds, which one precedes and brings forth the other is not easy to discern." *Calvin: Institutes of the Christian Religion*, dd. John T. McNeill, trans. Ford Lewis Battles, The Library of Christian Classics, XX (Philadelphia: Westminster Press, 1960), p. 35.
34. *History of Dogma*, trans. Neil Buchanan, (New York: Dover, 1961) 1, 17.

Watching Theologians Make Theology: a Guide to Good Taste

By W. Fred Graham

*A*NYONE WHO STUDIED under James Kelso very long came from that exercise with a tendency to shy away from the practice of theology. At least half-convinced that most systematics was just "pagan Greek logic" and that Methodism had succeeded because Wesleyans "sang their theology" (and thus escaped the devilish task of writing it out), the student also knew that simple biblicism wouldn't suffice, since neither the angels of God nor our sainted professor cheered when Samuel hewed Agag to pieces with an axe. What to do? Under Kelso's tutelage you were forced to know your Bible—some fellows even knew it in the original!—but any theology beyond St. Paul was suspect. It was only much later that this student discovered Luther's pungent description of philosophy, which supports Kelso's jaundiced view of a lot of theologizing: it is, Brother Martin quipped, the devil's whore.

With the ancestry of theology thus clearly limned, there still remains the stubborn problem of understanding and communicating our faith, for men, created by and through the Word, will not be dumb and deaf. They will try to understand how the Power that grasped Isaiah, Peter, St. Francis, and themselves is related to the rest of life. What follows is an attempt to describe how men make theology. The first section examines by means of the metaphor of salad-making the various ways theologians toss together a theology. In the second section, we look at various ways people who think about theology do so in relation to natural science, that great usurper of the throne of theology, once the Queen of Sciences.

INGREDIENTS IN A THEOLOGICAL SALAD

I hope to describe the making of theology in such a way that any reader can then pick up a book about theology and tell what ingredients went into its making. This means I must first describe the ingredients which go into theological concoctions, and then point out a few of the ways in which those ingredients are mixed to make particular kinds of theology—each with its own main ingredient and seasoned with others to produce different salads. Just as watching a cook throw the salad together makes clear why it tastes the way it does, so attention to what the theologian puts into his work will help explain why it comes out the way it does.

First, then, the ingredients. They are only four in number, and are as easy to remember as lettuce, onion, garlic, and jello. In older days the primary one was the *tradition of the gospel,* which includes both the Bible and the various ways earlier Christians tried to understand its message for their own times. A few years ago it would have been necessary to distinguish the Bible from ancient confessions, creeds, church pronouncements, and the like, and it still may be helpful in assessing the weight given to each by Protestant and Catholic or Orthodox theologians. But they cannot be clearly untangled, as a reading of Karl Barth makes clear. Although that most Protestant of theologians proclaimed a theology of the Word (that is, one in which the biblical tradition was the basic ingredient), yet he had to wrestle in almost endless fine print with what the church had said about and done with that Word in centuries past. So while a separation can be made—obviously the Incarnation is taught in the Bible and the Assumption of the Blessed Mary is only tradition in a secondary or derivative sense—yet few theologians are writing about the "Glories of Mary" these days, while a clear preference for the Bible is found in theologies tossed together by modern Catholic theologians. So this tradition of the gospel—an attempt to make clear and be faithful to ancient biblical and confessional standards—can be seen in many theologies, particularly those which admit some obligation to Karl Barth, the Reformers, or to James Kelso.

The second ingredient is the leaven of *secular categories.* (Purists who say that leaven does not belong in salads are ruled out of order and out of the kitchen.) I wanted to say *philosophical categories,* since those have in the past been the kind used most often—Roman Catholics used Aristotle and Protestants used Kant and Hegel. But a broader term is needed in a day when the last word from Esalen Institute or the most recent broadside from the radical left is regarded by some as genuine theological material. It was over-use of this category by scholastic theologians and opponents in debate that occasioned Luther's expletive about philosophy's job portfolio which we noted above.

The third ingredient is one we shall call *ordinary experience.* No theologian can be entirely deaf to the common experiences of average people in his culture, so a theologian of the Word cannot merely repeat the Bible but must use analogies to show that what he is writing about makes some sense to the reader he wants to attract or inform. Now, of course, it is sometimes hard to know whether you are getting ordinary experience or a secular category (our second ingredient) in the mixture you are reading. For instance, I read a book recently in which a minor theologian said that the "youth culture" must be understood as the guide for writing theology today. (He meant the loving, feeling, "greening" facets of that culture, not homicidal Mansonites or committed Jesus People, of course.) Now he may mean that the thought forms of the counter-culture the young are supposed to represent constitute a new intellectual ingredient, a secular category, which the theologian must make the theological salad's main ingredient. If so, then he is referring to our second ingredient. Or he may only mean that youth's experience is the ordinary experience of modern men—or soon will be as they grow to maturity and responsibility—and theologians cannot write around that experience, but must try to speak to it.

The fourth category is an odd one—most theologians have usually left it out—which we may call *religious experience*. This is a tough one to analyze very well, since it may mean something wild and ecstatic (like the gift of tongues) or the calm, continuous assurance of some people that God is dependable. In the Middle Ages this latter assurance may have been the ordinary experience of Europeans, but in our secular age, where an invisible, sacred universe is not made real in daily life, this is not so, and a distinction between ordinary and religious experience must be made.

All right, there they are, our four ingredients: the tradition of the gospel, secular categories, ordinary experience, and religious experience. Let's observe a few mixtures just to get the hang of it. As I wrote earlier, it is the Barthians who keep emphasizing the Word of God, our first ingredient. They reject any mixing-in of secular categories, arguing that each one only leads to a new idolatry which men will later realize to be false, and when they reject that ideology they will also reject the theology which clings to it. For example, if you use Hegel, you soon end up tying the gospel to the myth of progress, which runs pretty much counter to the New Testament and to any ordinary reading of history. Or if you depend too much on religious experience or ordinary experience—well, remember what Calvin said about the human mind being a regular idol-factory and Jesus' sharp raps against the traditions of men. A lay theologian who writes theology with the gospel tradition uppermost is the French Protestant Jacques Ellul. His *Meaning of the City*,[2] in which he calls the city man's chief pride and greatest idol to himself, is a recent example of a theology in which the biblical tradition is the main ingredient. Readers hooked on modern novels might agree with me that John Updike's stories carry a conviction that the dis-use of this ingredient is the great sorrow and sin of modern man. Though quite different in character, two of Updike's novels, *Rabbit Run* and *Couples*, have the same abandoned state of modern autonomous men who hear no lifegiving Word. The preachers in both novels haven't a clue, for the same reason.

Theological cuisines based heavily on secular categories are many and varied, and only a glimpse can I give. Paul Tillich, for example, answered the sense of meaninglessness many moderns share by presenting the gospel hitched to idealistic philosophy.[3] John Cobb,[4] Schubert Ogden,[5] and Ian Barbour [6] pour in lots of Whitehead's process philosophy and mix it with the gospel tradition. A problem with both Tillich and the process servers is that the amateur reader may find their philosophical categories shredded and tough. At the other end of the kitchen, death-of-God theologians have used secular categories provided by existentialism, language analysis, or Hegel-cum-Nietzsche, and came out with a mixture which received great early notices (their salad days!), but which later gourmets have pronounced flat and tasteless.[7] Modern man has a discouraging tendency to develop a jaded palate before he has been served a main course.

The reader must be warned against lumping all these theologians together, as if they were tossing together similar theologies. They are not. All they share is a propensity for making secular categories their main component, or at least to pour lots of it in the mix. Some give up on the gospel tradition entirely (like a chef's salad without lettuce), while others try to make that tradition stand out as even more flavorful by their use of a secular category as salad base or a major ingredient.

The hardest to measure ingredient is ordinary experience. It is also unstable, and different cooks employ it different ways. C. S. Lewis, for example, used to combine it with a rather secular logic to woo unbelievers to the gospel tradition. Langdon Gilkey, brilliant Methodist layman, tries to analyze the way people talk about their ordinary experience to show the unconscious sense of purpose, hope, and meaning our talk contains. This leads, he argues, to a new basis from which to proclaim theism in an agnostic age. Here ordinary experience is subjected to a secular category, a philosophical grinding, called "phenomenology," which shucks off the surface husks of ordinary experience to get at the fruit below. The purpose is to set people on the way toward the gospel tradition. The only one of our four ingredients Gilkey rejects is religious experience, which he believes is unusable in a secular age.[8]

The last ingredient is the one my reader will recall that I regard with suspicion. Religious experience is the cooking sherry of modern theological cuisine—just as good and just as dangerous. Cooks who rely on it too much are notoriously undependable, regardless of how inspired they may be. Now few first-rate theologians try to write theology with massive quantities of this stuff. William James tried it at the turn of the century in his *Varieties of Religious Experience,* and everyone paid him homage and called his book a classic and hurriedly tried to find other ways to make a good theology salad. Masters and Houston (not to be confused with the clinical sexologists, Masters and Johnson) have made a small effort on the basis of their experiments with drugs and meditation.[9] That is, they have walked into the kitchen and swigged the sherry, but they haven't found the other ingredients and do not yet seem to have found a bowl to pour things in.

There is a lot of religious experience going on these days.

On campus we have Campus Crusade for Christ more successful than ever, the so-called "Jesus Movement" now appearing
east of the land of sunshine and earth tremors, the growing
number of readers of books by Keith Miller and other advocates
of modern religious experience. But so far theologians have
left this ingredient in the cupboard with the deadly nightshade
and arsenic. It may not be long, however, before many of
their students will bring it with them to seminary and the
professors will need to question its absence from their own
divine concoctions.

That's it. Except for the mixing bowl, which I think needs
just a word. You see, a great problem with modern man is
that he has no adequate world-view or even a good working
set of priorities by which he decides what is true, what is
real, what is valuable in this pluralistic, chaotic, rootless age
of ours. We may call this mental framework or world-view
a "myth", by which we do not mean it is something untrue
but something which works like an old Greek or Indian myth
to help man understand who he is, where he has been, where
he is going, and how to get there. Or, since a myth is usually
a story, we might say that we need a "metaphor" to do the
same thing, since to speak of God as "Father" is probably
better termed a metaphor than a myth. We shall keep both
terms around and see which works better for us. The myth
or metaphor is what I mean by the mixing bowl—the hardly
conscious assumptions about the world and man and the divine
into which we pour our ingredients, whether we are professional theologians or amateur seekers. Some theologians—
usually theologians of the Word—assume the old metaphors
still work (God as loving and just Father, death and resurrection, eternal life, etc.). Others think the old conceptual
framework won't do, so they create a new one or use a secular
one—the myth of progress, the myth of political action as
bringing in the Kingdom (a finely mixed metaphor), the myth
of education as salvation, the myth of the global village, and

so on. Others just pour out the ingredients, and they run all over the table because the cooks have rejected the old battered bowl of classical Christianity but have forgotten or neglected to put a new one in its place. That's why some modern theologies seem so formless, just pieces of this and that slithering in the jello of impulse on the flat tableland of secularity.

SCIENCE AND RELIGION: FOUR METAPHORS

Of the four ingredients out of which theologies are made, the greatest care should probably be taken, not with religious experience (despite its volatile nature), but with ingredient two, the secular categories which we enlist to make our salad sell. And of all the secular categories, the method and content of the natural sciences is a chief competitor with Christian theology for the minds of men and is thus capable of co-optation as a secular category in making theology. Indeed, some unexamined preface, such as "science tells us . . .," probably constitutes the unexamined mixing bowl that many modern people use in tossing their world-view together. A brief look at the struggle between science and theology may help remind us why this is, and then we can examine ways relationships between the two are often understood.

BATTLES FAR OFF AND LONG AGO

For many educated people the ability of science to discover truth while theology defends its errors is a chief intellectual stumbling block to belief. History records a number of battles between science and theology; and in each of these, the religious point of view has had to retreat, to compromise, to put up increasingly futile, jerry-built battlements in its desperate fight to stave off total defeat.

125

We shall look at only two of these battles, ignoring the skirmishes about lesser or less-clear issues (e.g., with the Freudian geography of the *psyche*) and begin with the origins of the scientific epoch in the work of Copernicus and his publicist Galileo and its culmination in the discoveries of Newton. Everyone is familiar with the work of these men, and a brief résumé should be sufficient to show their impact on religious thought. Copernicus, in his attempts to update the old Julian calendar, which had gotten ten days behind the seasons, decided early in the sixteenth century that calibrations would be easier to figure if he assumed that the earth revolved around the sun, rather than using the traditional, common-sense method of calculating periodic epicycles (cycles within the larger circuits) of the various heavenly bodies in their march about the planet Earth, the presumed center of the universe. In the next century, Galileo, in addition to his own work with motion and astronomy, argued strongly for the Copernican view that the sun was the center of the observable universe but was finally forced to recant by the church. However, his submission could not change the facts. The earth was reduced from its former glory as center of all universal attention to being merely the third ball out from the blazing center of things, and man's exalted position was reduced correspondingly. What Newton did was to show how the laws that bound earth to sun, and moon to earth, and each thing to every other thing could be understood. In sum, Copernicus and Galileo argued that the earth and man were not so very important to the universe as the Bible seemed to posit and as feudal Christianity validated in society. And Newton showed that the whole heavenly system could be thought of as a giant machine held together by invisible but powerful forces of a physical nature operative through the ether of heavenly space. (That ether was an erroneous concept was not made clear until long afterward and would not have invalidated the metaphor anyhow.)

Theologically this did several things: it cast doubt upon the accuracy of the biblical perceptions about the importance of man and his home in the divine scheme of things; and it tended to remove God from direct intervention in the operations of nature, since all that is required of him is that He construct the machine in the first place and put it to running. There is little or no need for divine intervention in the process once it is putting along smoothly. The result of such a picture of the universe was to remove God from the system and cast Him in the role of divine architect or celestial watchmaker, who does not stoop to intervention, even miraculous intervention, in the mechanism He has made. The reader will perceive that I am referring to the theological position called Deism. But it is a short step from Deism—which understands the need for a divine Maker—to atheism, which regards an unnecessary God as perhaps no God at all. This is the import of the famous response of the French scientist La Place to Napoleon, who had asked him what God's role was in the system of nature: "I have no need of that hypothesis." In other words, why should we need to imagine a Creator of the machine, our universe? Perhaps it has always just existed.

But if the Copernicus-Galileo-Newton Revolution was a blow to the sacred cosmos, what the English scientist Darwin did with his Theory of Evolution was a good deal worse. The time was more than a century and a half later, for Newton had written his major work in 1687 and Darwin did not publish till the eve of our Civil War, his *On the Origin of Species* appearing in 1859. Newton, a layman, was religious enough to believe that his commentaries on the biblical book of Revelation were more important than his scientific discoveries. Darwin, trained originally in theology, was interested in almost nothing but the processes of nature and their examination by scientific medhodology. (However, the co-discoverer of the evolutionary hypothesis, Alfred Russell Wallace, remained a Christian, albeit a heterodox one.) Again the scientific information is known to almost everyone: Darwin argued forceably and with examples and logic that the different kinds of living creatures populating the earth are the result of chance variations, some of which were better adapted to the environment than others and so survived to reproduce and dominate. He lacked only a mechanism for the variations—a lack made up for by later discoveries about mutation in gene and chromosome formation.

It would be unfair and untrue to say that Darwin had no support from religious circles for this theory, for there had been for more than half a century a segment of Christian society which held a progressive belief about historical change—a very optimistic belief—which tied in perfectly with Darwin's scientific ideas. But on the whole his discoveries were understood to undermine the biblical belief that God had made everything in a very short period of time and that the separate "kinds" of creatures mentioned in the Creation story in Genesis were special divine creations, most especially man himself. Darwin saw all of life as a seamless web from the simplest organism to complex man, and he observed no place for special divine intervention in the process.

Without going into theological responses at any depth it can be seen that Darwin had changed the Newtonian metaphor from that of an unchanging machine to that of a progressive, self-changing, and self-perpetuating machine, or perhaps organism, with progress proceeding in an unedifying manner captured most sharply by Tennyson's phrase, "nature red in tooth and claw." [10] Some found Darwin the final reason for pronouncing the end of theology, and atheism proceeded apace. Others, correctly perceiving that science would destroy traditional religious and social world-views, resolved to deny that his theory was aught but theory, and demonic guesswork at that. Still others tried to accomodate God to this complex world-view and said He was that which worked through the changes of evolutionary history to bring about the emergence of a creature capable of responding to the divine in more and more appropriate ways. This synergistic view is a very common one in theological circles insofar as theologians pay attention to scientific discoveries at all these days. Let us turn now to an examination of theological approaches to the world-view of modern science and see if we can move ourselves a step toward a theology for a secular world, a world dominated intellectually by respect for scientific method and discovery.

FOUR METAPHORS DISCLOSE FOUR VIEWS

The first two views will take little of our attention—not because they are not respectable views, but because they are of little help to religious people in a secular society. The first is outright atheism or unshakable agnosticism, where the universe is seen through the metaphor of a vast cause-and-effect, physico-chemical mechanism, an accidental world with no purpose except the blind purpose of a machine, which is simply to function. There is no room here for religious thought, unless religion be scorned as a desperate creation of man which shields him from an indifferent universe, as argued, for example, by Freud in his *Future of an Illusion*. Occasionally people who think this way betray in their speech or writing that they think this mechanism is not quite mechanistic after all and has some sort of built-in purpose or even personality, which lack of rigor pulls them toward some sort of pantheism. But such aberrations from scientism are not our interest, for strictly speaking an accidental mechanism is just that—a mechanism without spirit, heart, or purpose.

In this view the four ingredients of theology tossed out in the first section are pared to two, and those two are rigorously interpreted. The biblical tradition is scorned as irrelevant and religious experience labelled as only misunderstood or "sick" ordinary experience, while secular thought itself must be rigidly scientific at its base. A thorough-going behavioral psychology travels this path—at least in its Skinnerian version—but Marxian thought (which *claims* to be scientific through and through) seems to most outside observers to be scientific only in its economic and social analysis, but mythical in its pre-historical underpinnings and especially its future hopes. Here it reveals its rootage in biblical thought which begins with myth and ends in apocalyptic projections (e.g., the millennium, the New Jerusalem), but deals realistically and empirically with the present.

The second view is almost the opposite of scientism in that the observable cause-and-effect universe is held to be merely the invention of human minds. Now this may be understood in an extreme way as denying objective validity to the universe—sometimes Hindu or even Christian Science thought seems to veer in this direction. But usually people holding this view do not deny objective validity to the universe—they believe it is there—but they simply deny that our understanding of it has any necessary correlation with the way it is. For them the scientific metaphor of cause-and-effect mechanism is only a handly tool for observation, and we might just as easily replace it with another one, except that we now have a "habit" of thinking that way. I think this is what Theodore Roszak [11] means when he laments our subservience to the "myth of objective consciousness"—that we have become enslaved to one particular projection from our minds, one perceptual framework, and we embrace that projected picture of universe-as-machine while rejecting other possible projections we could make if we would. Put in this less extreme form the reader will see in a moment that this view is somewhat congruent with the two positions which will follow.

From the extreme metaphors of universe-as-mechanism and universe-as-unprovable-projection, we shall turn to two views which are more common today within western theology. The first of these comprises various attempts to preserve both the scientific point of view and yet mix the theistic with it.[12] If we can imagine God as both orchestra leader and writer of the scores the various musicians play, we may have an approximation of the metaphor which such thinkers are working with. However, we must also grant autonomy to the musicians to depart from the score if this view is to hold together, for both evolutionary history and human history show that some species or events or people play such dissonances that they self-destruct while the larger beat of life goes on.

The French theologian and paleontologist Pierre Teilhard de Chardin [13] probably is still the best representative of this effort, since most others who think in this direction either do so scientifically with Teilhard, or they cross the boundaries into philosophy and work with a similar model provided by Alfred North Whitehead. Teilhard tried to achieve a synthesis of science and religion by showing that evolutionary history has a direction, and that direction is toward the increased complexification of matter, which produces or is accompanied by increase in "soul" or "psychic energy" or "the within of things" or "consciousness". He used these terms interchangeably. For example, a dog has a more complex nervous system than a frog and correspondingly has more consciousness. For Teilhard, God seems to have two roles: (1) He is the Omega Point toward which global self-consciousness is heading, and the metaphor of God as Goal is probably better here than Orchestra Leader, although He does direct the orchestra of life by attracting all things toward Himself; (2) but God is somehow—and it is not clear how—involved within the process of evolutionary change itself. Teilhard assumed a strictly scientific explanation for evolutionary change—mutation, chance variation, survival of the most fit for the environment—but in, with, and under it all, God is at work, correcting, maintaining, increasing the supply of consciousness on this globe as the physical complexity of its creatures increases as well. For Teilhard, the end product—self-consciousness or reflexive consciousness in man—was worth all the aeons of patient work, the dead end products such as dinosaurs (matter is not lost, after all), and the present risky situation of that fragile biped who knows that he knows. Evolution is finally conscious of itself on earth and will begin to converge now on God as Omega Point, the conductor and writer of the immensely complicated score which is being played even as it is being written.

In this theology a secular scientific category, evolution, has become the major ingredient in the theological enterprise. The gospel tradition has diminished in size, but it does provide us with the major term for God—Omega—and in Teilhard's personal life that tradition was very important. It is my observation that it influenced the way he lived his life more than the way he thought his life. Ordinary experience is not emphasized in Teilhard's work, and religious experience seems best understood as occasional glances of understanding between the conductor and some of the players who are specially tuned or, perhaps, turned in His direction. It is possible for a kind of mysticism to be part of this way of thinking, for the God who is located not out in space but forward into time is also patiently helping us rewrite the score of our own lives, and Teilhard seemed to live in the continual presence of God (see his *Divine Milieu*) amidst study, exploration, imprisonment (by the Japanese in China during World War II), and rejection by the Catholic hierarchy.[14]

Our final way of looking at the relationship between scientific and religious thought is that of the theologians who stress the biblical tradition to the exclusion of other salad ingredients. To such thinkers divine involvement in the natural world is neither affirmed nor denied but is regarded as irrelevant to theological thought or to religious faith. God is simply not understood to be examinable nor explainable on scientific terms—which does not negate the value of science but believes it to be an inappropriate medium for divine revelation or human theologizing. I suspect that such theologians are uneasy with the way others pick and choose from nature in order to arrive at knowledge of God. One can hear them ask, "What does the demise of the mighty dinosaurs tell us of God? Or the disappearance of our cousin Neanderthal? Might we not get from evolution something other than a picture of God as Father and rather decide that he is a rascally tyrant of the first order? God has not bidden us to find Him in the stones and bones, but in Jesus Christ, or in the history of His dealings with the People Israel?" For this theology, God has awakened in the human heart some understanding of who he is through stirring the imagination of certain men (prophets) to contemplate their own history, and the only way we can meet Him is to open ourselves to what they have written and thereby find the key to open our hearts to God's spirit. As for science, it is free to go its own way without fear that God may be hiding in the interstices of matter or spooking the protons as they wheel about the minuscule space of their nuclear orbit.

Here the metaphor that occurs to me is of a Householder who built a residence long ago but considers the people in it vastly more important than the house. If those people want to get to know their Householder, there is a much more direct way than by studying the house itself. The Householder wants to know them, is constantly with them, will welcome them "face-to-face" to a better home when they are finished with this one. This is not to say that study of the house is not worthwhile. After all, the Householder did make it—though he's in it only as an artist is "in" his painting—and it's up to those who live in it to care for it. But it's not the way one finds the Householder. You might say that in this theological metaphor, the Householder's past career is of only minor importance to his guests.

Of the four ingredients—gospel tradition, secular categories, ordinary experience, and religious experience—in this model only the first and last are of prime importance for faith, and men can't do much about the religious experience. All one can do is to be faithful to what the Householder has provided in the special record collection of His prophets and trust that the Householder will finally meet him too.

Where does that leave us? All these positions with their different metaphors are—perhaps unfortunately—attractive to me. The first one and the last one have the advantage of leaving science to the scientist but the disadvantage of assuming that there is either no God or that God has pretty narrow interests. God as orchestra leader and score writer does better with human history than it does with the emergence of different "lower" creatures throughout evolutionary history on earth, since presumably creatures without free will should not have been able to make the grievous mistakes evolutionary history seems to display for us. The problem with the second metaphor, that our minds have simply invented the cause-and-effect universe—which many readers will identify as variations on philosophical idealism—is that it exalts human imagination to the point of denying scientific objectivity or realism. Most scientists do not think they have merely arrived at a satisfying way of regarding the physical universe but maintain they have actually and really discovered something about the-way-it-is. Still, that position helps remind us that it is possible to be so wedded to one pair of spectacles that great parts of life are disregarded because they do not easily fit the cause-effect pattern. The archetypal and mythological, the non-rational and inexplicable, ESP and poltergeists may finally be of more importance to secular man than the rational and analytical. It is certainly true that right now secular man is prejudiced in favor of the scientific, often to the neglect of his personal wholeness.

James Kelso will read this essay in his honor, shake his head, and exclaim, "See? See, I told you. Pagan Greek logic is all words and structure. But where is the power of the gospel?" Without going that far—after all, I had other professors too!—

he has a point. Any mixing of theological ingredients and any metaphor based on an accomodation with science which negates the chief biblical metaphors of God as Father, Judge, and Redeemer are finally unhelpful. For the chief problem of life and the great glory of biblical faith is not, What is God?, but what is God for me? That was Luther's great question. And when that question is ignored or denied, then theology falls under the Reformer's indictment: it is, indeed, the devil's whore.

NOTES

1. You may think that my hesitancy here disproves my thesis that merely by watching what is put into a theology you can understand and appreciate it better. However, it really shows not that he was too fast and subtle for this theologian-watcher, but that he mixed his theology carelessly.
2. Jacques Ellul, *The Meaning of the City*, tr. Dennis Pardee (Grand Rapids: Eerdmans, 1970).
3. Paul Tillich, *Courage to Be* (New Haven: Yale Univ. Press, 1952); *Systematic Theology*, I (Chicago: Univ. of Chicago Press, 1951).
4. John Cobb, *Christian Natural Theology* (Philadelphia: Westminster, 1965); *God and the World*, (Philadelphia: Westminster, 1968).
5. Schubert Ogden, *Reality of God* (NY: Harper & Row, 1966).
6. Ian Barbour, *Issues in Science and Religion* (Englewood Cliffs, N.J.: Prentice-Hall, 1966).
7. Paul van Buren's *Secular Meaning of the Gospel* (NY: Macmillan, 1963), combined the first two, while Thomas Altizer, *The Gospel of Christian Atheism* (Philadelphia: Westminster, 1966), poured in the latter heady brew.
8. Readers not ready for Gilkey's massive *Naming the Whirlwind the Renewal of God-Language* (Indianapolis: Bobbs-Merrill, 1969), might try the gentle, humorous, "simple" use of ordinary experience in sociologist Peter Berger's *Rumor of Angels* (Garden City, N.Y.: Doubleday, 1969)—same salad, but less of it and easier to digest.
9. R. E. Masters and Jean Houston, *Varieties of Psychedelic Experience* (N.Y.: Holt, Rinehart and Winston, 1966).

135

10. Although in reality survival of the fittest does not mean survival of the most cruel or predatory but survival of that which fits its niche in the environment best. Rabbits, we know, do better than wolves and incomparably better than sabre tooth tigers.

11. Theodore Roszak, *Toward the Making of a Counter-Culture* (Garden City, N.Y.: Doubleday, 1969).

12. I say theistic rather than Christian or Jewish because such views concentrate primarily on how we can understand God's interaction with the natural world, so that the Christ-event or Israel's Peoplehood is bracketed or unexamined or assumed while this effort is going on.

13. Cf., Pierre Teilhard de Chardin, *The Appearance of Man* (N.Y.: Harper & Row, 1966); *The Future of Man* (N.Y.: Harper & Row, 1969).

14. Cf., Teilhard de Chardin, *The Divine Millieu* (N.Y.: Harper, 1960).

James Kelso
and
Contemporary Theology

By Addison H. Leitch

In the providence of God and Calvinistic happenstance, it was my privilege to be a student of James Leon Kelso from 1933 to 1936; and about ten years later, we became colleagues on the faculty of Pittsburgh-Xenia Theological Seminary, where we were together for fifteen years. In such circumstances men get to know one another pretty well, and he knows as well as I do that if a *Festschrift* is a collection of scholarly papers, then I don't belong here. But I am happy to note that *Festschrift* may more exactly be called a "festival writing," and I am happy to join a festival any time, especially as this kind of festival is "issued by admirers," says Webster, and I certainly belong in that crowd.

Something else needs looking into here: what exactly is meant by putting Kelso together with contemporary theology? This we shall see as the paper progresses and perhaps sustains its thesis. The thesis builds itself on two emphases in his teaching which impressed me in my student days and which create in my thinking now all kinds of parallels with what has been happening in the contemporary theological scene. There will be many reminiscences these days about some of the legendary events which may or may not have taken place in classroom and in personal conversations, and I will not join in that sort of thing now; nevertheless, there are these two indelible memories, and I reiterate, they relate him to contemporary theology.

The first of these from happy memory was that marvelous ploy he invented for "copping out" in the classroom when student questions became too pressing or student spirits became too rebellious. Every professor needs something for his second line of defense, and the genius of Kelso's invention was that it was not only Biblical but full of sweet reasonableness. He would say to his antagonist, "The trouble with you is that you just don't know your Bible." How true. And what could the poor student say to that, knowing as he surely did that he really didn't know much about the Bible and suspecting that Kelso knew a lot more, the ground for the student's argument had shifted into the great unknown, and he stood disarmed. He couldn't quite get up the nerve to say, "I do so know the Bible." More seriously, however, this defensive measure was for the sake of something else. Kelso was always strenuously Bible-centered; he himself knew how much more is yet to come out of the Book. He was, therefore, impatient with theologies or systems or definitions or religious clichés which could block off the student from the Bible itself. What we are too sure of knowing may block us off from knowledge. This is a nice thing to chuckle over now; it was always a tender spot with him.

The second of these is the memory of his emphasis on the Holy Spirit. It seems to me that he said things like this: "This is the day of the Holy Spirit," or "We have to come to a new understanding of the Holy Spirit," or "We are probably as wrong about the Holy Spirit as the Jews were about Christ." The Holy Spirit keeps a man's theology sort of open-ended. You had the feeling that when Kelso was groping for how to get the thing said, it was because he always knew there was so much more out there than anyone had yet managed to get said.

How innocent we were in Pittsburgh-Xenia in 1933-36. I really believed that Alf Landon would defeat Roosevelt in 1936, and it was a complete landslide in the opposite direction. But a "good U.P." was a Republican in those days, and it was hard to hear anything else. Theologically, Barth had broken on the scene in 1919, and Sir Edwyn Hoskins brought him over into English in 1931. Meanwhile, the British had been working over Barth in the German, and studies were already widely available on Barth in English. Close at hand were Brunner and Niebuhr. I recall having heard Niebuhr mentioned once in three years, and I never heard the name of Barth or Brunner, not to speak of Bonhoeffer, almost an exact contemporary of mine, who was already in deep trouble by the late thirties. Dr. McNaugher in New Testament made us familiar with the theologians of his own student days— Denny, Davidson, Rainey, and the like—and for this I have been constantly grateful. Dr. Karr in Systematic Theology had enough material for three hours a week for three years in what can best be described as an extended catechism built on our text book. A. H. Strong, built in turn on Warfield, Charles Hodge, and perhaps James Harper, although Harper always insisted that he had nothing to say which Hodge did not have in his three volume work. Again, I am grateful, for we were given a complete framework; we systematically covered all the subjects, we found out how the theological land lay, and agree or disagree, we had a corpus from that day forward with which to work. But no contemporary theology. It may be they didn't think it would be good for us, and with the amount of philosophy we had going for us then they were probably dead right!

In the midst of all this Kelso was a contemporary theologian (easy now, there is still much to be said!) as I read him now. If the debate today, for example, is between propositional theology and existential theology, where would you put him, especially if the propositions were built into structures based on "pagan Greek logic!"? His appeal was always away from the systematizers to another look at the Bible and especially the use of that Bible, not so much as something to argue about or prove, but to obey. And his emphasis on the Holy Spirit upon the word raised all kinds of existential possibilities. It was Seeberg who was quoted as saying "The Holy Spirit is the Achilles Heel of Protestantism," and he must have meant what we all can observe: put the Bible into the hands of any man, tell him a little about the priesthood of all believers, and the first thing you know Luther has his "frantics" and the great liberator, Cromwell, has to become the great Dictator, because all kinds of people from the Peasants to the Independents have a way of getting out of hand. Churchmen always want lay movements, "but not *that* way." I think Kelso's sympathies were with the religious struggles of that common man, not the "assured findings" of the scholars. And more than that, Kelso, by reason of his own disciplines, was being forced into the stream of contemporary thought by his associates in archaeology. Archaeology is not just a question of digging and classifying; it is long conversations with first-rate minds, and the associates of Kelso, men like Vincent, Albright, Glueck, etc., were not your ordinary garden-variety fundamentalist. All kinds of things crept up in digs besides whether the walls of Jericho fell out or in, things like language, culture, comparative religions, the milieu in which contemporary theology likes to move today. Some of this came across to us seminarians away back then.

An outstanding professor of theology from a nearby "name-brand" institution said in a lecture recently, "There are no theologians today." (I do not name him to protect the innocent.) It is at least a helpful thought because we have so much catching up to do with the outpouring of theology in the last fifty years. To begin with, who can call himself a

master of Karl Barth? Arnold Come wrote in a book review
that he had spent eight to ten hours a day on his sabbatical
reading nothing but Barth's *Dogmatik*. And that is only one
portion of Barth's lifetime production. Then one may add the
names which immediately come to mind like Brunner, Bultmann, and Tillich, not to mention Berkouwer and Dooye-
weerde. In addition to basic works all of these men interlock
with one another in published theological discussions and
criticisms. Then there are almost endless articles, monographs,
and books written about the men and about their critics. What
has been written by and about the theologians of the last fifty
years will have to settle down and get sifted out. Perhaps
a great systematizer is in the wings ready to cover it all; we
need him. And what can one more say about the offerings
of the Niebuhrs, the Baillies, Oman, Farmer, Dodd, Bonhoeffer,
Altizer and Hamilton, Van Til, and perhaps a touch of P.
T. Forsyth, who was supposed to be the "Barthian before
Barth." There are lesser lights, too, who keep us stirred up—
Cox, Robinson, Cone, Schaeffer, Bea and Küng.

As one does in atomic physics now, or in astronomy, one
can get at the truth only by taking a stance, following a clue,
projecting an hypothesis, extrapolating from an *a priori* assumption or presupposition. There are necessary relativisms
and probabilities here. The dynamics are such that more may
come out at the far end than was fed in at the beginning;
it is always possible to dig up more snakes than you can kill,
or to change the figure, one needs to sit a tight saddle, but
that doesn't determine which direction the battle may take.

As to contemporary theology my own set of mind came
with the reading of Barth's *The Word of God and the Word
of Man* in 1935. This mind set was strengthened about the
same time by the reading of *The Barthian Theology* by John
McConnachie, which centered also on Barth's views on Scripture. Insofar as Barth is Neo-Orthodox he is Orthodox because
of the fact that his theology is Bible-centered, God-centered,

Christ-centered, and Sin-centered. He is "Neo," so far as the ordinary orthodox are concerned, because of the way he handles the text of Scripture. Even though the conservatives, the orthodox, and the fundamentalists are having their own problems in defining the authority of Scripture—the question of verbal-inerrancy gives them their problem—they are one in pulling away from Barth and his followers and their radical treatment of Scripture, their free use of the historico-critical apparatus, and therefore, their willingness to find myth, legend, cultural conditioning, and gross error where the conservative is arguing in the direction of sober truth and inerrant text.

Nevertheless, Barth is a Biblical theologian, and many who have followed him since have been so-styled. Barth's starting place (and Van Til's!) is the acceptance of canonical Scripture as the only basis of operations. What Barth does is to accept the findings of the higher critics and establish therefore, within the record, not the "words" of God but the "Word" of God. Anyone who is conversant with contemporary theology knows how this all goes and where it leads. One reads the Bible somewhat as he reads one of Jesus' parables; there is one teaching—one Word—in each parable, and the details of the story or the setting in which it appears are incidental. Thus the point of The Good Samaritan is that one is neighbor to the man in need who falls across his path; by the same method the Word in Genesis 3 is that man is a fallen creature in spite of the questions of serpents talking or God walking in the garden. One does not have to accept such an approach to the Bible, but he has to understand it if he is going to understand contemporary theology.

There is another principle operative which must also be understood. The clue to the Word in the words of Scripture is the Living Word, even Jesus Christ. He must shine through, come through, speak authoritatively by way of the words written. This is not foreign to some of the things said by Luther and Calvin, and the orthodox are aware of how Jesus Christ is the *logos* on Scripture as on everything else. What worries the orthodox, however, is how one may play fast and loose with the words and not somehow change the Word. But that is another question.

The capstone of the Barthian approach, however, lies in the action of this Word in the life of the individual. A man may hear the Word preached, find the Word in his devotional reading, or whatever; the important thing is that it is not really the Word of God *for him* until the Word shows action in his life—we are "epistles known and read of all men." And the Word comes alive in the believer in the situations in which he finds himself, the existential situation. Thus, the same verse or the same sermon may convey the same message to a doctor or lawyer or professor, but each in turn can be called upon to do something different because of the difference in his situation or from the day to day change in the existential moment when his decision is called for. This moment of decision is critical, judgmental (crisis) and so one walks by faith, hearing and obeying as God speaks to a man where he is, what he is, and what he ought to be doing. In all this there is escape from fixed requirements ahead of time growing out of codes of ethics, legalisms, catechisms, propositional or systematic theologies.

All of this is known in greater detail and with greater finesse by anyone who is the least bit acquainted with the writings of Barth. What is not so well known is that, whereas Barth's own emphasis was on the establishing of great theological supports for all this, others chose to move away from his theological concern to the more subjective application which his system allows. The whole system is criticized for being subjective, and the Living Word gets farther and farther away from the authority of the words until theology and Scripture are dismissed by radical approaches in favor of a call to action. "We know all that theology stuff and we know about the Bible, but in our day we have to be where the action is." And the action is "where cross the crowded ways of life." It is odd also, is it not, that in more fundamentalist circles Spirit-filled Christians have much more singing, much more sharing of their own views, and much less study of the Bible. "What do you think?" and "How do you really feel?" become the important questions.

Emil Brunner was the immediate follower, or better, the closest co-worker of Barth's, and whereas, at least for a spell, they differed on Natural Theology, in everything else they seemed to be in basic agreement. Brunner is easier to read than Barth; therefore, his more popular approach may be a good way of getting at Barth. His emphasis on the Divine-Human encounter pointed up the way in which man knows the will of God and how he is called upon to obey. Again the approach is "situational" or "existential." The emphasis is on the "encounter." It is *by way of* the Scriptures, whether preached or read, that the Living Word is manifested. But Christ comes as a Word from beyond, a challenge to my way of doing things, a call to newness of life in the life situation. It will not do for me only to read about God's law or God's ethic, it will not do for me to give even intellectual assent, it will not do for me to follow the pressures of church or society; what I find in Scriptures, or better, what finds me, is the living God. We meet face to face; there is real encounter, and in this crisis situation rebellion or obedience will follow. The immediate moment is critical and destiny is at stake. But see again how the Word has moved out of the Bible into the arena of wrestling and decision.

Reinhold Niebuhr, with his great social concern coupled with his radical view of sin, understood this arena of conflict with all its ambiguities, its great defeats, and its small victories. One does not have set before him a choice between absolutes, one does not choose right against wrong, for such clear choices are not given. This is not to say that right and wrong are relatives; it is to say that in the confusions of life and in the

cloudiness of a man in his own human limitations, his lack
of information, his prejudices and conditionings, and certainly
in his sinful condition, the choices are not all that clear. He
can only choose *in the direction of* the good and away from
the evil: one step enough for me! An election year is a good
time to understand this. Not to vote at all because the candidates are not as Christian as they could be or we would
want them to be, is an evasion of the responsible situation
into which God has called us as mature adults. But to vote
at all is to vote, not for God vs. the Devil (no matter what
the campaign speeches say), but to vote for the better (not
the best) man, knowing full well that, as Niebuhr inderlines
in so many ways, we are sinful men acting in a sinful society.
We therefore must repent of even our "good" deeds, for our
righteousness is indeed "as filthy rags." Again the emphasis:
what am I called upon to do in my situation, things being
as they are? The Holy Spirit plays on the Scripture, there
is an encounter, one must act. Variations of this theme came
later in a more popular way through Joseph Fletcher and his
situational ethics, and we have all wrestled with that one.

The same thread may be followed in Bonhoeffer and Tillich.
The interrelationships of Barth, Bonhoeffer, and Tillich are
a study in themselves as is also an understanding of the relationship of the early Bonnoeffer and his later *Letters and Papers
from Prison*. Tillich is a problem of total grasp and understanding, which very few have yet mastered. In Bonhoeffer, however, two things are clear: he did preach from the Bible, the
whole Bible, and he tried to be loyal to the Lutheran Church
while severely criticizing it; and he had his own excruciating
existential situation to deal with under the demonic pressure
of Hitler's tyranny. A pacifist by conviction, displaying the
highest levels of obedience in his personal and communal life,
he was nevertheless forced to an impossible decision: participation in the assasination plots against Hitler. The law says
"Thou shalt not kill." The obedient pacifist was shaken loose

from such absolutes because of a "higher" calling. Taking a page from Kierkegaard's book, he seized on the "teleological suspension of the ethical" and settled for the "penultimate" ethical choice when he thought the "ultimate" was not available to him. Kierkegaard used as his illustration Abraham's willingness to kill Isaac in a faith obedience to God which went beyond the law "Thou shalt not kill." Abraham's hand was stayed; so was Bonhoeffer's, strangely enough, and he never had the opportunity to kill. But note where his struggle lies: the Word of God to him over against and in spite of all other words—church, society, or Scripture. Highly subjective? What about Luther against the Church and the State? Do you only, Luther, know the truth? Well, "Here *I* stand, God help *me*, *I* can do no other."

Tillich warns us against Heteronomy, the dictation of any outside authority in our Christian action, and against Autonomy, the obedience to self alone; we are not to be other-centered or self-centered. We are to hold to Theonomy, God-centeredness. Again it is like Barth and Brunner, Niebuhr and Bonhoeffer—a swing to the confrontation of God in one's life, mediated by Scripture, pulled toward the New Being in Christ, but hardly bound to any fixed point, Biblical or otherwise. If one conjoins with this Tillich's teaching on correlation, this slant on things is even more demanding. "Correlation" means that theologizing consists in accepting the problems before us in all their ambiguities and frightful anxieties and discovering their answers in what theology offers. In other words, our approach to truth is not so much Biblically centered as problem-centered. The theological question is whether God has spoken to *my* condition. Again we see how the land lies.

Bultmann is a special case. He insisted that he was a Biblical theologian; his basic text is indeed called *Theology of the New Testament*. But he virtually dismisses the gospels as having any verbal dependability; he builds on the Pauline and Johannine writings only after he has put them in their cultural milieu—especially the influences of Gnosticism and hellen-ism—and his de-mythologizing portrays the end product of serious form-criticism. Nevertheless, once he has decided what the Bible is, he uses what he has. And he uses it as the others have used it: the divine-human encounter leading to personal obedience in the given situation.

There are others in this train. But there are others on another track too. Berkouwer, who has been the champion to whom conservatives, Calvinists, orthodox and the like have turned (when he was not too friendly with the Vatican!), has his own kind of correlation not to be confused with Tillich's. He, thinking of himself as the preacher's theologian, insists that theology must "correlate" with pulpit and pew. Thus, in his own way, he turns the edge of sharp theologizing by insisting that one's theology must be preachable and understandable, controlled constantly by where the listener is in his under-standings and problems. Predestination, for example, must not be pushed to any extreme which seems irrational to the man in the street.

Dooyeweerd [1] has become a kind of fad with "in groups" here and there who claim to understand him. It is something like the kind of fetish which surrounded Tillich in university circles, but the Dooyeweerd movement is hard to the right theologically. One need not here get into its difficulties (often affording special pleasure of those who claim understand-ing—like drawing maps for the Hobbits), which demand all manner of understanding of philosophy, history, logic, culture and the arts, political science, etc. (Schaeffer on a deeper level) which the ordinary reader cannot bring so easily to his task. One needs to recognize within the limits of this paper only one thing: in the tradition of Kuyper, Bavinck, Van Til, the Dutch School with headquarters in the Free University, there is a marked turning away from the place of Reason in theolog-ical matters. In the Faith-Reason standoff, which goes back at least to the Middle Ages, Dooyeweerd and his followers,

Reformed theologians all, condemn rationalism and all its works thereby showing parallels with the Barthian tradition and leading, as we have suggested now many times, to a theology which evades "proof" of the traditional kinds and turns the edge of propositional theology. Berkouwer and Dooyeweerd in their own ways are also a mark of the core which runs through all contemporary theology and which has been the concern of this paper.

It is ridiculous, of course to align James L. Kelso with any or all of these theologians. He would want to disavow much of what they have said; he might well wish to call a plague down on all their houses. But there he is, a man who insists, as they all do, that the truth is to come out of the Bible, that the truth will be much more and much grander than any theological statement about it, that the truth will be best known through obedience and not through definition, that there are limits to "pagan Greek logic" as against the "higher" logic of the Scriptures, and that the work of the Holy Spirit in the heart of the believer is to take of the things of Christ and show them unto us "for us men and our salvation." And the end is not yet; the best is yet to be.

May I suggest one theologian in closing, a man who has become a favorite of mine. He is Jacques Ellul, French Protestant Distinguished Professor at the University of Bordeaux. I commend his writing to you for this day in which we live. His book is the Bible, and he is open to all the new truth of God through the Holy Spirit. But he has this to say in a brief essay in *Theological Crossings:*

> The mark of the theological radicalism I have in mind is precisely its refusal to compromise with these theologies, which look (but only look) sound and are the expressions of the spirit of the times. It is *beyond* the crisis that we must find the true expression of the Revelation. Not an expression that is acceptable, adaptive, conformed

to the modern spirit, but an expression that is true because, on the one hand, it comes to grips with the problems of our society and its people, and, on the other, firmly upholds the *reality* of the Revelation in its fulness. Today my thinking centers on the search for a Credo for the church of tomorrow.[2]

So away with everything "up to date" or "relevant" or "timely". The truth is still beyond us, and the conservatives as well as the liberals know how bankrupt our day is. The Good Shepherd "leads us *out*" while we like to stay within the confines of our theologies or our "relevant" liberal shibboleths. It is no longer a time of "me too" in theological belief or social action. We are waiting on the Lord for something beyond anything we now know, and I think James Kelso has known this all the time.

NOTES

1. Cf. Herman Dooyeweerd, *In the Twilight of Western Thought* (Philadelphia: Presbyterian and Reformed Pub. Co., 1960). Dooyeweerd is a Dutch philosopher at the Free University Amsterdam whose attempts to harmonize Christian faith with his philosophy have won adherents among certain American and Canadian Reformed theologians, especially within the Christian Reformed Church.

2. Though Jacques Ellul is by profession a sociologist, his recent spate of writings have been theological in character. See for example: *The Meaning of the City*, tr. D. Pardee (Grand Rapids: Eerdmans', 1970); *The Judgement of Jonah*, tr. G. E. Bromiley (Grand Rapids: Eerdmans', 1971); *Prayer and Modern Man*, tr., C. E. Hopkins (N.Y.: Seabury Press, 1970); *The Theological Foundation of Law*, tr. M. Wieser (N.Y.: Seabury Press, 1960).

Truth-Telling: Illustrating The Moral Dilemma

By Wayne H. Christy

"Do you swear to tell the truth, the whole truth and nothing but the truth—so help you God?" The daily intoning of that oath in the courts of our land constitutes a legal device for trying to get people to tell the truth. The right to take the Fifth Amendment seems to define certain exceptions to the requirement just stated.

The existence of the terms: "truth-in-lending-laws," "credibility gap," "information freeze" suggests that there are areas of institutional life in America where failing to be totally open with others is common.

A COMPLICATED SUBJECT

A recent article in *The Readers Digest* was titled, "A Simple Short Cut That Will Set You Free." [1] Honesty was presented as the "simple short cut." As this presentation develops, the reader can judge the validity of any "simple short cut" in the area.

In a book of readings titled *Ethical Choice*, Robert N. Beck writes:

To say what is; to speak words which conform to thoughts; to act in the light of what one believes to be the case: such injunctions seem easy and imperative.

Despite all this, however, moral complications arise when we reflect on the imperative to be always truthful or to wonder about the principle (if any) that might justify truthfulness.[2]

There are numerous situations in which it is hard to know what truth to tell: How do you answer the questions of a dying man about his hopes for recovery? What truth do you use in response to the queries of a child about where babies come from? How do you respond to the safe-cracker who demands the combination to a bank vault? How far can governmental limitation of news properly go?

WHAT IS TRUTH-TELLING?

There is a difference between truth and truthfulness; between accuracy and veracity; between logical truth and moral truth. When we talk of the morality of truth-telling we are not concerned about statements whose incompleteness is caused by lack of knowledge. Such an assertion might be inaccurate, but it would not be immoral. Robert Beck writes:

Truth in the Moral sense is or involves an act of will such that one's words or actions agree with one's thoughts and one's thoughts are directed and guided by one's understanding of what is the case . . . Truthfulness is thus always a *personal* value.[3]

Helmut Thielicke adds an important idea when he insists that truth has to involve *a relevant statement that brings out meaning*. He says "Though it is true that man is a two-legged animal without feathers" that is not informative enough to be the truth about man.[4]

Sydney J. Harris relates a story told by Billy Phelps, popular

English professor at Yale, of a captain of a ship who wrote in his log, "Mate was drunk today." When the mate recovered he was angry and chagrined, requesting that the notation be removed because that was actually the first time he had ever been drunk on duty. "Sorry," said the captain, "in this log we write the exact truth." The next week the mate kept the log and in it he wrote, "Captain was sober today." [5]

WHAT IS LYING?

To push on toward a definition let us look at some definitions of what "lying" is. Is it failing to tell every fact that could be told if all were known? A dictionary definition of a lie is "A falsehood uttered or acted *for the purpose* of deception; *an intentional statement* of an untruth designed to mislead another." [6] To this H. H. Titus adds, *"Without his consent."* [7] A faked kick or a bluffed throw or a "tactful bid" are not subject to moral judgment.

The plot thickens when we notice a couple other modifiers. Helmut Thielicke, whose chapter entitled "Compromises and the Limits of Truthfulness" includes several illustrations from the times of German totalitarianism, says, "Lying is to deny the Truth *for egotistic reasons.*" [8] He would agree with Paul Ramsey when he refers to truth-telling as "communicating the truth to someone *to whom the truth belongs.*" [9]

THE ABSOLUTIST VIEW

The question we turn to now is whether morality calls for *always telling* the truth—"telling it like it is?" If truth-telling is an imperative, what makes it so? First, the absolutist view. St. Augustine is represented as saying "A lie is always and necessarily sinful," and St. Thomas Aquinas as writing, "A lie has the character of sinfulness, not only from the damage done to the neighbor, but also from its own inordinateness—it is not lawful to tell a lie to deliver anyone from any danger whatsoever." [10] Richard D. Cabot, states in his book, *The Meaning of Right and Wrong,*

> How can we ever be sure where a conscientious liar will draw the line? It appears to me, therefore, that the doctrine that *it is sometimes right to lie, can never* be effectively asserted.[11]

A famous philosophical defense of the view that truth-telling is a constant obligation is that of Immanuel Kant in his essay "On a Supposed Right to Lie from Altruistic Motives." Kant contended that "to be truthful in all declarations is a sacred and absolutely commanding degree of reason, limited by no expediency." [12] His primary argument for making the requirement for truth-telling unconditional is that "truthfulness is a duty which must be considered as the basis for all duties" that are based on agreements because the agreement would be rendered "useless if the least exception were admitted." [13]

Harold H. Titus uses an illustration that helps me at this point. "The counterfeiter injures the person who receives the spurious money *and who is unable* to pass it; he *also brings sound money under suspicion* and thus injures society." [14]

THE NECESSITY TO LIE

The fact is that in spite of some who have taken such an absolutist approach, most people today and many in the past have taken the view that there are times when something other than the full truth should be told. Some even insist that it pays to lie. You know—"Nice Guys Never Win." Machiavelli in his essay ironically titled "How Princes Should Keep Faith" argues that truth should be subordinated on occasion to other values—in this case to power and political stability. He sounds like a fifteenth century Leo Durocher when he writes, "Princes who have set little store by their word have, by their cunning, accomplished great things and in the end got the better of those who trusted to honest dealing." He concludes that "for this reason a prudent prince *neither can or ought* to keep his word *when it is hurtful to him.*[15]

Equally crass is Voltaire who wrote:

> Lying is a vice only when it effects evil;
> it is a great virtue when it accomplishes good.
> So be more virtuous than ever.
> *One must lie like the Devil*, not timorously or only occasionally, but confidently
> and constantly. Lie, my friend, lie! [16]

UNJUSTIFIABLE LYING

Most lying is certainly unjustifiable. There is no question that certain lies are wrong. Many times people use the lie to cover up some mismove. Durant Drake, insisted that "the selfish lie is never justifiable; the cowardly lie—lying to get out of unpleasant consequences—is wrong because cowardice is wrong." [17] This is the most common cause of lying. It has been a sin from the very first when Cain's answer to God's question "where is your brother Abel?" was "I do not know." [18]

Theilicke is offended by gross deception of children by adults, citing as an example "the stork bit" in response to a child's questions about where babies come from. He calls this "In no sense a white lie, but an out and out lie, bold-faced, blatant, unexcusable, and tasteless to boot." [19]

For a mother to explain her being in bed by the ruse that stork "bit" her is too much for Thielicke. He makes the thoughtful observation that an essential criterion of the genuineness of such an answer is whether the child has to unlearn it and start afresh when he comes to adult life. He comments that "it is the mark of truth that *one cannot grow out of it; one can only grow into it.*" [20]

Sometimes there may be two groups confronting each other, verbally, where there is no intention that honesty be a part of the conversation. Perhaps because of a lack of trust which leaves no hope for response, there is double talk. The groups conversing do not really communicate. Neither do they really address the issues in candor. This is the way I see the exchange of verbiage and euphemisms between the adults and the students on the current topics of no hours and open dorms on campus. *Deliberate rejection of candor is dishonesty* of a type which makes communication impossible.

THE JUSTIFIABLE LIE

Over against these cases where there is no adequate excuse for failing to tell the truth, there are occasions which many would judge to involve circumstances allowing for, or even calling for, something less than the truth. Titus sees that:

> a considerable majority of present-day moral philosophers agree that in the concrete situations of life, men occasionally face the alternative of sacrificing one value for another and that in some cases the selection of the greater value may mean the temporary denial of the obligation of truthfulness.[21]

There are three types of circumstances which seem to some to justify a lie.

One situation that for many ethical thinkers involves exception to the normal pattern of truthfulness is the case of probing by one who has no right to the truth. Does such a person deserve the truth? An example would be a Nazi storm trooper asking information about the whereabouts of Anne Frank. Drake calls such inquiries a "sort of moral burglary".[22] Thielicke shows us that when the inquisitor is one with whom fellowship has broken down he has forfeited his right to the truth. Such an enemy he says is not in a search for truth, but in a power struggle. To Thielicke a white lie told in such a situation can no more be called lying in the strict sense than killing in self-defense can be called murder.[23]

A second group of curcumstances that calls for tact rather than utter frankness is related to the conventions of polite society. Durant Drake says that "to thank a stupid hostess for pleasure she has not given is loving one's neighbor as one's self." He reports that he knew only one person whom he could count on not to indulge herself in these conventional false-hoods, and so far as he knows, that person has been unable to keep a single friend.[24]

Thielicke tells of a church sexton in a small country church which often had seminary students as pulpit supplies. The sexton had a formula for replying to students who asked him how he thought they had done. If the sermon was quite good, the reply was "The Lord has been gracious." If the service was only moderately good, he would say, "The text was dif-ficult."If the day had been a disaster, the kindly old sexton would allow that "the hymns had been well chosen." [25]

The same writer introduces a third area of exception when he cites occasions when "out of love for the other, I think I must spare him the hurt that telling the truth might inflict." Sometimes this tack is taken by bearers of bad news. In the Bible story when the boy Samuel was told by God of the dire fate of Israel and his friend Eli, the man Eli had to pressure the truth out of the reluctant boy prophet.[26]

"A Special Report" article in Life magazine several years ago was titled," Poignant Tissue of Lies." [27] It told of a well-in-tentioned conspiracy to protect an old couple from learning of the war-casualty death of their son of the Army Air Force. Philip Posa, a brother, decided to protect his 80 year old parents from the blow. This was possible because the old folks did not read English and seldom heard radio or T. V. By writing letters presumably from his dead brother and by writing replies for the parents to their son, he has kept up the deception, hoping that their deaths will come without their suffering the knowledge of their brave son's death.

The dilemma of whether to tell or to withhold bad news

is faced most often in hospital cases. Joseph Fletcher has long been interested in this subject. In his retirement from the Episcopal Theological School he is now working at the University of Virginia Hospital. Of this new assignment he has written:

> In medical care the problem of truth-telling is becoming thornier and thornier, due most of all perhaps to the technical character of diagnosis and treatment and the difficulty of communicating honestly without distortion.[28]

His early interest in this field of ethical dilemma resulted in a 1960 book, *Morals and Medicine.* In that book Fletcher takes seriously an obligation toward truth in the abstract, remarking that "deception has consistently been held to be a fault against virtue, and no moralist has ever attempted to defend it in principle." [29]

Dr. Fletcher's rationale for being forthright with a patient whose condition is serious follows this line:

1) As persons we are rendered puppets if knowledge which should be available is denied.
2) The facts of an illness are the property of the patient and are not to be withheld from him.
3) It is important that there be a mutual respect between patient and physician.
4) To deny the patient the facts of life and death is to assume responsibilities which he alone can take care of.[30]

A few years ago, an important practitioner in the Children's Hospital of Philadelphia, Dr. C. Everett Koop, wrote "What I tell a dying child's parents." "Because most people feel that doctors don't tell them everything, I try to be as candid as possible. I try to answer questions before they are asked." [31]

TWO APPROACHES TO ETHICS

This topic of truth-telling is important to me as an illustration—a kind of test case for comparing the contextual or situational approach to ethics with a system that places more emphasis on principles and rules.

SITUATIONISM

Paul Lehmann uses truth-telling as his first "for instance" as he distinguishes between his contextual ethics and what he calls an "absolute ethic." Joseph Fletcher includes any law against lying in his contrast between situation ethics and "legalism." I just do not find very many writers taking as rigid a stance as challenged by both Lehmann and Fletcher. Who says a Christian is required always to tell the truth, the whole truth and nothing but the truth? Some twenty-five years ago I wrote a series of articles for Sunday School studies on the Ten Commandments. One of the essays was titled "Truthfulness in all Things." [32] Today I could not write a commentary on the Ninth Commandment without referring to exceptional cases. Paul Ramsey speaks of "exceptions" and "a problem of compromise"—when one must withhold or deny the truth to someone to whom it is rightfully due under ordinary circumstances, for the sake of an unusual and overriding obligation. So has Christian ethics in almost all ages "justified" theft under certain circumstances—or assassination or war. [33]

Whether or not the law is sometimes intentionally violated is not the question. The questions are: What is the analysis of what is involved in the making of the exception? What is the role of the law? What is the place of the exception? What makes the act right or wrong? Is truth something for real or isn't it?

Paul Lehmann uses two illustrations. One involves a person selling a second-hand car—selling it under emergency circumstances in which he needs a good price for the car. The other instance reviews Lehmann's response to a dying friend who asked him, "What do the doctors say? Is there anything that can be done?" Lehmann's emphasis is on "Christian koinonia". He speaks of the "living word" and the "right word." He seems to be saying that what is important in the area of true or false is the relationship between the two men, i.e., the prospective buyer and the pressured car owner. Lehmann writes, "The business transaction becomes instrumental to their discovery of each other as human beings, and whether much or little is told about the car, *whatever is told is the Truth*." [34] Now right there he loses me. I am not saying that the developing of a koinonia experience is an unimportant thing, but Lehmann started to talk about "a lie" and about "truth-telling," and when he reaches his conclusion I think he is talking about something else.

In the other example, Lehmann starts by asking, "How white is a lie? how black can the truth, the whole truth, and nothing but the truth be? What in such a situation *is* the truth?" [35]

Then he proceeds to tell how he spoke compassionately to his sick friend about sustaining her Christian faith in the days ahead. Paul Ramsey's criticism of this is that Lehmann avoided her question and changed the subject. He "brought up the Truth when the truth was asked." Though Ramsey allows that that was "the most important thing to speak of in that hour or in any hour," he charges that Lehmann withheld the truth from the lady, and that in so doing he failed to treat her with adequate respect in her predicament.[36]

Another ethicist whose approach is situational is Dietrich Bonhoeffer, author of an essay called "What Is Meant by Telling the Truth?" He holds that "telling the truth means something different according to the particular situation in which one stands." He, with Lehmann, uses the term of "knowing the right word" on each occasion. He too espouses the "living truth." He tells of a child who replies, "No", when a teacher, in front of the class, asks him whether his father came home drunk often. Allowing that this "No" is a lie, Bonhoeffer puts the blame on the callous questioner and on the lack of sophistication in the child. Says Bonhoeffer,

> Yet *this lie contains more truth,*—it is more in accordance with reality that would have been the case had the child betrayed his father's weakness in front of the class.[37]

Bonhoeffer grants the possibility of two dangers in his system:

1) Thinking that truth is so variable that there is no difference between truth and falsehood, and
2) Always calculating as to *how much truth* to give a particular person.

To this writer these dangers are so real as to threaten the very concept of truth-telling.

In his most definitive book, *Situation Ethics,* Joseph Fletcher puts primary emphasis on a debate which is crucial in a study of situationism. This debate centers on the question of value. Fletcher is right when he says "the rock-bottom issue of all ethics is value." This is the old question of nominalism vs. realism. In our case, is truth in truth-telling something real? When you finish limiting and delimiting what is meant by telling the truth, is there then something there that is a value? I think there is, and I insist on reasons for retaining the value. I do not grant that taking this stance necessarily makes me an absolutist or a legalist.

The key to Fletcher's approach, held in common at this point with Lehmann and Bonhoeffer, is rather than being real in itself, like a noun; trueness is actually a name, a predicate, a manner of describing a particular approach or way of acting. Fletcher writes that "there are no values" at all, there are only things (material and non-material) which happen to be valued by persons." This brings him to say that:

The rightness of an act, then, nearly always and perhaps always, depends on the way in which the act is related to the circumstances.[38]

About truth-telling in particular, he writes:

> For the situationist what makes *the lie right is its loving purpose;* he is not hypnotized by some abstract law, "Thou shalt not lie." If a lie is told unlovingly it is wrong, evil; *if it is told in love it is good,* right . . . Right and wrong, good or bad are things that happen to what we say or do.' Whether they are veracious or not depends on how much love is served in the situation.[39]

AN ETHIC OF RULES AND PRINCIPLES

Paul Ramsey's objection to Lehmann's contextualism is helpful. Ramsey holds that truth can be defined as "communicating the truth (and, of course, intending to do so) to someone to whom the truth in question belongs." [40] He goes on to grant that, "to tell the truth *requires,* it would seem, both a certain correspondence and integrity *between thought and speech* and a *co-respondence* and integrity between *the speaker and other persons.*" [41] Ramsey allows for making exceptions to principles such as "Thou shalt not lie," but holds that the principle should be seen to have a reality which calls for adherence to it most of the time.[42]

Nicolai Hartman, writing on "Truthfulness and Uprightness" brings out an emphasis that seems to me necessary.

> From the point of view of truthfulness, the "necessary lie" is always wrong. There may be times when someone—physician prisoner, possessor of confidential information—"must resort to a lie" but if they do so they make themselves guilty on the side of truthfulness.
> ....
> A morally mature person might see some value and take upon himself the responsibility for the lie. But these

situations do not permit of being universalized. They are only extreme cases in which the conscience is heavy enough . . . For it is inherent in the essence of such moral conflicts that in them value stands against value and that it is not possible to escape from them without being guilty.[43]

Thielicke brings out an important point when he makes this distinction: "Whoever retains an awareness that in certain fields and situations some crookedness is inevitable is still under a restraint which no longer applies to the man who no longer makes any distinction between crooked and straight, evil and good." "Having to sin" is basically quite a different idea from that of eliminating the concept of sin altogether.[44]

CONCLUSION

I am uneasy with the situationist approach as an ethical formula for Everyman. Though the concern of its advocates is supposed to be for persons, I happen to be such a pessimist that I think the only person that most people are concerned about when the chips are down is one's self. I just do not see most people making altruistic decisions occasion after occasion. For many the "new morality" is rationalizing.

Neither do I think the Christian way should be legalistic. I see truth-telling in ordinary cases to be a way of life that makes for the best human relationships. Still we have seen that there are cases when it would be best for all concerned that the truth be withheld.

Recall Jesus' word to the rich young ruler who claimed that he thought he should get into heaven because he had kept all the commandments from his youth. He was told:

You still need to do one thing
Go, sell all that you have, give to the poor and follow me.[45]

162

The Christian life is something that goes beyond the keeping of commandments.

All the situationist commentaries that I read on the moral commandments are telling us how to tell less truth than the commandment says. For example, James Pike has a book in which he gives seventy-four cases, all liberalizing the law.[46] Are there no situations that call for more truthfulness than the law demands? I had a carpenter work for me who charged less than his carpenter's wage for a day he spent cleaning up. How about that kind of honesty?

I think Christian Ethics has to revive its emphasis on "Christian." It must relate to Christian Faith. If I can bring myself to a totality of commitment to God I will be on the road to a sound ethical life. Dietrich Bonhoeffer, a devout man, as well as an ethical theorist, stresses an approach with which I close.

> The commandment of complete truthfulness is really only another name for the totality of discipleship—There is no truth toward Jesus without truth toward man—We cannot follow Christ unless we live in revealed truth before God and man.[47]

110

FOOTNOTES

1. Elise Miller Davis, "A Short Cut That Will Set You Free," *Readers Digest*, (April, 1970), pp. 165-68.
2. Robert N. Beck, and John B. Orr, *Ethical Choice* (N.Y. Free Press, 1970), p. 3.
3. Beck and Orr, *Ethical Choice*, p. 4. Compare similar treatments by Nicolai Hartmann in Beck, p. 39, and in Joseph Fletcher, *Morals and Medicine* (Boston: Beacon Press, 1960), p. 39-40.
4. Helmut Thielicke, *Theological Ethics* (Philadelphia: Fortress Press, 1966), p. 522.
5. Sydney J. Harris, "Strictly Personal", Pittsburgh Press, N.D.
6. *Webster-Merriam Unabridged Dictionary*, 2nd ed., (N.Y.: C. G. Merriam Co., 1950).

7. H. H. Titus, *Ethics for Today* (N.Y.: American Book Co., 1957), p. 265.
8. Thielicke, *Ethics*, p. 530.
9. Paul Ramsey, *Deeds and Rules in Christian Ethics* (N.Y.: Scribners, 1967), p. 77
10. Joseph Fletcher, *Morals and Medicine* (Boston: Beacon Press, 1960), p. 41.
11. As quoted by Fletcher, *Morals and Medicine*, p. 47.
12. Paul L. Lehmann, *Ethics in a Christian Context* (N.Y.: Harper-Row, 1963), p. 127.
13. Beck and Orr, *Ethical Choice*, p. 19.
14. Titus, *Ethics for Today*, p. 266. Joseph Fletcher, before his *Situation Ethics* emphasis expressed a similar view in the phrase: "Lying troubles the waters of human relations", *Morals and Medicine*, p. 49.
15. Beck and Orr, *Ethical Choice*, p. 17. Helmut Thielicke cites Frederick the Great as using the same rationale.
16. Thielicke, *Ethics*, p. 520.
17. Durant Drake, *Problems of Conduct* (N.Y.: Houghton-Mifflin, 1914), p. 246.
18. Genesis 4:9
19. Helmut Thielicke, *Ethics*, p. 527.
20. Thielicke relates an extensive "fairy tale" about birth which illustrates what he sees to be truth legitimately adapted for the understanding of a child.
21. Titus, *Ethics for Today*, 1957, p. 268.
22. Drake, *Problems*, p. 248.
23. Thielicke, *Ethics*, p. 531. He adds that on this level of interrogation truth is not respected, but torpedoed.
24. Drake, *Problems*, p. 249.
25. Thielicke, *Ethics*, p. 549.
26. I Samuel 3:17.
27. Richard Stolley, *Life*, Unidentified issue.
28. Joseph Fletcher, personal letter to the author, January 9, 1971.
29. Fletcher, *Morals and Medicine*, p. 46.
30. Fletcher, *Morals and Medicine*, Chap. 2. "Medical Diagnosis—Our Right to Know the Truth." Remember Fletcher's later increased emphasis on "It all depends." In a letter to me he indicated that if he were rewriting the book, the chapter on "Our Right to Know the Truth" would be the most extensive rewriting.

31. C. Everett Koop, "What I Tell a Dying Child's Parents," *Readers Digest* (Feb., 1968), p. 143.
32. Wayne H. Christy, "Truthfulness in All Things," *The United Presbyterian* (November 15, 1943), p. 11.
33. Paul Ramsey, *Deeds and Rules in Christian Ethics* (N.Y.: Scribner's, 1967), p. 78.
34. Paul Lehmann, *Ethics in a Christian Context* (N.Y.: Harper and Row, 1963), p. 130.
35. *Ibid.*, p. 132.
36. Ramsey, *Deeds and Rules*, p. 84.
37. Beck and Orr, *Ethical Choice*, p. 46.
38. Joseph Fletcher, *Situation Ethics* (Philadelphia: Westminster, 1966), p. 58-59.
39. *Ibid.*, p. 65.
40. Ramsey, *Deeds and Rules*, p. 79.
41. *Ibid.*, p. 80.
42. In a chapter in a later book Outka and Ramsey, *Norm and Context in Christian Ethics* (N.Y.: Scribners, 1968), Ramsey took seventy pages to establish that: "It cannot be shown that Christians or just men should never say Never," p. 134.
43. Beck and Orr,*Ethical Choice*, p. 41.
44. Thielicke, *Ethics*, p. 539.
45. Luke 18:20
46. James A. Pike, *You and the New Morality* (N.Y.: Harper Row, 1967).
47. Dietrich Bonhoeffer, *The Cost of Discipleship* (N.Y.: Macmillan, 1959), p. 155.

PART THREE

Church and Ministry

Introduction

BY ROBERT A. COUGHENOUR

"*B*EYOND RELIGION lies Christianity." While no definition is attached to the word "religion," the meaning of the line is clear enough. Religion is a man-made system of beliefs and practices. No matter what the practices and creeds of other "religions," from an enlightened Greek "paganism" to the mystical versions of Eastern "faiths," Christianity is "beyond" them, because it is the revelation of God to men, not man's own construction. This quotation from James Kelso's unpublished notes was found in two different contexts. One context for the quote was in a sermon on the uniqueness of the church based on the uniqueness of her message. The other setting is a meditation on the Lord's Supper. While the matrix of each is different, taken together they display Kelso's belief in the "two marks of the church" according to Reformed theology: (1) where the gospel is rightly proclaimed, and (2) where the sacraments are rightly administered, there is the Church.

James Leon Kelso loves the Church, but he harbors no illusions about its earthly perfection. More than once he commented something like this:

> Of course there are sinners in the Church. No better place for them. Where else can they learn to stifle their hypocrisy and learn to obey Jesus Christ?

Kelso noted that "the disciples failed, even between the Lord's Supper and the cross."

> Judas betrayed him, Peter denied him, and all forsook him and fled. Even after the ascension his servants often failed him. Look at Peter's failure to greet Gentiles at the Antioch supper Paul told about in Galatians. Look how harsh Paul had to be with the Galatian saints. Remember, Christ himself rebuked the churches of Asia (Revelation to John 1-2).
> Of course, these are not reasons to slack in obedience; to deny the charge given to the Church "to go into all the world."
> Peter denied him but was recommissioned to feed his sheep.
> John Mark fled the garden, but was recommissioned and became a believing Evangelist.
> Paul tried to crush the early church, but was commissioned her greatest soul-winner.
> Build your earthly ministry around the Communion table (the focus of the church). Here's where saints (redeemed sinners) acknowledge their sins, their fellowship, their new power, their renewed charge to evangelize the world.

James Kelso has always been a churchman. His services as pastor in Indiana, for forty years in the church's seminaries as Professor of Old Testament and Archaeology, as an elected Moderator of the United Presbyterian Church of North America, are eloquent testimony to his churchmanship. But, in addition to these posts of leadership, Dr. Kelso shares, even at this writing as he has for many years, his enthusiasm and learning with a weekly Adult Bible Class of his church home, the Beverly Heights United Presbyterian Church in Pittsburgh, Pa.

Always a practical expositor of Scripture, Dr. Kelso passed along to his students hints he believed were useful for preaching. For example, note the following excerpts from a longer presentation entitled, "A Year's Preaching from the Old Testament:"

I. O. T. Persons who have a Message for Today
Practical Men—Moses (Faith must have its organized church; Faith must have its creedal statement; Faith must have its social program.)
     —David (Church must produce a good State; Church must have its music; Church must have its cathedral.)
Underdogs—Joseph, by compulsion
                  Jonathan, by choice
                  Habakkuk, by circumstances
Far-sighted Men—Isaiah (Remnant of Church seen long before, and "gates of Hell will not prevail against it).
     —Jeremiah (A vision of a pure spirituality—the law written on the heart).
Seldom-mentioned "Big Saints"—Enoch; Eldad and Medad; Jonathan; Joel.

II. O. T. Problems with which the Church still struggles
False Israel/True Church. The Church is a hospital. All have, and *still* sin.
Family/Marriage and Divorce. Church program too often splits up family. Have a stay-at-home-with-the-family night once a month.

III. O. T. Practices and their meaning for Today.
Sacrifice/It cost money; it had public confession; it had a church dinner; it pre-figured the personage of Christ.
Full gospel (social gospel)—No longer I who live, but Christ who lives in me. He helped the sick, the unfortunate, handled "psychiatric" cases. (Foreign Missions are most successful when they imitate Christ; most successful when they use Old and New Testaments).
Church
    a. The gates of Hell have not prevailed against it.
    b. Always a mixture of saints and sinners (proportions varied).
    c. God always used it (even in Judges; even the "bad figs" in Palestine when the rest were taken to Babylon).

171

In 1922, the first year of Dr. Kelso's published writings, three of his four articles dealt with the missionary experience of Paul—his mission and ours to evangelize the world. In 1972, *fifty years later,* in a paper circulated at the Denver meeting of the General Assembly of the UP Church in the USA, Dr. Kelso wrote the same message as that of the 1922 articles, ". . . busy yourselves with evangelizing a lost world. . . ." This observation demonstrates one of the major concentrations of James Kelso's life—the command of Christ to "go into all the world"—his constant stress on world evangelism.

Because of his archaeological treks to the Middle East and because of the strong United Presbyterian missions in Egypt and Pakistan, James Kelso developed a special interest—more accurately, a passionate attachment—for the Arab world. A strong anti-Zionist position coupled with a belief that God has given to the Christian Church the responsibility of being God's People under the New Covenant, in addition to personal experiences of injustices in Palestine, led Kelso to an articulate pro-arab position on the Middle East question. Let me hasten to add that Kelso is always careful to distinguish between anti-Semitism, which he abhors, and anti-Zionism. Zionism, for him, is itself anti-Semitic owing to its political rather than religious base. However, his position is more pro-Christian than it is either anti-Zionist *or* pro-Arab.

His deep concern and that of Mrs. Kelso led them both to offer aid to displaced Palestinian Arab families in 1949. Dr. Kelso worked with the chief United Nations representative in helping Arab refugees while in Jerusalem in 1949-50. Mrs. Kelso personally raised thousands of dollars for the children of Arab refugee families.

All considered, James Kelso's attitude displays what he believes is absolutely necessary to a Middle East solution: a forceful proclamation of the gospel demonstrated by helping the helpless: feeding, clothing, giving shelter, and seeking justice for those wronged.

James Kelso's emphasis on pastoral care is one further mark of the man. His "pastor's heart" was clearly seen in his demanding, but gracious, attitude toward students experiencing difficulty in his courses.

Kelso's desire that pastors of the church pattern their ministries on a biblical understanding is shown by his message titled, "A Pauline Pastorate," from which these representative quotations are taken:

> Read II Corinthians 5:20-6:10 25 times.
> Master its content!
>> I. Think like Paul. Be an ambassador for Christ.
>> That means, be an imitator of Christ as Christ was of God. Christ lives in me. For me to live is Christ. Practice imitating Paul.
>> II. Plan like Paul!
>> Try to work out his strategy and use his tactics. Get into the big cities; get with the people where they are; Stress the relations he stressed: Man to God, man to man in the street, man to man in business, man to man in the homes.
>> III. Work like Paul!
>> Don't concentrate all your work on your tongue! Earn your salary! You need time to study your Book!
>> Earn your church workers' respect.
>> Forgive your church workers.
>> Discipline both yourself and your church workers.
>> IV. Suffer like Paul! (Master 6:4-10)
>> "He that spared not His own Son" demands a willingness not to be spared on the part of his clergy.
>> V. Pray like Paul!
>> VI. Praise like Paul!
>> VII. The Climax of all Paul's Ministry: to present every man perfect in Christ. Paul imitated Christ! Imitate Paul!

A further example of concern for the spiritual development of his seminary students is Kelso's stress on true humility and against false piety. One of his favorite epithets for those suspected of an over-weening pride in their "humility" was the warning, "Be careful you're not an HTT!" Any tendency in his students to be "Holier-than thou" thus challenged could scarcely survive.

Many of James Kelso's articles were written for publication in religious periodicals as well as in the professional journals of his day. He believed that one must take advantage of every media if the message entrusted to the church is to be proclaimed vitally and truthfully. In addition, Dr. Kelso kept in touch with scores of persons through newsletters. He encouraged good clear reporting, insisting that descriptions of Christian activities, especially from the mission fields be candid and well-honed to provide the "folks at home" with a spur for participation in the Church's ministry to the world.

The essays of Part III were selected to emphasize James Kelso's instructive influence in world evangelism (Donald Black's essay, "Into *All* the World"); his penchant for pastoral care (the essays by Bruce Thielemann, "The Comradeship He Commands," and Robert M. Urie, "Christianity and Counseling"); his support of Christian journalism (James A. Gittings' essay, "A Press in Chains"); and finally, his abiding devotion to the broad dissemination of biblical science and the great truths of the Gospels as displayed in "An Annotated Bibliography of Writings of James Leon Kelso" compiled by J. Harry Fisher.

Into All The World

The Call to Mission in the Contemporary World

BY DONALD BLACK

*T*HE MISSIONARY MOVEMENT has had the messenger at its center. Dr. James Kelso's deep commitment to the evangelistic task of the church was well known to those who participated in his classes, and his support of the worldwide missionary task was evident in his interest in the missionaries of the church. This essay will examine the missionary task from the perspective of the part which the missionary has played.

The New Testament gives adequate support to a perspective that begins with the messenger. God's mission becomes incarnate in particular people.

> "So the Word became flesh, he came to dwell among us." "As the Father sent me, so I send you." "You will bear witness for me in Jerusalem, and all over Judea and Samaria, and away to the ends of the earth."

The Acts of the Apostles is a series of events centering on the early messengers—Peter and John, Philip and Stephen, Paul and Barnabas, Paul and Silas. In the epistles Paul gives references to his own missionary experiences and on occasion centers on the missionary task.

> . . . everyone who invokes the name of the Lord will be saved. How could they invoke one in whom they had no faith? And how could they have faith in one they

175

had never heard of? And how hear without someone to
spread the news? And how could anyone spread the news
without a commission to do so? And that is what Scripture
affirms, "How welcome are the feet of the messengers
of good news!" We come, therefore, as Christ's ambassadors.

The history of the church's expansion has similar emphases.
Whether it is Augustine and his monks arriving in Britain or
Carey sailing for India, the missionary outreach of the church
is centered on the messenger.

REVIEWING A PASSING ERA

Most of our images about missionaries grow out of what
we call "the modern foreign mission era," beginning in the
19th century, expanding in its late decades, and growing into
its greatest period during the first quarter of the 20th century.
The basic patterns and assumptions had little change until
the Second World War. Many images and psychological attitudes about missionaries are holdovers from those days, and
a review of what some of the assumptions were will help us
understand which elements have continuing value and which
factors are undergoing change.

Missionary service has been a combination of individual
response and group involvement. The individual response has
been to a call from God heard against the backdrop of some
human need. The group involvement has been a means of
checking the validity of that call, of sharing a fellowship for
spiritual strength, of guidance in fulfilling the call, and of
providing material needs.

INDIVIDUAL RESPONSE

The modern missionary movement has its roots in the pietis-
tic revivals which swept Europe and North America in the

18th and 19th centuries. It has been fed by the knowledge that God through his Holy Spirit lays his hands on individuals, holds before their eyes a vision, sets their hearts aflame to fulfill his great work.

> Whatever strains there may have been in relationships, whatever mistakes there may have been made, whatever wrong headedness, the fact that most of them became missionaries was the result of an inward call and their motive was a genuine desire to serve. . . . there is an inwardness to the missionary call which comes to many unexpectedly and with a compulsiveness they cannot resist.[1]

This call was heard in a theological context. Although there was a broad spectrum of theological emphases, certain basic beliefs dominated those who heard the call. They believed that the triune God is a God of love; that human beings have sinned and rejected that love; that Jesus Christ is the divine Lord and Savior of all people, who must now be called to be his disciples; that the Scriptures are the Word of God, the inspired record of God's revelation; and that the church is the continuing body of Christ to be established in every nation.

The missionary call has an outward direction.

> The Christian missionary is one who is possessed by a divine passion to share the truth of God with the entire world.[2]

Perhaps so in the ideal, but quite often this call has been focused on a particular situation. One of the former Secretaries of the Commission on Ecumenical Mission and Relations, Dr. Glenn Reed, tells how his call to mission service grew out of a seminary prayer group which began intercession for the Anuak tribe in the Sudan. Certainly the modern missionary

movement was a response to God's calling in a concrete historical situation by men who were shaped by their own period
of history. It was a time of exploration and adventure; and
the lure of the unknown, the romance of the exotic, the challenge of difficult tasks were undoubtedly mixed into the motives by which those missionaries made their response.[3] These
were never the dominant drive for those who kept at it, for
only a deep personal commitment to the true goals of the
task could help people endure the frustrations which beset
even the most successful.

The elements common to the historical situation in which
the missionary movement was carried out were:

1) World cultures on the whole were considered to be static.
People lived in world compartments which were not likely
to change. The cultures had been shaped by centuries of
interplay between land, people, and the gods. So westerners
pictured Africa as black and primitive, the Dark Continent;
Asia as yellow and passive, the domain of Buddha, Confucius,
Mohammed; South America, along with southern Europe, was
Latin and Roman Catholic; the rest of Europe and North
America was white and a mixture of Protestant, Catholic, and
Orthodox. This pattern described how things had been, no
marked change was anticipated.

2) The description of cultures listed above emphasizes the
religious aspects. Part of the world view of that day was a
concept of western Christian civilization. The missionary
movement had its geographical dimension; missionaries were
sent from Europe and North America into Asia and Africa
and the Pacific Islands. They were going from the Christian
West to the non-Christian lands. When a "mission field" was
defined within the Christian West it was usually a special
"alien pocket," such as the American Indian or the former
slave population in the southern U.S.A.[4]

This cultural and geographical dimension has led some to
reserve the name "missionary" for those who cross some national or cultural or language barrier for the sake of the Gospel.

The missionary represents one of the gifts which the Spirit manifests in every age and in ever new forms. He is one who is possessed of a divine passion to see the Gospel penetrate into the lives of men to the ends of the world and to see all the world united in Christ. The missionary is one who thus feels the call constantly to go out from his own particular *oikos* to those beyond, and lives in holy discontent and restlessness because of this calling.

As the missionary goes with this intensity of concern, his life is a sign of the cosmic dimension of God's redemptive work and thus of the supra-national character and calling of the church. It is also a sign of the power of God to draw all men unto himself despite divisions and to the fact that the Christian is always a stranger in the world in which he lives.

The one indispensable characteristic of this *gift* is the concern of the missionary to go out from his own local group, class, or nation to those who are beyond.[5]

The new situation makes this view more difficult to defend, yet there is an element of moving into an unfamiliar context for the sake of the Gospel which must not be lost.

3) The world view of a western Christian civilization assumed that western education, western medicine, western agricultural science, etc., were really benefits of the Gospel. When the missionary founded a school or a clinic he was sharing and dispensing the fruit of the Christian way of life. In some cases these institutions were seen as instruments of evangelism, a point of contact where students studied the Bible and attended chapel. From another approach, they were seen as integral to the Christian witness. Mission programs included these means of serving society because they would meet obvious needs—would liberate people from the darkness of illiteracy, the bondage of superstition, the lethargy of malnutrition, the agony of disease.

David Livingstone plunged into East Africa as a British consul at large. In defending his move away from official missionary appointment he wrote:

Legitimate commerce breaks up the isolation engendered by heathenism and the slave trade and surely if we take advantage of the very striking peculiarity of the African character (i.e., their fondness for barter and agriculture) we shall eventually bring this people within the sphere of Christian sympathy and the scope of missionary operations.[6]

4) The resources for such a mission would be found in the affluent West—both the technical expertise to run such educational and social service institutions and the money to support them. Although many such institutions met their operational budgets from fees and government grants, the support of the missionary workers, charity work, and scholarships was often sought from the western supporting churches. The pattern was one which defined mission in terms of economic condescension, from the "haves" to the "have nots." The resources for mission appeared to be in the missionary's control.

These elements from the historical situation of the missionary movement were shared by other parts of the society. Colonial administrators were introducing western education and social processes and often sought the assistance of missions in fulfilling their goals. Commercial interests were seeking people trained in western methods to work in their branches.

Kenneth Cragg has traced some of the problems that developed out of this world view and historical context. He has shown how the parallelism of the modern missionary era and the colonial era provided more tension and less collaboration than is usually pictured, but he also relates how this very parallelism in time added problems for the missionary. The imperialism of the West was a fact, and the missionary could not escape it. Neither could he escape the fact that westerners were almost all white, and consequently, his religion became the "white man's" religion, his Lord the "white man's" God. His civilization and his desire to share its benefits required

ERRATA

For Me To Live

Page 22, line 2: *For* nᵉhōšeth *read* hᵉhōšeth
Page 39, note 10, line 2: *For* 'iš *read* 'îš
Page 45, line 3: *For* malkₑkehem *read* malkᵉkhem
Page 45, line 24: *For* 'shtwrt *read* 'shtwrt
Page 72, line 1: *For* γονη *read* γυνη
Page 72, note 16: *For* ΚΣφαλη *read* κεφαλή
Page 243, line 11: *For Biltiotheca Sacra read Bibliotheca Sacra*
Page 267, line 22: *Read* ἐχουσία

institutions, organizations for decision making—all established on western lines.[7]

Arend Th. van Leeuwen has accepted this world view and claims it is God's strategy in history. The Judeo-Christian view of man in the western world has given rise to a truly secular view of life that dispels the false views of the world inherent in other religious approaches. Thus in the colonial era, the activity of missionary, administrator, and merchant all establishing elements of the western Christian way of life was thought to be God's way of destroying all false religions (including the religious views Christians have attached to the Gospel!) and preparing the way for men to build a new humanity.[8]

GROUP INVOLVEMENT

These images of a missionary's call and labor viewed in a particular historical context apply to the group response as well. The group was often participating when the call was discerned. The first missionary journey of Paul and Barnabas was the result of a call heard when five prophets and teachers were observing a fast. After testing their discernment through further fasting and prayer, a commissioning service was held and the early mission movement was launched.[9] John Mark was not mentioned in this group; he both appears and disappears later. His failure to pass this "on the job screening" not only brought him Paul's negative vote for the second journey—it broke up the team! Shades of things to come!

The group involvement in the call is a common experience. The first movement for mission in the U.S.A. was the result of a now famous "haystack prayer meeting" that led to the founding of the American Board of Commissioners for Foreign Missions. An extreme case would be that of Andrew Gordon, first missionary to the Punjab, India, from the Associate Presbyterian Church. He was elected by the Synod to be its first missionary, although he had not volunteered and was not even a commissioner to the meeting. But when word reached him of the Synod action, he gave it prayerful consideration and accepted it as God's call.[10]

This interplay between the group and the individual has been an important part of the entire movement. Very early the missionaries in the field began to suggest the type of person needed—sensitive, flexible, persevering, committed.[11] And as one generation's vision became the next generation's institutional burden, requests sought professional competence—teachers, doctors, printers, evangelists. The group (by now a Mission Board) had the task of checking the validity of the call when volunteers applied or actually recruiting people to fill request lists. At times the process has appeared to limit the call to the group process—the priority for selecting is for those who fit the requests. The initiative has shifted to the field. To combat this danger, most mission agencies try to keep some money available for the committed and talented person who does not fit the pattern but who feels he has a call to serve.

Until the end of World War II the missionary was the local congregation's window on the world. Henry Venn, early leader of the Church Missionary Society, urged his missionaries to keep writing reports and letters for the sake of the church's understanding of how the gospel was affecting other parts of the world.[12] With America's military and economic involvement, with the affluence of American society and the ease of travel, with television media, this window on the world is no longer exclusive. But the missionary can still provide a special perspective on the world, for his contact with the other society and his approach to its culture is different from that of the tourist, the military, and the commercial traveler.

From New Testament days to the present there is the concern for intercessory prayer, more effective when more informed. Paul shared his problems with the Corinthians in order that they would continue to pray for him.[13] He closes his letter to the Ephesians with a request for prayer that he will speak the right things in a bold spirit. And the fellowship of prayer that the missionary movement has developed has been a constant source of strength to the life of the church.

In a sense the missionary has been an anchor for the supporting group in a changing world. The churches in the West can not fully enter into the experience of living in another culture. They can not fully understand the pressures on the congregation in a Pakistani village or the financial security problems of a teacher in India. They can not know the complexities of life in an Islamic culture, but they do know "our missionary" in Beirut.

> He has a theology that is sound, he knows how we think,
> he will represent us, for we sent him.

The relationship is one of security.

One of the difficult problems confronting the churches in the West is their poor preparation to understand some of the angry voices from Asia, Africa, and Latin America. Indeed, they have not been prepared to hear similar voices from those parts of our own society—blacks, Hispanic Americans, Indians, Asians—who feel they are one with the world's dispossessed. Yet, the involvement these churches have had with churches in the "third world" should have prepared them.

But what sort of involvement? In many cases they have been involved with their own messengers; they have identified with those who come from their own society, who are like them, and with whom they can identify without any cross cultural experience.

We are caught here with a tension. The burden of this essay is that mission is incarnate in people. We have looked at the situation from the perspective of the missionary and the group who offer support. What of the future from this perspective?

MISSION ON SIX CONTINENTS

The phrase which describes the perspective for mission today is "mission on six continents." It was coined as a challenge for those who had thought of mission in terms of a movement from the Christian West into other areas of the world to begin to comprehend mission as a movement from all parts of the worldwide fellowship of Christian believers to the places in society where a witness for Jesus Christ can make an effective contribution to the mission of the church.

Within this context the missionary activity takes on some new aspects.

There will still be a place for the messenger, and the response to God's call will still be a combination of individual response and group involvement. The definition of missionary quoted from *An Advisory Study* is still valid (above p. 179).

The authors continue:

> If the definition given above of this special missionary vocation is correct, no single factor is more important for the future of the Christian world mission than the development of adequate forms for the expression of this vocation in the life of every Christian church. In a church which is alive and growing, and discovering how to relate itself creatively to the world around it, the missionary intention will express itself in patterns which are constantly being renewed by the Holy Spirit so that they may be most effective expressions of this *charisma*.[14]

God has brought into being at this point in history a worldwide fellowship of Christians. This fact has gained general acceptance over the past two decades, and the churches now see themselves as one church among many churches in all nations. The churches in the West are prepared to join hands with the churches in Asia, Africa, and Latin America to fulfill God's call to mission in those areas. And this view repeats the pattern of the past—it is still a movement from the West to the former mission areas. The response to God's call must become the western churches' acceptance of Christians from former mission areas as peers in the task of mission in the West. Experience in recent years shows that the sophisticated society of the West has great difficulty in accepting such an approach to mission.

The problem is more than one of humility. Westerners have for so long operated mission on the assumptions of an affluent technical society that has the answers other people need (the "haves" to the "have nots") that they can scarcely discover any points in their society where fresh insights from another culture might make a contribution.

When westerners are freed from the world view that cultures are basically static and accept the dynamic view of a world in cultural and social movement, when they are freed from the concept of mission moving out of the West, they are then given a vision of messengers flowing from every part of the Body of Christ to those places where each can make his best contribution.

The world view from this latter perspective has no society which can claim to be Christian. All societies will have a cultural base with certain religious presuppositions, but the social upheavals of our day are making these less significant. And the movement of people across national lines are providing new elements in every society.

The messenger is one called by God to pick up a particular challenge and confront society with the meaning of the Gospel. He may or may not leave his nation, but in any case he will carry out this task with the understanding that others in another segment of the world and the worldwide community of Christians are involved. There will be times when the locus of the task will shift, but the issue will still be the same.

For years concerned whites worked at serving the black community in America. They were often at odds with the white community, and in a sense, had made a cultural leap.

When the civil rights movement began many whites flocked to help. Then the Black Power movement and the search for a black identity revealed that many of these efforts by whites were a block to this search. Whites that wanted to be involved in the race issue were told to pick up the battle in the white community. But they are still called to deal with the race issue, and the lines of communication must be kept open, so that each group is working toward the same set of goals.

The same cry is being made in the international scene. People who work in Latin America are told that the real battle is to change the attitudes and practices of the U.S. Government and business community, for it is their policies which keep South America from basic change. The North American that feels the call to Latin America may work in each society for a period of time. Personnel support practices are being revised to make such flexible service possible.

We have been describing a more flexible pattern of service—one individual moving between cultures. A certain amount of concentration will still be required, for within this framework there is still need for one who digs deeply into the cultural patterns, the language, and the issues of a specific nation to make himself knowledgeable and acceptable.

One of the contributions those who cross national and cultural lines can make is assistance in discerning the issues for mission. The church in any land is tempted to seek security, to identify with the society, to shun any issue which will lead to persecution or restriction. The call to mission may be to address certain issues, and any church will avoid an invitation to conflict. The call to mission may well come to some small group who are a threat to the established order both within and without the church. How other churches can relate to such groups that are not "in" with the ecclesiastical structures becomes a point of tension. But the churches cannot act as though they are limited to the institutional ecclesiastical structures for meeting a specific need. A true test of church response will be the ability to open the structures to groups who catch a vision and begin to deal with a specific need.

One of the problems in our time is that though the true resources of mission are not limited to the affluent West, western financial support is needed for this flow of messengers among the worldwide fellowship of the church. The ecumenical movement is developing channels to move such people.[15] The United Presbyterians may not be able to identify the person in Asia or Africa their money supports, but they will also have someone from the worldwide fellowship of Christians living and working among them.

There will be a new definition of the issues to be addressed as the church responds to people's needs. Where a former generation responded with schools, clinics, hospitals—a present generation may deal with community action, land reform, legal aid for the poor, self-development programs for a minority. Where the church sees these approaches to help people find their place in society, their dignity before God and man, they become important ministries for mission.

Finding support groups within the situation will be a continuing problem. The foreign mission movement had highly organized "missions" in each country for each mission group. It was composed of the missionaries and provided a psychological base as well as an administrative structure. Over the past two decades these "missions" have been disbanded, and the missionary's support group where he works is no longer a fellowship of his own cultural compatriots; he is in the arms of the church. The church as a structure cannot always provide what is needed, and adequate substitutes have not been found. For those from other nations in the U.S.A. churches are proposing a similar fellowship, an "international caucus" to give a stronger voice and a place for common thinking and discussion.

One theological perspective for mission on six continents is that God was in Christ reconciling the world unto Himself. The ambassadors of reconciliation come from every part of this world; they share the experience they have had in Christ, the gifts God has given their church, the knowledge they have gained through living in God's world, and the insights they have about the meaning of the Gospel of reconciliation. The churches that have lived under political restrictions can share what it is to be powerless in a society; those that have faced rapid industrialization can share the impact of this change on worship and nurture. Those that have come from affluence can show how this creates condescension; those that live with poverty, how it creates tension.

And each can share his belief about Jesus Christ, for a new rich experience awaits the church when she deals seriously with her mission on six continents and feels the drive of mission into *all* the world.

NOTES

The quotations are from the New English Bible: John 1:14; John 20:21; Matthew 28:19; Acts 1:8; Romans 10:13-15.

1. Douglas Webster, *Yes to Mission* (London: S.C.M. Press, 1966), p. 27.
2. T. Romig and A. Crouch, *The Missionary* (N.Y.: World Horizons, 1965), p. 1.
3. H. Richard Niebuhr, "An Attempt at a Theological Analysis of Missionary Motivation," *Occasional Bulletin,* Missionary Research Library, 14, No. 1 (January, 1963). The reader can make his own interpretation of such mixed motives. Missionaries may appear less pious because they did share the element of adventure so common to the day, or God may appear more practical because he used such common clay!
4. In some cases missionaries were sent to work among Roman Catholics, but usually by groups who considered that church apostate. South America was not considered a "mission field" for years since the Roman Catholic church claimed 95% of the population. It is only since 1950 that the Catholic Church itself has recognized the fallacy of that position. Most Protestant missions and churches in South America have strong anti-Catholicism in their attitudes, mostly a reaction to their pre-Va-

tican II experiences. Post Vatican II experience has been one
of adjusting to new openness and new relationships on both sides
with much progress still to be made.

5. *An Advisory Study*, Commission on Ecumenical Mission and
Relations of the United Presbyterian Church in the U.S.A., New
York, p. 48.

6. Quoted by George Seaver, *David Livingstone: His Life and
Letters* (N.Y.: Harper, 1957), p. 299.

7. Kenneth C. Cragg, *Christianity in World Perspective* (N.Y.: Oxford, 1968), pp. 19-30.

8. Arend Th. van Leeuwen, *Christianity in World History* (Edinburgh: Edinburgh House Press, 1964).

9. Acts 13:1-3.

10. An interesting account of the problems of this approach is related
in Andrew Gordon, *Our India Mission* (Philadelphia, 1886). At
least twelve "volunteers" were sought by this process of listing
names before Andrew Gordon agreed to go.

11. The famous Edinburgh Missionary Conference in 1910 listed
these characteristics: Docility, Gentleness, Sympathy. See G. M.
Seteloane, "The Missionary and his Task," *International Review
of Missions* (January 1970).

12. Max Warren, *To Apply the Gospel* (Grand Rapids: Eerdmans,
1970), p. 98.

13. II Corinthians 1:8-11; Ephesians 6:19-20.

14. *An Advisory Study*, p. 75.

15. A special Committee on Ecumenical Sharing of Personnel has
been organized within the World Council of Churches. It plans
to work on the philosophy that the missionary force in any area
should be international, interracial, and interconfessional.

The Comradeship He Commands:

Comments On Inter-personal Relationships and The Clergy

By Bruce W. Thielemann

> Truly, shepherd, in respect of itself, it is a good life; but
> in respect that it is a shepherd's life, it is naught. In
> respect that it is solitary, I like it very well; but in respect
> that it is private, it is a very vile life. Now in respect
> that it is in the fields, it pleaseth me well; but in respect
> it is not in the court, it is tedious. As it is a spare life,
> look you, it fits my humour well; but as there is no more
> plenty in it, it goes much against my stomach.
>
> Elizabethan Song

PROFESSIONAL LONELINESS

THE FOLLOWING is the product of eleven years of professional
loneliness and two years of professional comradeship. It is an
attempt to document certain ideas with regard to the necessity
of strong bonds of kinship and love among ordained clergy.
I have no doubt that all that I write here is equally or almost
equally applicable to Christian men and women in every walk
of life. However, I make no claims in other directions, for
my own experience has been that of a clergyman and I want,
insofar as it is possible, to make these words not only the
study of a theme, the presentation and support of a thesis,
but also the record of my own professional relationship hegira.

In his letter to the Christians who lived in Galatia, Paul

issues these instructions: "Bear one another's burdens, and so fulfill the law of Christ." [1] The sense of Paul's line is obvious to even the most unsophisticated Christian. We are under obligation as disciples to demonstrate love to one another. Supportive words of Scripture spring readily to mind:

> You shall love . . . your God . . . ; and your neighbor as yourself.[2]
> .-./ as you did it to one of the least of these my brethren, you did it to me.[3]
> For this is the message which you have heard from the beginning, that we should love one another. . . .[4]

Paul is here calling us to the recognition of not a new legalism, his principle reason for writing the Galatians is to eliminate legalisms from faith, but to call our attention to a life principle which is to be always evident in the family of faith. Even as Christ took the cross of mankind and made it His own, so we are to take up the hurts of other hearts, the sufferings of Christians and non-Christians, and make them our own. Discipleship means nothing less than this.

Discipleship, however, does mean considerably more than this. Although the call to burden bearing is quite explicit in this word of Paul's, there is another implicit dimension to these words which is less often noted. In order to bear another's burden you must first be aware of it, that is, before bearing must come sharing. Prior to any conscious assistance rendered to another there must be an equally conscious recognition of need. On the face of it, this is far from a profound revelation. But, I submit it is one we have quite forgotten. To bear for someone you must first know what needs to be borne; and this means, quite obviously, that if you would have your burdens borne by others of the household of faith you must be willing to share, to tell about, to reveal, the weight that presses you. It took me eleven years to begin to recognize the truth of this.

We often think of Paul as a great burden bearer. Almost everyone of his epistles carries expressions of concern, words of wise and prudent counsel, pledges of prayer support and the like.[5] We do not so often notice that Paul was an equally great burden sharer, never hesitating to express his needs to others that he might know the support of their love, prayers, and deeds. In his letters to Rome and to Colossae and in his letters to the Corinthians and Thessalonians he specifically requests their prayers.[6] He pleads for hearts to be open to what he is called upon to endure.[7] He reveals the pain of the "thorn" which is his [8], he asks for barriers to be broken down [9], he urges Timothy to hurry to his side [10]. Paul never hesitates to give to his brothers and sisters in Christ the gift of his own need, his own weakness, his own vulnerability.

Surely one of the most obvious evidences of the sin of the world is the fact that most men determine to conceal rather than to reveal themselves.

> . . . self-concealment is regarded as the most natural state for grown men. People who reveal themselves in simple honesty are seen as childish or crazy as was Billy Budd, in Melville's novel, or Prince Mishkin in Dostoyevsky's *The Idiot*. The assumption that concealment is a more natural state for man than candor has given rise to many stratagems for getting inside a man's defenses. These run the gamut from attempting to get a man drunk, to asking him to report his dreams or to tell what he sees in some inkblots.[11]

Should such stratagems be necessary in the Christian community? It seems to me that Paul demonstrates, assumes, and teaches exactly the contrary. He expects not an effort to conceal ourselves from each other but, rather, a consistent effort to reveal ourselves for our mutual upbuilding in ministry. The necessary pre-requisite for self-disclosure is, of course, love; and this is precisely the attitude which is to be of the essence of Christian fellowship. When love is in one's heart for another one should not only be striving to know the other but also to display love by letting the other know oneself. In other words, one of the most obvious ways in which to make your love real to a fellow believer is to let that fellow believer into your life that he or she might begin to love you. I shall go so far as to say that it is this openness to bearing for another and sharing with one another, this trusting self-disclosure with concomitant gentle service, which most clearly distinguishes the Christian community from the world. "By this," Christ said, "all men will know that you are my disciples, that you love .one another." [12] This love is more than picking someone else up, it is also permitting oneself to be hugged and lifted also.

Do not mistake my meaning. I am not at this point arguing that we are to be ceaselessly engaged in calling ourselves guilty sinners, in belching up and out our confessions and self-recriminations. Such conversations can be a substitute for really honest self-examination and revelation.[13] I am saying only that to give oneself to others without permitting others to give themselves to you, to affirm other's needs but to deny your own needs and/or to deny to others the right to affirm you in your needs, is a denial of yourself, of others and of God. Basic to my thinking is the proposition, which we shall be noting shortly, that we become and remain our true selves only in the act of relationship and, therefore, when we reject, conceal, hide, ourselves from others we are rejecting not only them but also ourselves. We so refuse ourselves that we have virtually committed suicide. Beyond that, by denying our authentic needs, selves, we reject our neighbor also. We give him only bits and pieces, not the whole self. I would even go so far as to suggest that inasmuch as we understand ourselves to be made in the image of God, the denial of ourselves to ourselves by denying ourselves to others—this deliberate insistence on seeing less of us than we really are—is clearly a refusal to see and know as much of God as we can see and know of Him.

Writing as a Christian to other Christians it is legitimate for me to assume that we are agreed that we gain more in giving than in receiving. This basic principle applies to personal relationships as well as to the benevolent budget of the local congregation, and such giving includes not only the offering of one's abundance but also of one's poverty. This, it seems to me, is of the essence of Christian community. Such being the case, it behooves the leaders of the faithful to demonstrate this bearing and sharing relationship. The clergyman should be the example of openness to his people, but most of us are not. Because we are not, we do damage to ourselves, to our people and to our faith.

As I have analyzed my own experience and allowed others to do so as well, I have discovered at least some of those things in me and in my work which have led me to try to go it alone at the very time when I am trying to see to it that others do not have to go it alone. The foremost of these would be confusion between myself and my role. My role is essential to my life. It is basic to my total experience and brings me both joy and sadness—but my role is not me. A role is a gathering of behavior patterns which must be produced in certain appropriate contexts while at the same time all behavior irrelevant to the role must be concealed. What I have been learning to remember is that it takes a person to play a role. The person is not the role, and indeed, the role may in no way provide all the opportunities for self-expression that the person needs and desires. This is crucial. I become more and more convinced that most people so identify with their roles that they lose themselves or become, and this is especially tragic, fearful and anxious about themselves. This separation or alienation from the self is at the root of the "neurotic personality of our time" as described by Karen Horney.[14] Test the sad reality of this state of affairs by asking a person who he or she is. Almost without exception the response will be the identification of a role! Query: "Who are you, Bruce?" Response: "I am a minister." The reply is a denial of self. It may answer the question "what" but not "who". Jourard comments:

> There is a Faustian drama all about us in this world of role playing. Everywhere we see people who have sold their souls (or their real selves) for roles: psychologist, businessman, nurse, physician, this or that.[15]

For me the "this or that" is "minister," and I am bold enough to believe that I am not the only minister in the Church who regularly tells others not who he is but what he is. We develop a series of interpersonal behavior patterns that leave us feeling good for the moment but over the long stretch deprive us of our very being, separate us from the fellowship of belief, and force us to lonely Calvaries where not even a mother, a young disciple, or a dying sufferer like ourselves is present to watch, to cry, to plead, or to care. This kind of rigid role adherence has been called "character armor" by Wilhelm Reich.[16] The designation is well chosen. It is worn to protect us from anxiety producing self-confrontations and from equally threatening revelations of the self to others.

Let me be more specific by illustrating how this mechanism is developed by ourselves and encouraged by our congregations. Take the question of authority. Most of us have ambivalent feelings about authority. When we feel "put down" by authority we resent the one in authority and may even attack the position of privilege. When we feel "supported" by authority we draw closer to it in a desire to share its status. We seek some special, preferential attachment. What clergyman has not been called to the proper exercise of the authority of his role and been resented and attacked for it while at the same time resenting and attacking himself for it? Yet the one thing we will not do is to confess to our attackers that we are just as unhappy about the situation as they are and ask them for their understanding and compassion. When so attacked we buckle on the "armor" instead of taking it off and showing our soft insides—bleeding. On the other hand, how often do we say to the congregational "preacher-praisers" that we don't want to be loved as a preacher but as a person. I'll never forget the older lady who told me how much she loved me (I felt great) and then went on to say she loved all preachers (I felt terrible). My disappointment was obviously rooted in the fact that I needed personal affirmation from her, not some kind of reverence for "reverends". But I didn't say this to her lest she be offended or not understand. I just walked away wounded. In both of these instances, you see, the role was played at the expense of the self, bearing but no sharing.

Closely related to the above but of even greater consequence is the pastor's role as leader in the faith. The leader in any organization or group confronts authority problems, but the leader of a congregation, the pastor, also exercises a leadership in faith which sets his direction and example on a different level from that of other leaders. Most ministers who are open enough with me for me to really know are more troubled about this dimension of their leadership than with any other. We, I stand with them, are deeply disturbed by the difference between the faith we have and the faith we think our leadership requires us to have. Have you ever had the experience of being asked, "Are you a Christian?" You respond (note the role inserting itself again), "I am a Presbyterian minister." Then you are greeted with this reply, "That is not what I asked you. Are you a Christian?". Most clergy I know would resent that second question; and they would resent it not because it is unfair, which it isn't, and not because it is brutally direct, which it is, but because it pierces role-armor and forces a man to reveal a little of his inner agony over his believing and unbelieving. How often, when we look within ourselves, do we discover the very same questions we so easily answer from the pulpit or lectern? Further, if we are able to get far enough to ask this honest question, How much of what we do is for our own glory, and how much of it is for God's? When your faith is also your profession, it is hard to know how much of your faith is yours apart from your work, and how much of it is yours because of your work. The problem intensifies when one recognizes that the pastor's leadership in faith requires him to be constantly giving demonstrations of it. He must regularly be stepping out where angels won't go on tiptoe. He does this in the pulpit, with Church boards, at the side of the sick and at the grave. He must always radiate "the sure and certain" hope and, at the same time, come to terms with the shadowy doubts he labors so diligently to hide. To the people he leads, "Lord, I will never forsake Thee"; in his own heart as he goes down under the waves, "Lord, save me." [17] Again, the problem is one of confusing the self with the role, struggling to live up to the image. We want to be what we are expected to be, and this leads to controlled behavior. Such conduct is predicated on the assumption that the outer implies the inner. We know that isn't always true. We know our outer certainty may be our attempt to quiet inner doubt. This is sad. It is sad because once again we are denying our real selves and because doubt is never dispelled by untruth but only by utter honesty. We encourage and even demand this honesty in our people but often do not require it of ourselves. We are ready to bear the pain of another's doubt but unwilling to share the pain of our own.

We are unwilling to share the pain of our doubts even with those in our same role, our brother clergymen! Consider the following excerpt from William E. Hulme's book, *Your Pastor's Problems:*

> The most likely father confessors are fellow pastors. Here, however, the minister runs into the problem that these men are often his peers, even in age, and also at times his competitors. These are men in the same vocation, working in the same community, and often involved in the same problems. Men are reluctant to admit that they need help and even more reluctant to ask for it. The same sense of failure that other men experience when they ask for his help, the minister himself experiences when he seeks help for himself or his family. . . . The minister partakes of the masculine defensiveness of our culture. Let's face it—big boys don't cry.[18]

It would appear that Hulme assumes the principal reason for lack of deep interpersonal relationships between clergy to be the fact that most clergy are men, and men don't like to admit their inadequacies. To a certain degree this is probably true. Any fair appraisal of our culture indicates that it is considered unseemly for men to demonstrate emotion or failure anywhere except at a football game or after missing a putt on the 18th! This societal attitude is dead wrong, of course, and also deadly. The failure quotient of men is just as high as for women, and a man is no less an emotional creature than a woman.[19] Research has shown that men are less open than women.[20] This means men have more secrets than women. Keeping more secrets increases inner tension, anxiety, fear and stress. The result is more rapid physical and emotional breakdown.

> The experience of psychosomatic physicians who undertake psychotherapy with male patients suffering from peptic ulcers, essential hypertension, and kindred disorders seems to support this contention.[21]

The fact that men are less open to others and also less open to receive from others cannot help but be a factor in the inadequate relationships which exist between clergy.

But there are at least two other dimensions of this sad

situation which must also be noted. The first of these is a sense of professional inferiority. The clergyman today is bombarded on every side with that which tends to emphasize the unimportance of his role and, worse, his inadequacy in it. This is the day when science has become a faith and when those not "producing" in statistical and material terms are belittled. There was a time when the parson was the "person" in town, the best educated, most articulate, and consequently, most admired. That day is gone. Today the average clergyman has persons in his congregation who are more learned, more travelled, and just as articulate as he is. Moreover, these persons are engaged in work which society calls "worthwhile" in distinction from the man who keeps the old folks happy and tells stories on Sunday mornings.

At the same time that the culture refuses to take him very seriously, other factors conspire to accentuate his sense of inadequacy. His businessmen let him know that as a financier he is an ignoramus. His record of failures in counseling others convinces him that he was never taught adequate psychological counseling techniques. His inability to match the eloquence of the nationally known preacher on radio and television (whose only task it is to prepare his weekly broadcast or telecast) underscores his conviction that he is a dismal preacher. Simultaneously, there arrive on his desk stacks of instructions, directions and exhortations from his denominational headquarters telling him what he is not doing and what he ought to stop doing. Bearing in mind that the minister is generally a sensitive person anyway, a person given to self-deprecation and especially aware of his divinely given responsibilities, it does not take much of this to make him feel very inferior.

Now, add to this a measure of professional jealousy. It is altogether regrettable, but there is in the ministry the same desire to come out on top that there is in every line of work. What is more, there is the same tendency to believe that those who get to the top or closer to the top than we do have had certain "breaks" or streaks of "good luck" which have given to them the success we rightfully deserve. Daniel D. Walker has correctly noted that the ranks of the clergy, like the ranks of every other profession, are full of disgruntled men who feel their true worth has been unrecognized and who are, consequently, especially loath to admit any personal weakness or need to another clergyman.[23] Bitterness is the poorest of all soils for nurturing the growth of meaningful inter-relationship. Indeed, bitterness almost inevitably works to the detriment of the one caught up in it. It causes a bad situation to become worse, so that the clergyman passed over by "success" for one reason or another, just or unjust, by his anger, frustration, hostility, and wounded pride, becomes progressively less likely to know the "victory" he longs for. Thus, locked into the cell of his own self-pity and feeding upon the bile of his own cynicism, he turns more and more away from the counsel of others, especially his clergy brothers, and ends more lonely, isolated and negative than he was before. It is a sad story, but no man in the ministry for long has failed to experience it in observing the life of one clergy comrade or another, or more tragically, in his own. A particularly subtle manifestation of it may be seen in this all too common circumstance—a member of a congregation seeks counsel from a minister of another congregation and then in openness tells his own pastor about it. All too often the pastor looks upon the episode as a rejection of his leadership and of himself as a person. Instead of being grateful that he and a brother minister can together render intraprofessional assistance to the troubled person, too many men will see the seeking of outside counsel as a judgment upon themselves. They accuse themselves of one inadequacy or another, or they attack the "success" of the clergyman consulted either by direct comment or inner bitterness, and in either case, the result is the same. No authentic communication, inter-relationship, sharing, with either the parishioner or the other minister occurs. It gives me no pleasure to record this all too common circumstance, but candor demands it of me, and if it has no other virtue, it is, at least, the truth.

Put it all together and the picture is discouraging. Unable or unwilling to separate himself from his role, the average clergyman suffers intense inner dis-ease. Because of some or all of the following reasons he shares little with his people and less with his clergy brothers:

1. his constant questioning of the legitimacy of his leadership and especially of his spiritual guidance and adequacy;
2. his being locked into a male-dominated profession which, limited by its masculinity, tends to reveal less to and to hear less from others;
3. a sense of inferiority given him by society and his own hyper-sensitive appraisal of his own work;
4. a sad delusion which leads him to believe that he is the only preacher with such problems.

To his catalogue of sins and failures, real or imagined, he adds one more which is very, very real and very, very costly. He tries to go it alone. He does not share, and as I have already pointed out, by not opening himself, he denies himself, the fellowship of the faithful and the very God in whose image he is fashioned and in whose service he is supposed to find his peace. He does not share and, consequently, must bear his burdens alone.

And to be alone is hard on a man. There is, perhaps, no experience a man can know that is as deforming or destructive to the self as loneliness. We begin our earthly pilgrimage in closest relationship to our mothers, whom we see as virtually an extension of ourselves. This primitive we-group is understood by the infant to be the nature of things, and it pleases him so long as the mother responds to his demands. But now, and please forgive the brevity of these reflections, the experience of separation occurs. For some reason and for some time mother is apart from the child or unresponsive to it, and the child is aware of it. This separation brings with it an intense experience of loneliness, of isolation. The intensity is removed with the return of the mother, but the infant is never the same again. Fear and distrust are known for the first time. They have rudely intruded into the growth process. The perfect trust of the we-group is gone forever, and for most persons it never returns. To this point in his life the child has been a pragmatist; that which works for him is good and that which furstrates him is not good. But now, with the first doubting of the unalterable dependability of the we-group, the child begins to move from his original pragmatic life to the kind of living which will gain for him the cooperation of others. Pragmatism has been exchanged for hedonistic utilitarianism. The Golden Rule becomes the norm, do good and good will be done to you, or in language more appropriate to the age, be good and good will be done to you. Again the self is focusing on itself; it is furthering its own interests and is blithely assuming that to get along in this world all you need do is cooperate. Then comes the blow that hurts most; it is suddenly and very painfully discovered that those with whom we cooperate do not always reciprocate. It only has to happen once and the lesson is forever learned—some people will use our cooperation only to take advantage of us. With the recognition of this all previous conclusions pass away, and a basic distrust of others takes its place. Other people have let us down and are, therefore, not to be trusted. It becomes progressively more difficult to demonstrate the naïve confidence which was previously ours. We become alienated and, inevitably, lonely. We find it harder and harder to share because basic to sharing is trust, and trust is gone for us. Our playing the game by the rules has shockingly led to our being turned into fools, and we do not want to make this mistake again. We will no longer give ourselves away to benefit ourselves or others. We will live our own lives, and so donning our "character armor" we prepare for battle—and loneliness is a battle, a battle which at the least wounds and at its worst kills.

THE JOURNEY TO OTHERS

The journey away from loneliness is the journey to others. It is the pathway to the kind of bearing and sharing relationship with others that Paul describes as the life principle of Christ. I have now taken a step or two along this path and am ready to testify to its beautiful reality. A personal illustration might be in order at this point. I was overcome with a deep loneliness and need to share and also somehow sensitive to a similar need on the part of a brother clergyman in a neighboring city. I called and asked for a luncheon appointment. He tried to put me off, offering a series of unimpressive excuses. I persisted because my own isolation was disturbing me. I needed a bridge to somebody else's island. He proposed a date a week off. I pressed for that very day, and finally he relented. Three hours later we met for lunch, and I felt obligated to explain my need and to thank him for his willingness to share it. He looked at me without a word for at least two minutes as if coming to a decision and then shared the fact that the night before he had learned for the first time of his son's heroin addiction. His world had fallen in, and when I had called he was bearing the burden of this crushing revelation alone. He had put off, resisted, my luncheon request, thinking it better to bear his burden by himself, afraid to share it, and only my persistence had saved the day, or better, only the aggressive expression of my need, of my vulnerability, had encouraged him to share his. A beautiful relationship has begun and continues to deepen and to mean more and more.

Three cardinal principles of Christian comradeship are clearly evidenced in this single experience. First, we notice what I have spent many paragraphs above trying to establish—the tendency we have as human beings to try to go it alone and, more specifically, as clergymen to avoid revealing our weaknesses, failures and defeats to one another.[24] Had I met this man upon the street I would have greeted him, and he would have greeted me. I would have asked how "things were going," and he would have replied "great! and with you?"; I would have answered "never better," and like two lonely, lonely ships we would have passed in the night of our own needs!

Second, notice that his ability to share with me was directly dependent upon, or better, excited by, my ability to share with him. There appears to be a law of reciprocity in self-disclosure. There is a definite connection between one's willingness to be vulnerable and the degree of vulnerability offered to one by another. Warm, open, people warm and open other people. Jourard calls this connection or principle the "dyadic effect".[25] We observe it in almost all of our social relationships and single it out here only because it is the determining dimension in the kind of sharing and bearing we so much need. Before anyone will lean on you, you must be willing to do some leaning. I use the word "lean" quite deliberately. Dr. Paul Tournier in his *A Place for You* devotes an entire chapter to the idea of leaning. He calls the chapter, "The Need for Support," and after establishing the fact that we are all entangled in unimaginably intricate webs of inter-relationship and inter-dependence, he goes on to argue in later chapters for an ever greater openness on the part of the Christian toward God and toward other Christians.[26]

Third, the first act of sharing entered into by my clergy brother and myself was but the prelude to a friendship which is now more strengthening than I have words to describe. Suffice it to say that when we see one another, as we do quite regularly now, we come toward each other with a little run and leap at each other's extended right hand! I have more and more of these relationships, and they mean more and more to me.

Dr. William Glasser has pointed out in his influential book, *Reality Therapy,* the manner in which individuals fulfill their basic needs. He writes:

> . . . we must be involved with other people, one at the very minimum, but hopefully many more than one. At all times in our lives we must have at least one person who cares about us and whom we can care for ourselves. . . . One characteristic is essential in the other person: he must be in touch with reality himself and able to fulfill his own needs within the world. A man marooned on a desert isle or confined in a solitary cell may be able to fulfill his needs enough to survive if he knows that someone he cares for cares about him and his condition.[27]

I would amplify this truth as follows: knowing and sharing with persons who are in touch with reality enough to know us and share with us is splendidly supportive. You can endure almost anything if you are in a bearing and caring relationship with one or more persons who understand that part of being in touch with reality. The secret of meeting one's needs is to learn how to be open with and trustfully dependent upon others who will in turn become progressively more open and dependent upon you. We clergymen will be a lot happier when we learn this.

Two other aspects of ministry are immensely strengthened by entering into the comradeship Christ commands. Such a comradeship has an immediate and significant effect upon one's preaching. On a certain occasion T. Dewitt Talmadge, the great evangelist in the southland, preached in his own pulpit on a Sunday morning and in another pulpit the same evening. He used the same message on both occasions. In the morning the sermon was of tremendous effect, but in the evening it was of little or no effect. A friend who had heard both preachments and who observed that the presentation was almost identical on both occasions asked Talmadge why the results were so different. Talmadge responded with a sentence no preacher or congregation should ever forget, "Poor preaching is God's curse on a prayerless congregation". We all know that other factors can lead to poor preaching but if every other important factor is present and the prayer support of the people is missing the preaching will still be of little effect. The converse is true. A very ordinary preacher can become a man of great pulpit power if his people will pray for him and his needs. But how are they to know of his needs if he does not share them? How are their prayers to have the specificity Scripture enjoins if he hides himself behind his role and never reveals the cracks in his feet of clay? Or, to put the point in the terms used above, how can there be the openness on the part of the congregation, the willingness to admit needs and to hear God's word spoken to them, which effective preaching requires if the preacher himself has not demonstrated the same openness with the congregation which he expects of them? There is a very definite "dyadic effect" between a preacher and his people in preaching as well as personal relationships.

Communication is sometimes described as empathy or resonance. It occurs in much the same way a set of unstopped piano strings will reverberate or respond to the same tone to which any one of the strings is pitched. You can sing to such a piano and it will sing back to you. Preaching should be like this! The note the preacher sounds should be echoed, picked up, responded to, by the congregation, but this will never happen if the preacher's note is muffled, cracked, distorted by his efforts to conceal his own personal triumphs and tragedies. It will never happen if the congregation, the strings, are stopped, not open to the openness of the preacher. The one begets the other, and as preachers, the act of sharing vulnerability must begin with us. I was taught to shun the personal illustration. I was taught error! Let yourself and other people walk through your messages; your people will discover your humanity. They will respond to your openness with their own and will pray for your needs in the pulpit and elsewhere.

206

There is, I am convinced, no more important lesson to learn about pulpit ministry than this; our task is to announce what the Spirit says to us and we just cannot do this until we are ready to admit who we are and where we are. This is costly, of course, all will not respond alike, but the freedom is worth the price, and the prayer power of your people will enable you to reap pulpit harvests for God of which you have only dreamed. God honors openness with openness—it is His way of doing things, His life principle for Christians.

Finally, and obviously, the bearing and sharing of which I write has great relevance to one's counseling ministry. If it is true that the goal of the counseling relationship is self discovery, then it stands to reason that such discovery can only be built upon truth and discovered in an atmosphere of truth. Truth is not honored when the pastor-counselor plays a role, thus erecting barriers of falsity between himself and the one he is seeking to help. Tournier puts it in these words:

> The psycho-therapist's consulting room is a place for truth. It requires of me the same attitude to truth as it demands of the patient. If I want to help him to become himself, to show himself as he really is, surely it is necessary for me to be myself and to show myself as I am. Even if I hid my private thoughts he would feel them.[28]

Glasser expresses the point with reference to the frequent complaint of a patient that he is unable to assert himself because of his psychiatrist. He notes:

> It is because of the difficulty of becoming involved with a therapist who, instead of establishing a close personal relationship with the patient in his own capacity, sometimes plays the role of someone else and sometimes acts as himself.
> The psychiatrist must reject the untherapeutic concept of transference, relate to the patient as a new and separate

person with whom the patient can become involved. . . .[29]

At the risk of overworking this conviction, I quote Jourard on the matter also.

> It fascinates me to think of psychotherapy as a situation where the therapist, a "redeemed" or rehabilitated dissembler, invites his patient to try the manly rigors of the authentic way. The patient is most likely to accept the invitation, it has seemed to me, when the therapist is a role model of uncontrived honesty. And when the therapist is authentically a man of goodwill, he comes to be seen as such, and the need for sneaky projective tests or for decoding hidden messages in utterances vanishes. The patient then wants to make himself known, and proceeds to do so. In this defenseless state, the interpretations, suggestions, and advice of the therapist then have maximum, growth-yielding impact on him.[30]

Commenting on the work of nurses specifically, Sidney Jourard amplifies what I am here maintaining with particularized application.

> I believe that professional training encourages graduates to wear a professional mask, to limit their behavior to the range that proclaims their professional status. Thus, nurses are supposed to look and sound like nurses, doctors like doctors, as well as to do the work delegated to persons in those roles. Patients are exposed not to human beings who have expertise, but to "experts" who are dehumanized and dehumanizing. To spend time in the company of those who will not relate at a human level cannot be health engendering, either for the patient, or the professional.[31]

I submit that what applies to nurses or doctors also applies to clergymen.

Can we not agree that most people who seek counseling

do so because they have been unable to relate significantly with others? Are they not coming to us in the majority of instances because they are locked persons unable to disclose themselves successfully? If this is so, how can we seriously imagine that what they need to learn, how to share, can really occur in an environment in which their "coach" refuses to disclose himself and instead of teaching by demonstration as well as word adopts a role and refuses to come out of it? I recognize fully that what I assert here is subject to misinterpretation because I have no space in which to expand this thesis but I would submit that on the very face of it the matter is clear. Techniques may be used, but they must always be used in the context of the truthful revelation of the self, else the truth will rarely, if ever, be discovered.

CONCLUSIONS

The sum of the matter is this; the life principle of bearing and sharing is to be basic to our lives as Christians. As clergymen we have the privilege and responsibility to demonstrate it with special power. The refusal to do this isolates us as persons and forces us into a lonely world where we are not happy. The refusal to do this also deprives our people of the kind of preaching, counseling pastor to which they are entitled. it gives them, instead of a man or woman like themselves with the need to minister and to be ministered to, a man or woman locked into a role which separates and does not unite. It gives them a fence mender instead of a bridge builder. And this is the great need of clergy and laity alike—bridges of love which will span the waters of loneliness and distrust which separate us. Such bridges are built on the twin pillars of bearing and sharing, and these bridges alone will unite isolated island personalities into an archipelago which will then extend itself into a continent and as continents open to one another they become a kingdom and the name of that kingdom is *The Kingdom of God.*

The Apostle Paul clearly speaks the word we so desperately need to hear, "Bear one another's burdens, and so fulfill the law of Christ. . . ." But to this word we must bring understanding and the first premise which must be clearly understood is this—in order to bear for another the other must first share his need. This is basic and this, my clergy brother, applies to you and me just as much or more than it does to all other men. As noted before, sharing is not easy. It is quite often painful. The pain comes from different directions. It comes from those who use what you share against you. It comes from those who brand your honest efforts as weakness and as testimony to your personal inadequacy. It comes from those who assume that your speaking of the joy and power you have found in vulnerability is some kind of boast, some kind of arrogant expression of your strength and their weakness. These persons will be quick to brand your openness as supercilious and condescending. By so doing they testify beyond dispute to two different realities, their own frightened loneliness and their insensitivity to your need. If your words threaten them, be gentle, for only tenderness will open them. If their charges express their inability to understand your burdens, then keep on "keeping on," for someone somewhere will eventually understand that you speak of these things because of your continuing need for openness and love. Someone somewhere will hear the lonely hurt which is evidenced by your preaching the gospel of self-disclosure and when this special one hears you he or she will say, "I understand and I will help you with my openness." On that day the pain of the effort will seem as nothing when matched against the inestimable beauty of knowing that at least one other person knows you are His disciple by your trusting love.

NOTES

1. Galatians 6:2. All quotations from Scripture are from the Revised Standard Version.
2. Luke 10:27.
3. Matthew 25:40.
4. I John 3:11.
5. Romans 15:25; 16:1-2; I Corinthians 4:14, 15; 7:1; II Corinthians 13:14; Philemon, and many other references too numerous to mention.
6. Romans 15:30; Colossians 4:3; I Thessalonians 5:25; II Thessalonians 3:1.
7. Philippians 4:10.
8. IICorinthians 12:7.
9. I Corinthians 1:10 ff.
10. II Timothy 4:9.
11. Sidney M. Jourard, *The Transparent Self* (New York: Van Nostrand Reinhold Company, 1971), p. viii.
12. John 13:35.
13. Earl A. Loomis, *The Self In Pilgrimage* (New York: Harper & Row, 1960), p. 90.
14. Karen Horney, *The Neurotic Personality of Our Time* (New York: Norton, 1936).
15. Jourard, *Transparent Self*, p. 31.
16. Wilhelm Reich, *Character Analysis* (New York: Orgone Press, 1948).
17. I do not think it coincidence that more clergymen identify with Peter than with Paul. We would all like to be Pauls for our own sakes and to please our people who expect us to be Pauls, but in reality we know ourselves to be what we are, Peters.
18. William E. Hulme, *Your Pastor's Problems: A Guide for Ministers and Laymen* (Minneapolis: Augsburg, 1966), pp. 113-114.
19. For an excellent study of the American male as he confronts the erroneous and unrealistic expectations of contemporary society see Brenton, Myron, *The American Male* (New York: Coward-McCann, 1966). See especially chapters 2, 4, 5 and 7. I regret that I do not have space to develop this theme here as there is no doubt that the 20th century American clergyman is expected to be an "all-round guy" and that not only is not possible, it is not, by contemporary American definition, even to be desired.
20. Sidney M. Jourard, and P. Lasakow, "Some Factors in Self-

Disclosure", *Journal of Abnormal Social Psychology* (1958), p. 56.

21. Jourard, *Transparent Self*, p. 36.
22. *Ibid.*, p. 39.
23. Daniel D. Walker, *The Human Problems of the Minister* (New York: Harper and Row, 1960), p. 47.
24. It is interesting to observe that we are no better at sharing our victories than we are our defeats. We seem to harbor a continuing fear that even reference to our successes, let alone rejoicing in them, will sound like arrogant boasting. We, thus, isolate ourselves not only in shadow but in sunlight. How can we "rejoice with those who rejoice" if we do not share our own rejoicing and encourage others to announce their rejoicing to us? Preachers need the benefit of one another's acclaim just like everybody else. We need other's shoulders to cry on but also other's hands to slap our backs!
25. Sidney M. Jourard, *Self-disclosure: An Experimental Analysis of the Transparent Self* (New York: Wiley, 1971).
26. Paul Tournier, *A Place for You* (New York and Evanston: Harper and Row, 1968) p. 170 ff. Dr. Tournier's many books on the subject of this paper are well known. Few men have contributed as much to the meeting of the Christian's personal needs as Dr. Tournier. Those interested in this area of study could do no better than to begin their reading with his works.
27. William Glasser, *Reality Therapy: A New Approach to Psychiatry* (New York and Evanston: Harper and Row, 1965), p. 7.
28. Tournier, *A Place for You*, p. 84.
29. Glasser, *Reality Therapy*, p. 52.
30. Jourard, *The Transparent Self*, p. 134.
31. *Ibid.*, p. 178.

Christianity and Counseling

By Robert M. Urie

THE PURPOSE of this essay is to present a series of personal thoughts concerning Christianity and counseling.[1] Our first assumption will be that Christianity needs no definition for purposes of this paper and we will therefore proceed immediately to a definition of counseling. Following that definition, we will pursue several avenues or issues that inevitably arise from that subject. Finally, there will be an attempt to relate traditional Christianity to counseling in a reasonably coherent statement of the key issues.

An adequate definition of counseling must deal with several elements in one way or another. Counseling is between two persons, one of whom is in a mental, psychological, or spiritual condition of stress; while the other person is perceived as being in a position of adequacy or helpfulness. The one who receives counseling must do so with a significant degree of willingness and self-volition as he feels or recognizes his state of need. There must be a sense of trust between counselee and counselor, while a climate of privacy and absolute confidentiality will also prevail. The last element in this definition, but one that must be considered very early in the chronology of a counseling relationship, is a clarification of goals that are meaningful and acceptable to both parties. Now we will examine these elements of counseling in more detail.

First, it was stated that counseling is between two persons;

this immediately raises the question of group counseling. It is our conviction that group counseling can be understood in two ways. Either it is a case of a group having its needs cared for as if the group itself were a single counselee, or the counselor is in fact dealing with one counselee at a time in a series of short contacts as the interplay moves from one member of the group to another. In the first instance, when a group is treated as a conglomerate individual with several needs the needs of individuals cannot be met in a counseling sense. This of course, does not mean that persons cannot improve, or learn, or gain in self-understanding in group sessions, but such gains are more properly called educational rather than counseling gains. Our definition is quite arbitrary at this point and is of course open to debate.

In the other interpretation of group counseling, the counselor deals with each individual in the group on a one-to-one basis for varying periods of time. That this is possible and quite common in actual practice is a well-known fact among counselors. As the counselee and counselor begin to communicate with each other in a group, the psychological setting changes until it seems as if no one else were there. The counselee forgets his surroundings, and a sense of privacy may be established in which the counseling process is in every essential the same as one conducted in a private office with only the counselor and counselee present. As this relationship or process-within-a-group increases in effectiveness for the one counselee, the counseling value as such for the remainder of the group decreases. Again, as indicated earlier, other members of a group can learn, and to some extent, vicariously suffer and grow as they observe and listen to the one-to-one counseling; but their participation is something quite different from counseling in the usual sense. If, on the other hand, they literally interrupt the one-to-one process to interject their own needs, insights, or questions, then the initial contact will be broken and that particular counseling process will cease.

We stated further that one of the two parties in counseling is in a state of mental, psychological, or spiritual stress. This is simply to say that counseling must be about something and deal with a perceived need on the part of the counselee. There are schools of therapy which hold that help can be applied to unwilling subjects and that improvement is just as likely to occur whether or not the subject has agreed to participate. We suspect that these more radical approaches of reality therapy, chemotherapy, or any of the behavior modification schools are dealing with a different area of concern than that included in our definition of counseling. While this paper is not the place for an examination of the problem, it does seem that there is a broad philosophical and possibly ethical gap between those various therapies and the counseling we have in mind. Our basic premise once again is that there is a perceived need on the part of the counselee and a subsequent willingness to bring this need to a counselor.

A counselor, on the other hand, is one who is perceived by the counselee to be in a state of adequacy or potential helpfulness. This does not mean that a counselor must be a person who has no problems himself. Neither does it mean that he has overcome all self-doubts, fears, and frustrations about his own life. A good counselor has probably experienced all of these feelings during his own lifetime and may well continue to be faced by them as a professional counselor. So what is the difference between counselor and counselee at this point? The difference is one of degree, of emphasis, and of priority. Essentially, the counselor is one who experiences feelings of inadequacy to a considerably lesser degree than a counselee at the time of contact between them. The counselor has in some personally effective manner already dealt with his personal problems before entering into the counseling relationship. He either has handled his own problems or has developed an effective life-style that enables him to assign emphases or priorities to his various doubts and fears. When he then enters into a counseling relationship with a fellow human being, his own needs or problems are assigned to a relatively low priority level at that point in time. The counselor therefore is correctly and accurately perceived as one who is in a position of personal adequacy and potential helpfulness. A responsible counselor is one who can accurately evaluate his own situation during counseling and shall also terminate a relationship when his own needs assume more than a secondary priority.

Priorities in the counseling relationship lead us to the statement of goals or understandings between counselor and counselee. Early in the chronology of a counseling relationship there must be a frank understanding of what is expected by and from each party. Counseling literature is replete with exhaustive case histories in which too much was expected of the counselee or the counselor. On the one hand, counselees have been expected to provide all of the coherent verbal material in the session, with the counselor offering nothing but monosyllabic grunts of affirmation or question. Other counselors, only slightly less restricted, have responded with endless and mechanical restatements of everything said by the counselee, "You feel that. . . ." On the other hand, there have always been counselors who felt compelled to offer diagnosis, interpretation, information, and advice to a counselee even before there has been any adequate understanding of the individual's actual needs. It is, therefore, imperative that a frank understanding be reached very early in the relationship.

An adequate understanding of goals may be nothing more than a simple statement to the effect that this counseling session or series of sessions is not intended to be psychotherapy. It might be an agreement to deal with a definite problem area, such as vocation, parent-child relationship, or relationships with peers. It might be an agreement to deal with a feeling of loneliness, or fear, or anger. The agreement or understanding between counselor and counselee may even take the form of a written contract in which the person seeking help agrees to attend a given number of counseling sessions and the counselor agrees to reserve specified time for that purpose. In addition to the perception of content or subject area and the assumption of responsibilities by both, there must be a deeper understanding. This can be verbalized, but it must be experientially grasped rather than intellectually understood by counselee and counselor. It is an understanding that "I" as counselor cannot save "You" as counselee. While the counselor does have professional skills, personal adequacy, and a sincere commitment to the needs of others, the final responsibility remains with the counselee. If this were not true, we would have a Subject-Object relationship in which the growth and progress of each counselee would depend sole solely on the techniques and efforts of the counselor; and the failures would also become personal failures of the counselor. In either case, we have lost the essential understanding of humanity and man's need for self-actualization. A counselee is not an object to be treated in any manner, bad or good, by the counselor. Even though we have clearly indicated that a difference in skills, adequacy, and personal coping ability may exist at a given time, the counseling relationship is still a person-to-person relationship in the most fundamental sense. What the counselor offers is a climate of acceptance and understanding in which this person can himself begin to understand and to accept himself. It is imperative that an understanding of these fundamental aspects of the relationship be reached at a very early point in the counseling. To proceed otherwise is to foster dependency and to risk even greater problems of confrontation and disappointment later on in the counseling relationship; situations in which the counselee can say, "Now look what you've got me into".

Another element in our definition of counseling deals with the willingness of a counselee to enter into the relationship. Friends, relatives, and other interested parties can suggest counseling and may even arrange appointments, transportation, and other details. But at the point when a counselee actually sits down and begins to share himself in any significant sense with a counselor, it must be on an open and completely willing basis. The importance of this principle cannot be over-emphasized, not so much for the benefit of counselees, but in consideration of the counselor's time. It is unlikely if not impossible that counseling by our definition can take place apart from the willingness of a counselee to enter into that relationship. Otherwise, as indicated earlier, we have a Subject-Object relationship in which one is doing something to the other and the counselee loses the very qualities he is seeking to increase or enhance in his own life. It is a psychological-philosophical contradiction to coerce a person into counseling for his own good.

A sense of trust between counselee and counselor is also a critical element in a definition of counseling. Out of this trust come the related matters of privacy and confidentiality. First, the counselee must see his counselor as one with whom he is absolutely safe in any sense of the word. He must believe that he can say anything and share any emotion that is honest at the moment without fear of betrayal to other parties, or of ridicule, judgment, or condescension from his counselor. At one level, this means that the counselee is safe to share his true feelings about his wife, his employer, or his God without fear of having it repeated by the counselor outside the counseling relationship. It means that he is free to express his darkest fears, doubts, or despair; knowing that they will never be used against him by the counselor in any way.

As an aside, the question of privacy does not depend upon counseling facilities or physical arrangements. Experience clearly demonstrates that counseling privacy can be obtained in a wide variety of settings—from the panelled pastor's office to the crowded campus cafeteria. We have even suggested that a sense of counseling privacy may be experienced in the midst of a group of people, all of whom are seeking the counselor's attention. The sense of privacy evidently arises from the personal contact between counselee and counselor in which full attention is given to each other. Any awareness of the presence other group members is retained with a sense of shared concerns, of trust, and hence, of confidentiality.

We do not mean to imply that our terms should be understood in an absolute sense. Adequacy, helpfulness, willingness, needs, and privacy are all relative to the situation in which they occur. We explained for example, that the adequacy of the counselor was relatively more than that of the counselee at this time. Likewise, the counselor is perceived to be relatively or potentially more helpful than other persons at this time. The terms "willingness," "needs," and "privacy" are closely bound up together and relative to each other. A counselee becomes willing to enter into counseling and will seek it out as his needs for mental, psychological, or spiritual relief become dominant in his life. He will seek counseling when his discomfort becomes greater than the anticipated discomfort or embarrassment of sharing himself with a counselor.

It should be quite evident at this point that our definition or philosophy of counseling is based on a health model rather than on an illness or medical model. For this reason, we do not speak of therapy in or by counseling. Therapy is healing by definition. Healing requires the presence of ill health, disease, or pathology. These conditions, in turn, require diagnosis or labeling, followed by prescription and medicine. Practitioners operating under the medical model will use nonexplanatory labels such as "paranoid schizophrenic." But we do not then know, simply by hearing the label, what is wrong or how to help this individual. In our definition of counseling, we have emphasized the active role played by the counselee in seeking help and the importance of his active participation as a person throughout all phases of the counseling process. The counselor's model or philosophy will of course determine

219

his attitudes, techniques, and overall stance in the counseling relationship.

While this essay is not the place for a discussion of counseling techniques, we can address ourselves to their place in a counseling philosophy. Initially, we might say that over-emphasis on technique falls in the same category as diagnosis and labeling of patients in the medical model. Only now we are labeling the counselor instead of the counselee! There is no particular value in stating that one is client-centered, non-directive, reality oriented, behavioristic, psychoanalytical, or health-directed if we are simply referring to a set of techniques. The extreme focus on techniques has been facetiously illustrated by the story in which a nondirective counselor watched his counselee leap from the twentieth-floor office window while the counselor faithfully restated, "You feel that you would like to jump out of that window?" Techniques of any type may become ends in themselves whenever the counselor finds himself more concerned about how he is doing than by what is happening to his counselee. It is probably wise for a counselor to know generally the ways in which he can best relate to counselees. If he is uncomfortable in doing or saying anything in a particular way, he should not attempt to continue it just because it represents a widely-accepted technique of counseling. Techniques of counseling should remain secondary to the actual relationship between the two persons. It does not seem nearly as important for a counselor to describe how he worked with an individual as it is for both to say with conviction that something did happen for the betterment of the counselee.

We will not attempt to answer the question of art versus science in counseling, but as in teaching and many human-relations activities, there always seems to be a recognized gift, sought by many, held by few. There are varieties of gifts and professional roles. The counselor, like the teacher, should have some special gift for his work. Any reasonably intelligent person can learn all there is to learn about counseling in a few weeks at most. He can learn to describe and to practice a variety of techniques with considerable skill, but techniques do not a counselor make. The accumulated evidence now suggests, in fact, that training generally decreases the effectiveness of counselors. While that whole problem is still open in the minds of many knowledgable people, the point is that certain natural gifts are extremely important to counselors.

Since we have raised the question of gifts or characteristics for counselors, we will not further evade it by saying that such gifts are simply spiritual or indescribable. In keeping with our previous discussion of counseling, the counselor's gifts are quite apparent. To begin with, he has the gift of self-adequacy in any ordinary humanistic sense. It might even be appropriate to speak of wholeness or peace in the original Hebrew meaning of *shalom*. The good counselor is not filled with internal warfare or division within himself, but is all in one piece. At the core of his being there is a degree of serenity which neither expects nor requires that his counselee respond in a particular way. Having met his own mental, psychological, and spiritual needs satisfactorily up to this time, he is free within himself to let his counselee go about meeting his own needs as well. This gift of adequacy, for want of a better term, attracts the counselee in the first place and gives him grounds for believing that help might come from and through such a source.

In a more mundane sense, the counselor also has the gift or characteristic of trustworthiness. Arising from the same roots of character as does adequacy, the counselor can be trusted because he trusts others, himself, and God. Having lived his life thus far in a climate of trust by parents and other loved ones, he has in turn learned to give trust as naturally as breathing. He has learned that people are usually kind, generous, and helpful when trusted. As a result, when a counselee receives him into his confidence he keeps that trust in both letter and in spirit. His lips are sealed to the information that passes between counselor and counselee; his heart is sealed in trust of this person as a fellow human being. Because he has the gift of trust, he can also be trusted; he cannot and will not engage in any counseling activity at the expense of a counselee's fundamental dignity as a person. In practice, this means that a counselee experiences acceptance from the beginning of his counseling. The counselor is not committed to changing the counselee to fit his own image, and the counselee is therefore free to be himself in beginning his self-chosen process of problem solving.

There are many other lesser gifts of varying degrees of importance to a counselor-counselee relationship. Empathy, for example, is nearly always present in effective counseling. Insight, understanding of human nature, and interpretative skills are all of great importance. Common sense and judgment have never been adequately defined in operational terms but are surely crucial to good counseling. In spite of all, however, these gifts are in a fundamental sense secondary to the gifts of adequacy and trustworthiness. When these first two are present in the counselor's life, it is likely that the lesser characteristics will also be found to a considerable extent.

Two minor problems remain before we consider the relationship between Christianity and counseling. First, the matter of giving advice versus the giving of information. Second, the place of sharing in counseling.

Counseling, in layman's terms, has frequently been used as a synonym for advising. From that point of view, the counselor is simply the one who knows the most and is always ready to tell the counselee what he should do about his condition. People are frequently inclined to respond very favorably to this advice-giving because it allows them to place responsibility for the outcome on the shoulders of the counselor. In reaction to that danger, counselors have frequently refused to say anything which could be taken as advice. Adequate counseling probably involves almost no advice-giving in the literal sense. An effective counselor may pose a series of alternatives for consideration by the counselee, leaving the choice entirely in the hands of the counselee. The pitfall here is that by merely describing some alternatives, a counselor may be understood as favoring at least these choices, thereby being put in the position of giving advice. Out of concern for being misunderstood, counselors have occasionally retreated to the point where they will not even give information. This situation is just as serious as the opposite in which the counselor does all of the talking. It should be clear that a counselor is perfectly free, even obligated, to share all information he has when it is appropriate to the needs of the counselee. This involves a judgment on the counselor's part, such as information about an ill person's medical condition and the like. Generally, however, when a relationship of trust is present, the giving of information is a natural and positive part of counseling, not to be misunderstood as advice.

Sharing in counseling is a more difficult question and has no simple answer. By sharing, we are referring to what a counselor should share of himself with a counselee. The most appropriate generalization we can make is this: share as little as possible. By this we mean the less social interaction the better, the less the counselor speaks about his education, family, and friends, the better for counseling. Experience suggests that questions on these topics are typically defensive plays by a reluctant or manipulative counselee who is either not committed to the counseling itself, or who must be challenged as to his motives. On the other hand, this is not to mean that a counselor should not be free to answer any normal, genuine questions that a counselee may ask at the outset of counseling. Later on, in an established counseling relationship, requests for sharing of this type are more likely to mean that a too-sensitive area in the counselee's life has been touched or that he has simply gone as far as he can go in counseling at this time.

Another kind of sharing is the basis for counseling as we have described it earlier. This is the sharing of one's essential humanity with another person in a relationship of trust and concern. It is the sharing of feelings for his needs that have been presented in the context of counseling. It is the sharing of strength with the conviction that things will work out for this person just as the counselor has experienced the solution of his own problems in life. It is simply a sharing of one's own being rather than a recital of life's details. It is the sharing of an integrity that comes from the counselor's innermost self and cannot be hidden or faked. And this concept of sharing brings us finally but inevitably to the relationship between Christianity and counseling, for what one does not have, he cannot share; and what he does have, he must share.

From the standpoint of traditional Christianity in its authentic and positive manifestations among men, it would be difficult to imagine an activity more closely, intimately related to it than the work of a counselor. The Christian faith has given us assurance and a reason for our own wholeness. Through our faith in Christ, we have experienced forgiveness, peace, and trust. We are potentially helpful people because we ourselves have been helped. We are potentially trustworthy and accept people because we have experienced a sense of worth ourselves.

If we were to define counseling in terms of problem-solving alone, then there would be little difference between pagan-humanistic and Christian counselors. Thus, if we are dealing with a problem of sarcasm between two parties and restrict ourselves to problem-solving as such, any counselor can deal with the immediate issue equally well. A theistic background would not change the situation necessarily, and any counselor would attempt to deal with the apparent underlying hostility in the situation. We could list any number of examples in which a theological perspective adds little to the solution of a particular problem presented to the counselor.

As a matter of record, however, we have not viewed counseling in terms of problem-solving or psychological housekeeping. We have consistently emphasized the qualities of the counselor and the resulting qualities of the counseling relationship. We have emphasized the adequacy of the counselor, his trustworthiness, and his fundamental respect for the person of the counselee. These qualities are intimately related to the counselor's Christian faith.

Adequacy and potential helpfulness were given initially in the definition of counseling. From the strictly humanistic viewpoint this means that a person has learned to get along in the world, to recognize and live with his own limitations, and to relate constructively to other persons. Investigation of his motives or his philosophical foundation typically reveals a respect for the worth of man as such. He will generally hold that it is good to be helpful to others because people are more truly human when they are being helpful to one another. And he does not feel it necessary to go any further with the subject.

The counselor who is a practicing Christian may do and say many of the same things as the humanist; but his motives, his foundation, and his faith are different. The Christian, too, has learned to get along in the world chiefly because he sees it as his Father's world and, hence, good. He is not suspicious of the world but understands that God has made it and this is one aspect of the solid foundation which he offers to his counselee.

The counselor that knows Christ as his Saviour has also learned to recognize and live with his own limitations. But again, his motives differ from those of the humanist, who has a philosophical, perhaps fatalistic, view of his own weaknesses. For the Christian, limitations, weaknesses, and faults are expressions of his condition in sin. He is also mindful of his natural estrangement from his Maker and broken relationships are a recognized part of his own experience. On the other hand, he has also known forgiveness and acceptance by the grace of God, making a new wholeness of life possible. From this wholeness or peace, comes his true sense of adequacy which is wholeness in Christ rather than of himself. And from this foundation of acceptance and wholeness or salvation in Christ, the counselor is genuinely able to relate to his counselee in a helping way. The counselor rejoices in his own condition of freedom and shares this good news with his counselee by simply being a whole person. He is a resource, a help in time of need, because he has resources from beyond himself. He has been touched by the Holy Spirit and knows that he can and must share this great treasure. In this context, Christianity and counseling are hand in hand and the counselor reaches out to touch another life even as he himself once was touched.

NOTES

1. In addition to the Bible and the lives of hundreds of young people who have influenced my counseling philosophy, I am particularly indebted to the following writers:

Allport, Gordon W. *Becoming.* (New Haven: Yale University Press, 1955).

Combs, Arthur W., and D. Snygg. *Individual Behavior.* (New York: Harper and Brothers, 1959).

Erikson, E. *Childhood and Society.* Second edition. (New York: W. W. Norton, 1963).

Glasser, William. *Reality Therapy.* (New York: Harper and Row, 1965).

Harris, Thomas A. *I'm OK—You're OK.* (New York: Harper and Row, 1969).

May, Rollo. *Psychology and the Human Dilemma.* (Princeton, New Jersey: D. Van Nostrand Company, Inc., 1966).

Ohlsen, Merle M. *Group Counseling.* (New York: Holt, Rinehart, and Winston, Inc., 1970).

Rogers, Carl R. *Client-Centered Therapy.* (New York: Houghton Mifflin, 1957).

Whitely, John M. (ed.). *Research in Counseling.* (Columbus, Ohio: Charles E. Merrill Publishing Co. 1967).

A Press In Chains:
A Mission Unaccomplished

The sad estate of contemporary Christian journalism

By James A. Gittings

*I*N A LONG AGO LECTURE, James Kelso told of a dispute among archaeologists over the location of an Old Testament site. "We just kept digging", he told a first-year class at Pittsburgh Seminary, "and eventually we had the truth of it."

The distinguished Dr. Kelso's anecdote ought to provide a phrase descriptive of the efforts of Christian journalism in 1972. Ought to, that is, but does not. The Christian press is in chains. In America it has seldom been out of them. A fair case can be made for the proposition that America's clergy and its leaders, of whatever theological or denominational persuasion, have no understanding of or commitment to freedom of information when the Church is a subject of journalistic inquiry. Not once, but a dozen times a year, a reporter who loves the Church must thrust out of his mind a suspicion that suggests itself: the *church* is an enemy of truth.

Our generation prefers to look first toward structures for evidence of suspected malfunctioning. Publishing structures in the church provide the most visible indications that the religious press is not free. The first organs that spring to mind are denominationally owned or sponsored: *Together, The Epis-*

copalian Presbyterian Life, United Church Herald, Mission,
and so on. Such publications are free to report large and small
triumphs in church programming; they are free (subject to
cancellations of subscriptions by irate readers) to report on
social problems and controversies; they are free to engage in
mildly adventuresome reportage of intra-church disputes. In
practical terms, however, they are not free to report that a
general secretary has mocked a country pastor in open assembly; they are not free to inform their readers that a bishop
has been caught with his hand in the till; they are not free
to disclose that a highly touted social action effort has blown
higher than an ammunition dump in a bombardment; they
may not print that a mission treasurer has knowingly con-
travened currency regulations in an important Asian country.
Two rules are discernible: a church-owned publication must
not cover church leaders *seriously,* that is as public personalities, nor publish no-holds-barred articles relating performance levels and accomplishments, or lack of them, of church
workers, programs, and *structures.* Not when individuals being
covered have a clear shot at a publication's jugular vein during
the end-of-the-year joint budget conferences that are a feature
of modern bureaucratic life in the denominations.

A second group of publications in the field of religion labor
under disadvantages that are different than those of the denominational journals, but no less constricting. These magazines and newspapers, of widely varying levels of editorial
integrity, are published or underwritten by special interest
groups, institutions, and private persons. To mind spring *Christian Century, Christianity Today, Christianity and Crisis, Presbyterian Layman, Moody Monthly, Presbyterian Outlook,* and
others. Each of these publications is identifiable, within broad
outlines at least, with a particular theological point-of-view.
Ideological limitations become clear when one tries, for example, to imagine *Christianity Today* reporting critically on Billy

Graham or admiringly of the Berrigan brothers. Equally unlikely is the notion of the *Christian Century* taking apart Robert McAfee Brown with any notable degree of heat.

A further limitation of the independent Christian journals stems from their underlying conception of function. Most do not view investigative reporting as a primary responsibility. They are magazines of comment; editorializers. Beyond attending major church meetings, staffmen on these publications can do little more for their readers than to chat editorially, often with vigor, about information that has reached them from other media. The independents exist upon handouts, *a la* newsmen in a Pentagon briefing room, and upon clippings. Given the partisan foundations of their journals, editors of the independent publications print items of news that help their causes along, roundly deplore the activities of the opposition, and that's that.

Anyone who has worked for or with Christian publications will recognize that a degree of caricature is to be found in the preceding paragraphs. Church editors are not usually, everywhere, or in all newsroom crises, craven men and women. Nor are church executives normally of a mind to exact payment in dollars at budget-making time for personal pique over news reports adversely affecting their agencies. Still, the nubbin of truth in what has been said is a large one, and at least one statement can be made flatly: nobody in denominational journalism covers the church in quite the same way, or with the same chips-fall-where-they-may attitude that a good political reporter brings to city hall. Large official journals staffed to do the job are stopped from performing it by bureaucratic considerations; independent publications lack necessary personnel for the task and in any case have disavowed reportorial dispassion at the outset for the sake of assorted causes and indignations.

Reactions to descriptions of this state of affairs tend to take one of two directions. Some people are incredulous that a man is dismayed. They say, "Of course church journals have limitations in their freedom to examine the church; they are house organs, aren't they?" Such individuals will discover later in this article that damage to the church and to the cause of the Gospel results from easy adoption of a view that is more proper for industrial managers than for members of the family of God. A second group of individuals turns hopefully to the secular press. They ask, "Isn't it true that the quantity and quality of religious writing carried in daily newspapers is up?"

There has indeed been an improvement in the attention paid by the daily press to affairs of faith, and the quality of staffmen assigned to the religion beat has improved dramatically on many dailies. Again, however, structure militates against responsible journalism. The varied polity and interests of the churches to be found in a large city, the amount of space available in a general publication, and the limitations of appetite in the general readership—how *much* religious news they will tolerate, and *what kind*—combine with the prejudices of editors whose interests rest elsewhere to make all but impossible the attempt of a religious reporter to do a distinguished job on a daily. On the national level, the picture is also mixed. Numbers of people reporting religion for national publications remain small, though growing fast. The overwhelming amount of material from which selection must be made drives most such writers to the screening of handouts and to prolonged attendance at board meetings. As a result, the nation hears what the Church is *saying*, rather than learning first-hand of what it is *doing*.

Finally, there are national columnists dealing with religion. Two or three are excellent, and are emerging as Walter Lippmans of the chapel set. One thanks God for these men at the same time that he notes their inability to reflect upon all of the major trends, or even a decent minority of the trends to be discerned in the nation's variegated religious life. Others among the columnists are sad indeed as personalities and as commentators. A West Coast columnist spells out every day in his approach to church-related news the adolescent hostilities that plagued his relationship with a clergyman father. And there is a chap on the East Coast, a political columnist usually, who produces a column on religious trends four times a year. He hasn't darkened the door of a church in years, nor kept up his reading either.

For John and Mary Jones, believers of Boonesboro, and for the Rev. John Smith, of Raritan Center U.P. Church, the prevailing state of affairs in religious journalism poses a set of problems. Where shall such people turn to read hard and accurate news reports, unrelated to program concerns or theological quarrels, about the activities of their denominations? In what organs can they discover facts, unrelated to fund raising, about the progress of the Gospel among people outside the household of faith? It is clear that ordinary Christians and their pastors are left only with denominational organs, a source of clues to what their leaders feel is important; with independent journals for data cut to fit group prejudices; and with daily newspapers for such grab bags of information on religion as make their way amid market reports, war stories, and society notes to the printed page. The set of choices offered is a poor one; the City of God in its present earthly manifestations assuredly possesses no *New York Times*.

All of the foregoing would be merely pathetic, not tragic, if it were not for four additional factors.

First, the absence of a truly liberated religious press makes for difficulty and undue delay in rectification of mistaken Church emphases and blunders of program. It takes too long for the bureaucracy, in the absence of an informed public, to change course. Given present religious church structures, a journalist can present the most awesome and battering set of facts about a particular Church scandal or miscalculation only to find that his research is discounted as a recital of his publication's prejudices. There is no structural basis for a believer to trust his sources of information; there is no reason for him to act upon information that is suspect.

Second, the absence of a liberated press makes it all but impossible for the Church to deal effectively with scoundrels. The reference is not to morals cases of which, gossip notwithstanding, there is not a great number. For dealing with such matters in the ordinary run of affairs, church editors have adopted a standard—one of silence—that will be applauded by everyone mature enough to realize that they are not all bad men who find themselves in moral difficulties. Instead, the reference is to churchmen resembling a brace of individuals, now running about America with voices in full cry, who nourish for the courts of the church a hatred so violent that it can only be attributed to their having been forgiven too much and too often. The personal following of some of these individuals is large; they speak brilliantly, write well, and are personally imposing. Moreover, they earn their bread by impugning the political and social morals of church leaders. In secular journalism, the elaborate and unfulfilled prognostications of these men, the repeated and unsubstantiated character of the lies they spread, and the pattern of foulness, of plain bad character, revealed consistently in the personal lives of some, would long since have earned for them consignment to that editorial Oblivion from which editorial quotation proceedeth not. Alternatively, a secular press that learned eventually to deal with Senator Joseph McCarthy would find means to signal, with due attention to libel laws, that the witness of such men is corrupt. In Church, on the other hand, the vacuum in free journalism makes it possible for scoundrels to remain putative "fathers and brethren", to some of the flock at least, for a decade after decent men and women who are in possession of information on their antecedents have turned their backs upon them.

Third, the absence of a religious press that is serious and free makes it difficult for the Church to rise to meet great opportunities for mission. Two or three examples suffice: at one time the missionary community in an Asian country learned that a migratory tribe had been caught and sealed in an isolated valley during border disturbances between two nations. It was winter in the valley; the altitude at which the tribesmen huddled with their flocks under the guns of opposing armies exceeded nine thousand feet. Secular newspapers of the area were prevented by military censorship from mentioning the plight of the nomads, and the American delegation of the international press was represented at the time by two know-nothing correspondents in a city a thousand miles away. The missionaries and their mission board sat on the information that had come to them lest the publishing of it result in embarrassment to "ongoing mission program." Since the ongoing program amounted in the main to the operation of a mission school system which, to be fair, provided instruction for twelve to fifteen thousand village children, one devoutly hopes that the post-graduation accomplishments of the children are exalted enough to offset the three to four thousand tribal lives lost in the snows because a church feared to embarass a government. Similarly, the Government of India in 1947 occupied predominantly Muslim Kashmir in violation of the terms of an agreement by which the old British Indian *raj* was to be split into two nations—India and Pakistan—on the basis of the religious preferences of inhabitants in specified

233

areas. The fact that the Islamic religion ultimately proved too thin a fabric to bind ethnically diverse peoples into one nation (the reference is to the recent divorce of East Pakistan from West Pakistan) does not conceal the absence in more than two decades of church journalism of reminders of Indian treachery. We had, it was stated in the 'fifties, "too much at stake in India to risk partisanship," though the missionary community knew more about India's heavy handed handling of Kashmir's Muslims majority that almost any other non-Indian group. Let it be noted, too, that church journals failed over the years to speak with passion on the Israeli-Arab imbroglio, an subject of continual concern to the scholar whom this volume honors. The lone editor to follow the subject consistently in his columns (Al Forrest, of the *United Church Observer*, in Canada) has experienced fierce pressure from Zionists and from church officials who fear them. Forrest's temerity is credited by some journalists with causing the Government of Israel to set in motion the travelling representative of that government who, from time to time, appears in offices of Christian publications with free tours in his pocket for the bribeable.

At a distance of a decade, one wonders about these silences of Christian journalism. What might now be the evangelical situation among nomads of the southern Asia heartland if we had shouted to the world of fifteen years ago the despair of a marooned tribe? What might be our present-day situation in mission to the Arabs if our's had been a voice over the years reciting for the world the injustices being done to Palestinians? As for India, we read every time the Indian Government refuses a missionary visa the degree of respect and accommodation won by our silence about Indian aggression in the late 'forties and early 'fifties. It is not too much to say that the modern Church has walked down the Jericho road too, from time to time, and passed by on the other side. The world knows it has done so.

Finally, the absence of a religious press free enough to report patches and smudges on the robes of Christ makes it almost impossible for Christian journalists to effectively communicate good news about the *Good News,* the Gospel. Nor is this to be wondered at. How can an evangelical publication which has been uncritical and unrestrained in praise of almost every evangelistic effort to come down the pike expect to be believed when its editors state that something unique happened at the Dallas *Explo?* Or at the Cincinnati Celebration of Evangelism? Conversely, how can official church publications which consistently have turned up their editorial noses at non-official evangelistic efforts now convince readers that their objections to Dallas or Cincinnati arise from serious considerations related to the theology of missions or to the Church's understanding of proper evangelical tactic for this time?

At this moment, in Indonesia, the Church is growing at a rate that merits notice in any publication, Christian or otherwise. Reports also have it that the Indonesian Church growth is accompanied by signs and wonders reminiscent of the time of Pentecost. Yet, the Indonesian developments have not received a great amount of editorial attention other than in journals of charismatically oriented sects and special interest groups. Why not?

As it happened, this writer was briefly present in Indonesia at a time near the beginning of the movement of villagers to Christianity. I bear witness that the reports of growth are true, and I attest that such growth is sometimes accompanied by manifestations which I do not understand and which, if a believer prefers, he may ascribe to extraordinary activity of the Holy Spirit. Neither observation makes the point which is to be drawn.

The problem for a journalist in Indonesia at the time of which I speak lay in the determination of evangelical western and Indonesian leaders that the face put upon the new Christian movement in reports to the outer world should be one of a pure and unalloyed miracle, all grace and sweetness. In effect, church leaders insisted—and western religious editors went along—that God had chosen to break *into* Indonesian history rather than to work *in* and *through* it.

Actually, the situation for non-Christians of the Indonesian hinterland after the abortive coup of 1965 was extremely dangerous and politically simple. A Communist party with a broad constituency among the peasants had been smashed. In cleaning up the debris of the abortive Red revolt, the Indonesian Army demanded that every citizen register his religious preferences. To state that one had no religion became tantamount, in so-called "infected" areas, to an admission of Marxist sympathies, and sometimes resulted in death or imprisonment. Since it had been a predominately Islamic army that engaged out in the villages in the post-coup slaughter of Reds and their sympathizers, many a villager chose to affiliate with the Christian Church rather than with the religion of the murderers of his or her relatives. Pastors were besieged in some localities with hundreds of individuals who pleaded that their names be entered upon church rolls.

Left alone, without modification, the preceding paragraph amounts to an oversimplification quite as heinous as the 'spiritualized' accounts to be found in present-day pentecostal magazines. To convert the paragraph into situational truth one must clothe it in the terror of the time, with the rootlessness of burned-out populations, with the scenes of bloodshed everywhere to be witnessed, and with despair, and sadness, and a sense of the ending of old ways. Out of the incredible tragedy of those days there grew a willingness to try out the new religious option, even though it had arrived at the interstice of a penpoint on a CID questionnaire or at the end of a machine pistol tentatively pressed by a soldier against one's belly. And so, a few of the erstwhile non-believers lifted their hearts in prayer to the God of the Christians. Then it happened, now here and now there, and in the telling of it a chill that proceeds

from awe sweeps down the spine of an otherwise jaded writer.
Down from heaven upon the new communicants rained joy,
peace, assurance, healing, and other attestations of grace, first
upon the desperate few and later, increasingly as the years
since 1965 have passed, upon many who have followed their
lead. Such a redeeming by God of tragic events is miracle
enough for this reporter, and if told in something of these
terms might have been believed by thousands at home who
have ignored more exhuberant accounts of new accessions to
the Indonesian Church. Instead of linking the event to history,
however, most church journals found themselves reporting the
Indonesian miracle as a kind of hocus-pocus, thereby booting
into the dustbin of suspected propaganda a great Christian
story of our time. In handling the story in this way, most editors
were not altogether blameworthy. Lacking staff on the Indonesian scene, the editors had for background only reports
from Church leaders who, manifestly, did not trust the laity
to interpret the good news about the *Good News* in Indonesia
from accounts suggesting a political factor was present in the
growth equation.

To sum up: The Church keeps its press in chains. It does
not believe that the Christian press possesses a mandate to
take up editorial arms against wrongdoers in the church or
out of it and it prefers to screen or "manage" news reports
on all matters of substance. From the Church's dealings with
its press one must conclude that Christians view the Church
as an organization that must be protected from the curiosity
of theologically or structurally unsophisticated persons rather
than as a society whose patterns and adventures of change
and growth are to be recorded in purity and with savage
commitment to straight reportage.

Such a set of conclusions brings a writer back once more
into the classroom of the great man to whom this book is
dedicated. One hears him speaking of one of the Old Testament
prophets and stating, "He knew his duty; his only problem

lay in finding the courage to be obedient." There are many
hopes and designs for a more free religious press in the future
that could be spread out here, and at least one of them is
important: that a non-official, non-partisan press should come
into being, and that it should be staffed by reporters and editors
who will cover the Church like city hall. For now, however;
for *right now;* James Kelso's indictment of the prophet applies
also to those of us who are Christian journalists. We know
our duty; it is to report that truth about Christian affairs that
is part of a larger Truth which makes us free. God grant us
the courage to write our stories straight, and give us editors
who are hard-nosed enough to see that they are printed.

Annotated Bibliography of James Leon Kelso (from 1922-1972)

By J. Harry Fisher

<u>1922</u>

"The Hebrew Tabernacle as a Work of Architecture," *Bibliotheca Sacra*, January 1922, pp. 62-71.

> The Hebrew made his temple monotheistic to conform with the spiritual demands of his life. He made it portable to conform with the physical exegencies of his day, but he also made it beautiful as a final tribute of his love to Jehovah.

> Coming to Palestine, he was not a creator but an adapter of what he had learned in Egypt. Thus, his Temple was aesthetic enough to honor God, practical enough to move with a shifting people, and exclusive enough to be distinctive from pagan religions.

"Paul's Roman Citizenship as Reflected in his Missionary Experiences and Letters," *Bibliotheca Sacra*, April 1922, pp. 173-183.

> Paul was not only called to be an apostle to the gentile world, but was endowed by his Roman citizenship to be the ideal evangelist. His Roman citizenship gave him

opportunity to converse with government officials and proconsuls, and also saved his life when jealous Jews accused him of treason. Paul also incorporated into Christian theology words of the Roman language such as "adoption," to describe man's new relationship with God.

"The Roman Influence in the New Testament," *Bibliotheca Sacra,* July 1922, pp. 310-320.

The New Testament abounds with the impact of Roman Culture, law, business, religion and politics. Jesus Christ and Paul used the Republic's assets to spread the gospel to 85,000,000 people who lived on 2,000,000 square miles of land.

"Key Cities in Paul's Missionary Program," *Bibliotheca Sacra,* October 1922, pp. 481-486.

The cities which Paul selected to evangelize were chosen for several reasons; their political and economic strength, their prime location as centers of business and commerce, as well as being places where there would be a cross section of religious and philosophical ideas. The cities were also citadels of corruption, pleasure, and evil. In the midst of a people whose chief ambition was honor, wealth, and pleasure, Paul sought to prove that the salvation of one soul is greater than winning the whole world.

1925

"The Three Major Themes of the Old Testament," *Bibliotheca Sacra,* April 1925, pp. 164-168.

Man (biography), Men (history), and God (theology) are the three outstanding subjects of the Old Testament. The ancient covenant honestly depicts men of contrasting worth while looking onward and upward to the MAN— Jesus Christ in whom Old Testament biography reaches its climax.

The Old Testament conception of history is that man

(nations) receive God's approval when their national actions are done in terms of God's will for all the world. This theme expands into a theology of God's Providence and Grace.

1928

"Amos—A Critical Study," *Bibliotheca Sacra,* January 1928, pp. 53-63.

The fascinating personality and life style of a bold prophet is vividly portrayed in this critical study. A comprehensive outline accompanies valuable insights into the lives and customs of the people to whom Amos preached, making it a valuable tool in understanding the "Prophet of Social Righteousness."

1934

"Some Recent Archaeological Studies," *Bibliotheca Sacra,* April 1934.

Three significant discoveries added greatly to the archaeologist's understanding of the Bible. The first was the A. Chester Beatty papyrus which revealed earlier and more complete records of the Bible. Secondly, Dr. Albright's final work at Gibeah gave us more understanding of this area's role in the history of Israel, and finally, Dr. Nelson Glueck's work in Moab as well as his survey of 150 different sites in the Northern Transjordan, which prepared the way for further excavations.

"Recent Discoveries in Bible Lands," *The Sunday School Times,* March 31, 1934, pp. 207-210.

Six significant discoveries have aided us in trusting the accuracy of the Bible. The purchase of eleven MSS. by A. Chester Beatty; the excavation at Eleush near Athens, which revealed a rival mystery religion to Christianity that survived until the fifth century A.D.; a new type of alphabet unearthed near Syria which helps us to better understand the patriarchs; a new trade route; and further excavations at Gibeah, revealing paintings in an old Synagogue indicate that the "Book" of the Christians is accurate.

"Abraham's Journeys in the Light of Archaeology," *The Sunday School Times,* June 23, 1934, pp. 411, 412.

One is able to follow in the footsteps of a great feudal lord who owned vast flocks and numbers of retainers. Special emphasis is given to the unearthing of the mystery surrounding the military invasion recorded in Genesis 14. The key Hebrew word of the passage, *hanikim,* had been translated by conjecture to mean "trained men." However, archaeology unearthed the real meaning of the word, "chariot warriors." The invasion now makes sense.

"Watching the Archaeologists at Work at a New Site," *The Sunday School Times,* September 1, 1934, pp. 551, 552.

Seldom do those who have to stay at home get such a clear picture of the actual methods of the archaeologist as they will find in this article. In an unusually vivid way, Dr. Kelso gives us the Biblical background of the site where excavations have recently been begun and takes us over the ground itself and into the workshop where he and his colleagues are studying numerous interesting finds.

"A Visit to Houses Built in the Time of the Judges," *The Sunday School Times,* September 15, 1934 pp. 579 and 582.

Here is an interesting mingling of the past and present; a description of houses millennia old as we see an age of simple living through ornaments, kitchen utensils, and tools of the family and shop.

"Bethel's History Written in the Dust," *The Sunday School Times,* September 29, 1934, pp. 609, 610.

The troubled history of the old Biblical town, whose modern name is Beitin, is traced through its victories and defeats, as well as devastation wrought by fire and sword revealed by excavation.

"Looking Over the Summer's Excavating at Bethel," *The Sunday School Times*, October 6, 1934, pp. 623, 624.

Ancient Egyptian and Syrian coins, tiny Canaanite idols, cylinders written in hieroglyphics, carved bone work, and farm implements are but a few of the items unearthed at this summer's excavation at Bethel.

"The Kyle Memorial Excavation at Bethel," *Biliotheca Sacra*, October 1934, pp. 415-420.

The findings at Bethel on this expedition were numerous and significant, coming from a period slightly antedating the days of Abraham and extending to the time of the Mohammedan conquest. Highlights of various periods in the city's history help one in understanding the vital role Bethel played in Palestinian life.

1935

"King Solomon's Copper Mines," *The Sunday School Times*, February 2, 1935, pp. 67, 68.

Heat that subdues man and beast and withers all green things; statuesque lizards frightened into lightening-like motion; black and white Egyptian vultures wheeling in the dazzling blue overhead; and rocks—these are what one finds in the gorges near the Dead Sea. Amid such scenes the slaves of Solomon chipped out precious ore to fill the King's coffers. Ancient mining camps are also described which must have been one of the main sources of the great King's enormous wealth.

"Tracing the Rise and Fall of the Moabites," *The Sunday School Times*, March 9, 1935, pp. 155, 158.

Moab generally spelled trouble for the people of Israel. The infamous origin of the people is recorded in Genesis 19, and thereafter the name is associated with fighting, divine curses, and idolatry. Some of their idols and high places are described as well as insights into ancient Moabite civilization. At the same time the author gives interesting sidelights on other Old Testament peoples and cities which were then being studied by archaeologists.

"Locating and Excavating Ancient Palestinian Cities," *Bibliotheca Sacra*, April 1935, pp. 170-178.

The difficulties in locating a site to excavate, the study of biblical and non-biblical sources, the field trip, the securing of permits to excavate, and the actual work at the excavation give the reader an inside view of the voluminous amount of work involved in an archaeological excavation. The author allows the reader to share the thrills of discovering Revelation in the dirt and mortar of Palestine.

"A Visit to a Capital City of Ancient Persia," *The Sunday School Times*, May 12, 1935, pp. 323, 327.

When Alexander the Great burned Persepolis he had no idea that he was preserving priceless records. But when the brick walls of the great palace buildings crashed to the ground, the debris buried a wealth of matchless sculpture on the lower walls. Thousands of carved figures were unearthed, and these portray the clothing, military equipment, and the customs of the people.

"Where Battles Raged in Ancient Palestine," *The Sunday School Times*, August 24, 1935, pp. 549, 550.

The financial problems of the thirties reduced the number of new archaeological excavations, but what was being excavated revealed the violence which often gripped that tiny parcel of land. The Hyksos and Egyptian periods in Jericho's history are recounted, Solomon's chariot headquarters at Meggido are discussed, the unearthing of the first Temple of Dagon is mentioned, and the high-places found at Petra are described in detail. Storerooms, storage jars, and queer drinking cups unearthed from the ruins indicate that the change of rule was accomplished by violence and bloodshed.

"Living Again in Bible Houses," *Bibliotheca Sacra*, October 1935, pp. 427-432.

Though it is seldom that the archaeologist is able to find two floors of a house, the floor plan of the first floor reveals much of the life style of the people who had inhabited the house. Jewelry, dice, weights, scarabs, and seals reveal a great deal about a city dweller's life.

1936

"Tracing the Story of an Old Enemy of Israel," *The Sunday School Times*, February 22, 1936, pp. 119, 120.

A new people moved into Asia Minor about 2,000 B.C. and by 1930 B.C. King Amittas of Nesas blended these little city-states into an empire which took in most of Asia Minor. The Hittites became involved with the Egyptians in either military or diplomatic contacts for centuries. The book of Exodus shows the Hitties as important members of the native population of Palestine which Israel had to dispossess. The history, conquests, commerce, language, and laws of the Hittites as well as their relationship to Israel are discussed in this article.

"The Older and Newer Phases of Biblical Archaeology," *Bibliotheca Sacra*, April 1936, pp. 181-186.

Whereas the early efforts of archaeology concerned itself with apologetics, the present archaeologist is developing theology. God is the hero of life as He works in the affairs of men. Therefore, the archaeologist stands in awe of God as his excavations reveal that only by God's power and grace was Israel ever to become a people.

"Ancient Letters on Pottery and Papyrus," *The Sunday School Times*, August 31, 1936, p. 567.

Twenty-five hundred years ago a military scribe wrote letters on fragments of pottery concerning signals used by the signal corps of his day. These ancient writings were translated and photographed. Of great interest were the large sections of the oldest manuscripts of Paul's epistles which had come to light.

1937

"Archaeology's Influence on Old Testament Exegesis," *Bibliotheca Sacra*, January 1937, pp. 31-36.

The author encourages exegetes to use the abundance of material archaeology has discovered which aids in the interpretation of the Bible. Background information about Canaanite religion helps us to see a greater contrast between the gods of Canaan and Yahweh. Social customs and Israel's unique system of worship will add new dimensions to the church's teaching and preaching as a result of the archaeologist's findings.

"An Early Neighbor of the Israelites," *The Sunday School Times*, March 28, 1937, p. 221.

Twelve years of bondage under Chedorlaomer, king of Elam, was enough for the kings of Sodom and Gomorrah and three other kings, so "in the thirteenth year they rebelled" (Genesis 14:4). The next year this same Chedorlaomer conducted an expedition, in the course of which he subdued "the Horites in Mount Seir, unto El-paran, which is by the wilderness." It was from this king that Abraham rescued Lot. The excavations taken at that time disclosed much new information concerning the Horites.

"Jericho, a Thriving City 1,000 Years Before Abraham," *The Sunday School Times,* May 1, 1937, pp. 315, 316.

> The most interesting aspect of the work at Jericho was the discovery that Jericho is the oldest continuously occupied city of the ancient world. Even more startling was the discovery of the fine civilization its people enjoyed. Though not using clay in their pottery around 4,000 B.C., they did use it in the construction of their houses—a building technique not used by the Greeks until 2,000 years later.

> Other areas of discussion in this potpourri of archaeological findings was the use of aviators and deep-sea divers at Tyre to discover a half-mile harbor; that the real estate boom in Jerusalem makes it prohibitive to excavate in that citadel of Judaism and Christendom; and an old MSS. of Deuteronomy.

"Early and Late Discoveries in Babylonia," *The Sunday School Times,* August 28, 1937, pp. 603, 604.

> From Genesis through Revelation, Babylonia plays a prominent role in the life of God's people. However, early attempts at excavating this ancient civilization produced few results that helped in understanding their customs and habits. Later work in Babylonian life brought the best results from the linguists, not the excavators.

> Rawlinson's work in deciphering cuneiform languages opened up studies of law codes, creation stories, and has helped in the chronology of the Old Testament.

"Egypt, the Birthplace of Archaeology," *The Sunday School Times,* September 18, 1937, pp. 651, 652.

> Two factors make Egypt the prime source of archaeological exploration; its exceptional climate—most of the area is extremely dry, which allows for preservation of ancient pottery and sherds. Also, the Egyptians' belief in the after-life provides the archaeologists with an oppor-

tunity to investigate old tombs where a person's personal possessions, parts of his house, and many of the small items he cherished would be buried with him.

Egypt is second only to Babylon in preserving literature which further aids the researcher in understanding the ancient world.

1938

"The Work Behind an Archaeological Expedition," *Bibliotheca Sacra,* January, 1938, pp. 63, 64.

An archaeological expedition is more than Bible knowledge, strong backs, and good intentions. If the excavation is to reveal all the site contains the skills of a variety of scholars must be employed: pottery analysts, linguists, surveyors, photographers, architects, and historians.

"Pioneers in Palestine Geography and Archaeology," *The Sunday School Times,* June 4, 1938, pp. 403, 404.

The excellent maps which Church School teachers and students enjoy are the results of the exacting work begun by two devout Christians in 1838. Edward Robinson and Eli Smith began their geographic studies of Palestine March 16, 1838 and supplemented that work with another trip in 1852. Miles of surveying, thousands of notations, much digging and sorting of finds, plus endless studies of old records have given us the maps we enjoy.

"Recent Finds In Bible Lands," *The Sunday School Times,* August 20, 1938, pp. 38-41.

Prehistoric work done in the Bethlehem area, the excavation of Lachish, Alan Rowe's discovery of the alphabet principle on an Egyptian scarab, the tremendous engineering feat of Tyre, and Sargon's trail of destruction are a few of the finds which are mentioned in this article.

"Unearthing Great Buildings of Moses Time," *The Sunday School Times*, January 22, 1938, pp. 63, 64.

Ammonite civilization had previously been considered unimportant, but the work of Dr. Nelson Glueck indicates its importance in the Trans-jordan. Before 1,800 B.C. and prior to Abraham's time, this nation contained a good Bronze Age population with excellent culture.

The potpourri of other articles concerns itself with "where Jehoshaphat's ships went to pieces," "coins found dating from the Roman seige of Jerusalem", "recent excavating at Megiddo" and a "mountain top heathen temple off the Dead Sea."

1939

"Biblical Archaeology Coming Out of Syria," *Bibliotheca Sacra*, January 1939, pp. 38-41.

Prior to World War I little had been excavated in Syria. However, since all the influence entering Palestine from the north must come via Syria, the value of knowing this ancient country was self-evident. Nations and people of the Bible either resided in or passed through Syria on their way to Palestine. If we are to interpret the Bible accurately, one of the best backgrounds is Palestinian history, and to know it we must know Syria.

1940

"A Resume of Recent Archaeological Research," *Bibliotheca Sacra*, October 1940, pp. 476-481.

After stating four propositions supporting the claim of

the Bible's uniqueness as being Revelation, Dr. Kelso offers an updating of what archaeology has been doing since World War I. Its major effect has been in revealing Palestine as the area providing the maximum of new data in the Middle East.

A detailed chronology of Palestine was worked out, customs and manners discovered, the religion of the Canaanite and Israelites unearthed and many Bible manuscripts found. These findings confirm the Bible story and demonstrate the unique supernatural nature of our faith.

"Solomon's Copper Refinery on the Red Sea," *The Sunday School Times,* March 23, 1940, pp. 237, 238.

Solomon's copper mine located in the small town of Ezion-geber had a large copper refinery which was built about 1,100 B.C. The mines to the north supplied the refinery with the raw materials to make their weapons of war, tools, and jewelry, which then could be sold on the Red Sea.

1941

(and Thorley, J. Palin) *The Excavation of Tell Beit Mirsim,* ed. W. F. Albright (New Haven: American School of Oriental Research, 1941, pp. 86-142)

The chapter written by Dr. Kelso in cooperation with Dr. J. Palin Thorley consists of two sections; the first dealing with manufacturing techniques used in ancient Palestinian pottery as illustrated by ware from Tell Beit Mirsim. The second section is a detailed technical study of pottery types from Stratum A.

1943

(and Thorley, J. Palin) *The Potter's Technique at Tell Beit*

Mirsim, Particularly in Stratum A., (New Haven: American School of Oriental Research, 1943.)

> This comprehensive study of pottery types found in Stratum A impresses one with its precision and detail. The study includes such items as small squat black perfume juglets and Astarte figurines.

"Some Sixteenth Century Copper Objects from Tell Beit Mirsim," *Bulletin-American School of Oriental Research*, 91, October 1943, pp. 28-36.

> An adze-head and a mace head were analyzed metallurgically as to their copper content. The result of this analysis indicates that the influx of tin used in bronze tools did not adversely affect the copper market or run copper out of business in the market place.

1944

(with Albright, W. F. and Thorley, J. Palin) "Early Bronze Pottery from Bâb Ed-Drâʻ in Moab," *Bulletin-American School of Oriental Research*, October 1944, 95, pp. 3-13.

> A description of the class, size, shape, design, and utility of the pottery found at Bâb Ed-Drâʻ in Moab.

(and Powell, Alfred R.) "Glance Pitch from Tell Beit Mirsim," *Bulletin-American School of Oriental Research*, 95, October 1944, pp. 14-18.

> The discovery of glance pitch raised four questions: (1) Is the pitch of this site from the Dead Sea? (Answer—yes), (2) Did the Dead Sea district in antiquity produce a plastic type bitumen and a glance pitch? (Answer—yes), (3) How did antiquity make a plastic bitumen out of this hard and brittle glance pitch? (Answer—by the use of vegetable oils, animal fats, or tree pitches. See Exodus 2:3), (4) For what purposes would this pitch be used? (Answer—a cure

for infected vines, to hold masonry in place and a multitude of other practical uses.)

1945

"Ezekiel's Parable of the Corroded Copper Caldron," *Journal of Biblical Literature,* 64 (1945) p. 93.

> Exegesis in its finest form as Dr. Kelso analyzes the key word "disease," to describe the reason Jerusalem and its people shall all perish as a result of God's judgment. His vivid vocabulary as he interprets modern man's same sin leaves a great impression in the heart and mind of the reader.

"Palestine Pottery in Bible Times," *The Biblical Archaeologist,* Vol. 8:4, December 1945, pp. 81-93. (Also published by the Smithsonian Institute, Washington, D.C. #3884, 1947.)

> Because pottery is able to withstand conflagration, making it easy to date, pottery becomes a chief tool for the archaeologist to understand and interpret the life-style of the city where he is digging. Pottery reveals a civilization's progress culturally, technically, and religiously.

1946

"A Ceramic Analysis of Late-Mycenaean and Other Late-Bronze Vases from Jett in Palestine," *Bulletin-American School of Oriental Research,* 104, December 1946, pp. 21-25.

> The intricacies of creating beautiful ceramic ware are detailed, beginning with their conception on the potter's wheel, through the painting, designing, finish work and their functiooal use in late-Mycenaen society.

1948

The Ceramic Vocabulary of the Old Testament, (New Haven: American School of Oriental Research, 1948.)

> This forty-eight page monograph is a study of the technical

vocabulary that is used in the Old Testament. It is an inductive study of ceramic material of all types from the raw clay through manufacturing techniques to finished goods in all fields. The unique feature of this vocabulary is that every word is examined from the point of view of both ceramist and archaeologist.

1949

"Activities of the American School," Bulletin of the American School of Oriental Research, 117, 1949, pp. 2, 3.

As director of the school in Jerusalem, Dr. Kelso's activities are reported.

1950

"Activities of the American School," *Bulletin of the American School of Oriental Research,* 118, 1950, pp. 1-3.

Clean-up of American school continued after the war. Surface explorations are made.

"Activities of the American School," *Bulletin of the American School of Oriental Research,* 119, 1950, p. 2.

School activities begin to pick up. Jericho to be excavated again by another team at a second site.

"Seminaries of the Presbyterian Family, *"Journal of Presbyterian History",* June 1950.

The heartland of Presbyterianism has three seminaries to train its young men for the ministry. The Reformed Presbyterian Seminary, 1807, is presently located in the former Joseph Horne mansion in Wilkensburg following a transitory existence in several states. Western Theological Seminary, founded November 6, 1827, was to be the Princeton of Western Pennsylvania and opened its doors in the session room of First Presbyterian Church of Pittsburgh. Its early history was a series of crises which were settled after the Civil War. The third Seminary is Pittsburgh-Xenia (now Pittsburgh Theological Seminary) and has a complex history resulting from mergers. The first seminary in the West (1794) was located north and west of Pittsburgh.

"First Campaign of Excavation in New Testament Jericho," *Bulletin-American School of Oriental Research*, 120, December 1950, pp. 11-22.

The first excavation at New Testament Jericho proved to be an archaeologist's delight. Four areas of work revealed much of that city's history. A Hellenistic tower guarded the Wadi-Qelt, while section two unveiled a civic center; section three, though briefly sounded, exposed structures of several historical periods. The least explored section, four, contained a building of small significance.

"Report of the Director of the School in Jerusalem," *Bulletin of the American School of Oriental Research*, 120 (December 1950), pp. 4-7.

As director of the American School of Oriental Research in Jerusalem in 1949-50, Dr. Kelso had the task of aiding in the clean-up of the school after the 1947-48 Middle-East War. He reports this activity as well as the academic and archaeological activities of the school.

1951

Excavations at Khirbet En-nitla Near Jericho," *Bulletin-American School of Oriental Research*, 121, February 1951, pp. 6-8.

A satellite excavation of the one at New Testament Jericho, possibly the Biblical Gilgal. The soundings revealed Byzantine or Early Arabic walls of unpretenious character. Also found was the ruins of a church built and destroyed four different times.

"Ancient Copper Refining," *Bulletin-American School of Oriental Research*, 122, April 1951, pp. 26-28.

This report is an interesting description of the developing processes the ancients used in refining copper. The analysis of ancient copper objects shows that the craftsmen of that day normally used a copper with a reasonably correct percentage of impurities or alloys, depending upon the particular purpose for which the object was to be used.

"New Testament Jericho," *The Biblical Archaeologist*, 14; 2, May 1951, pp. 33-43.

This ancient city rich in beauty and splendor afforded comfort and wealth to its inhabitants but was also a pawn in international politics. The cities geographic location made it a coveted possession as the citadels and fortifications found there indicate. However, the cities most notable fame is the role which it played in the life of Jesus Christ. It was the last city Christ visited before his death, the place he met Zaccheus, and where he healed a blind man. The author has a deep love for this city and especially the look up the Wadi Qelt—"It leads to the New Jerusalem."

"The Ghosts of Jericho," *The National Geographic*, 6, December 1951, pp. 825-844.

This is a descriptive narrative of the unearthing of New Testament Jericho written so laymen can understand what is involved in an excavation as well as vital information concerning the dating and historical significance of this old city. The colorful photos aid the reader in appreciating this excavation.

1955

"The Second Campaign at Bethel," *Bulletin-American School of Oriental Research*, No. 137, February 1955, pp. 5-10.

The excavation at Bethel II gave expanded insights into the development of pottery, building and economics. Most important was the volume of Roman sherds since they confirmed previous studies of Roman pottery at New Testament Jericho. The Roman forms at Bethel showed a fine evolution from the delicate early ware of the late first century B.C. on through the thickened pottery of late Roman.

"Excavation at New Testament Jericho and Khirbet En-Nitla," *Bulletin-American School of Oriental Research,* The Annual, Vols. 29, 30. 1955.

Chapters one to three, written by Dr. Kelso in collaboration with Dr. Dimitri C. Baramki, detail the pottery, masonry, plaster, and building construction of the two sites in a comprehensive manner.

"The Archaeology of Qumran," *The Journal of Biblical Literature* 74 (1955), pp. 141-146.

The discovery of the Dead Sea Scrolls led to four excavations of the area around the cave. The MSS. found are invaluable, being some of the greatest finds in Biblical research. Combined with the discovery of a secular community there is much new background material for Old Testament researchers as well as helpful information for those working in New Testament.

1956

"Excavations at Bethel," *The Biblical Archaeologist,* Vol. XIX, No. 2, May 1956, pp. 36-43.

Bethel, first called Luz, has a rich history dating from the early Bronze Age, 2200 B.C. and which ended in Arabic times. Its three thousand year history is dotted with many Biblical heroes. Most of its early history was dominated by Canaanite religion and culture, though in subsequent areas of its history its culture was that which it created. The findings of each age are highlighted to aid the reader in understanding the vital role this city played in the life of the Bible's people.

1957

"Archaeology's Role in Bible Study," *Christianity Today* (July 22, 1957), pp. 9-11.

A review of the part the continually growing science has on understanding, not proving the Bible.

1958

"The Third Campaign at Bethel," *Bulletin-American School of Oriental Research*, 151, October 1958, pp. 3-8.

The third campaign at Bethel had the disappointment of not discovering any direct trace of Jeroboam's temple. However, digging at various levels revealed the city's history from 1700 B.C. until the Byzantine age.

1961

"The Fourth Campaign at Bethel," *Bulletin-American School of Oriental Research*, No. 164, December 1961, pp. 5-19.

Disappointment again confronted the archaeological team as they searched for Jeroboam's temple. However, they did discover an old open-air sacrificial holy place of the Canaanites. This site may have been the holy place of the Jebusites at Jerusalem which David purchased as a site for the Temple to be dedicated to Yahweh. Most of the time was spent in studying the city's defenses which aided in dating the city early in antiquity.

1962

(and W. F. Albright) *"The Excavation at Bethel, 1934-1960"*, (Cambridge: American Schools of Oriental Research, 1962), 128 pp.

This culminating report on the Bethel excavations includes 120 plates of pottery and small objects. The initial chapters give a resume of all the data relative to the identification of Bethel and continues through all the major archaeological periods of the city's history.

"Bethel; la ville aux faux sanctuaries," *Bible et Terre Sainte* 47 (May, 1962), pp. 8-15.

This article in French recounts the findings of the Bethel excavations and includes, in large size, ten photographs, a map depicting Bethel's location, and a survey drawing of Bethel's ancient Northwest entrance gate.

Articles in *The New Bible Dictionary*, ed. J. D. Douglas. (Grand Rapids: Wm. B. Eerdmans Publishing Co., 1962).

Agriculture: The Importance of Palestinian seasons for agriculture is described as it involves cultivation, planting, irrigation, and harvesting. The major grain crops (wheat and barley) are mentioned along with fruits, vegetables and nuts.

Fortification and Siegecraft: Major cities of Palestine (Jerusalem, Jericho, Hazor, etc.) are noted as they represent the various methods of city fortification. The problem of water supply along with methods of siege are suggested.

House—Palestinian houses for the rich and poor are described with their use of stone and clay building materials. The history of Palestinian architecture is noted with descriptions of the most notable examples.

Trade and Commerce—A wide variety of goods were transported through Palestine which served as the bridge between the major nations of the ancient world. Trade routes, products, taxes and other particulars of trade and commerce are discussed.

Articles in *The interpreter's Dictionary of the Bible*, ed. G. A. Buttrick. Nashville/New York: Abingdon Press; 1962.

Bethel—Although the site affords no military advantage, the excellent water supply made the creation of the sanctuary city inevitable. Archaeological evidence is examined so as to reconstruct the political and religious history of this frequently mentioned site north of Jerusalem.

Jericho—The locations, history and significance as seen in the light of modern archaeology are noted as they relate to Old Testament Jericho, Neolithic Jericho, New Testament Jericho, and Roman/Byzantine Jericho.

Pottery—A discussion of the methods of fashioning clay into pottery, a history of the potter's craft (especially as it relates to archaeological studies) and the ceramic vocabulary as it is used in figurative and religious language are combined to suggest the significance which pottery had in the domestic, commercial, and religious life of Israel.

1966

Articles in *The Biblical World*, ed. C. F. Pfeiffer. Grand Rapids: Baker Book House 1966.

Gibeah—Saul's home town is described as the Tell-el-Ful located 3 1/2 miles north of Jerusalem. W. F. Albright's excavations of 1922-1923 and 1933 form the basis for the reconstructed history of this fortress site.

Jericho (New Testament)—Tulu Abu el-Alayiq, located one mile south of Old Testament Jericho and slightly less than that west of what is modern Jericho, is the site described as the location of Herod the Great's luxurious winter capital.

Metallurgy—The sources, uses and evolution of metallurgical technology are explained in the context of the prominence of the various nations of the ancient world.

Pottery—The techniques of fashioning clay into pottery for home, commercial, and religious usages are described here. The value of ceramics for the archaeological studies of Palestine is also noted.

Archaeology and Our Old Testament Contemporaries, Grand Rapids: Zondervan, 1966.

> Calling upon his rich knowledge of the past and his sensitivity to the present predicament of modern man, the author offers interesting contrasts and comparisons of Old Testament heroes with their contemporary personages. Poignant chapter headings—"Amos, a Salvation Army Preacher,"—"Penetrating Insights" . . . most of civilization has been simply a slow improvement in technology"; and practical advice—"Modern man has invented no new sins, nor has he found any remedy for sin, save Jesus Christ;" make this not only an interesting and valuable aid to the Christian's growth but a good resource for the life-styles and problems facing our ancestors.

1967

"Understanding the Bible Through Archaeology," *Church Herald* (December, 1967), p. 14.

> A brief demonstration that archaeology serves the purpose of aiding our understanding rather than "proving" the Bible.

1968

Archaeology and the Ancient Testament, Grand Rapids: Zondervan, 1968.

> The Ancient Testament is as alive today as when its authors recorded God's activity among men centuries ago. The author achieves his purpose of showing the superiority of Yahweh in contrast to the degrading, profane, and inferior gods men create and worship. Using a style familiar to his students, Dr. Kelso satirically, and at time facetiously, describes the misery and grandeur of man as he sometimes reacts, rejects, and too seldom responds to God.

"Life in the Pariarchal Age," *Christianity Today* (June 21, 1968), pp. 5-8.

> Abraham is a donkey caravaner whose Amorite background is clear. A brief look at the archeological evidences for the 1900's B.C.

"Perspective on Arab-Israeli Tensions," *Christianity Today* (June, 1968), pp. 6-9.

> A fair and objective historical presentation by one whose experience in Arab lands give him an "insider's" view.

1969

An Archaeologist Looks at the Gospels, Waco: Word Books, Inc., 1969.

> The Living Christ is alive in this vibrant account of first century life-styles, during our Lord's sojourn on earth. Contrary to the popular notion that first century life was backward—culturally and technically inferior—the reader discovers a rather sophisticated and advanced civilization to whom Jesus offered his gift of life and hope. It is the Christ whom the writer loves and serves, though, who is the dominant person and theme of this exciting book.

1970

"Inspiration of Scripture," *Christianity Today* (June 5, 1970), pp. 6-9.

> Always holding a high view of Scripture, Dr. Kelso states his position here as a professor of Old Testament and as a field archaeologist.

1971

An Archaeologist Follows the Apostle Paul, Waco: Word Books, Inc., 1971.

The first century world to whom Paul offered the gospel of Jesus Christ was one of crowded cities, travel, leisure, and new ideas. It was an age of competing religious and philosophical ideas as man sought meaning to life. It was a world modern man can easily identify with because it is so similar to the world in which he now lives. To this confused, searching, and fun-loving people, Paul introduced the radical truth—a man died and rose from the dead. That man was God's Son and you can know God through Him. The author's unusual archaeological experience in Roman culture and life presents to the reader the rare opportunity to be a part of that world.

The Case Against the Counterfeit Gospel. Pittsburgh, 1971.

In a brief any lawyer would be proud to present as his case, Dr. Kelso attacks the premise that "Social Action" is the gospel by repudiating such claims as outmoded; having been tried through the ages by pagans who did nothing to change men's hearts. The Gospel is men accepting Jesus Christ as Saviour and Lord and from this experience men will attack the social problems of his day. A heart of sin is man's problem and it was for this heart that Jesus Christ died on the cross.

"The Essence of Christianity is Evangelism," *Monday Morning* (May 3, 1971).

The article urges fellow ministers to put a stronger emphasis on evangelism.

1972

"Abraham as Archaeology Knows Him," *Perspective*, Vol. XIII, No. 1, Winter 1972.

Abraham's call by God to go to a new country was not an isolated incident in the Patriarch's life. There were economic and business factors which God used in calling Abraham to move into a new area. Dr. Kelso gives us new insights into Abraham the business man and also Abraham the spiritual genius who was to become the Father of a host of God's people.

UNPUBLISHED STUDIES

The Zondervan Pictorial Encyclopedia of the Bible, gen. ed. Merrill C. Tenney. Grand Rapids: Zondervan, 1973 (target date).

Forty-five entries written by Dr. Kelso will be included in this forthcoming volume. The largest entry is on "Occupations, Trades and Professions". Others of importance are "Samaria, City of," "Mizpah," "Samaritans," "Trade, Commerce and Business," "Travel," and "Wealth."

How to Study the Gospels Today
A Theological Seminary Many Laymen Want
A Supplementary Study on the Report of the Task Force on the Middle East
The Sins of the Conservative Clergy

Works Cited

PART I *BIBLICAL STUDIES AND BIBLICAL ARCHAEOLOGY*

BOOKS

Albright, W. F. and James L. Kelso *The Excavation of Bethel*, (New Haven: American Schools of Oriental Research Annual No. 39, 1968).

Albright, W. F. *Yahweh and the Gods of Canaan*. (London: Athlone Press, 1968).

Albright, W. F. *Archaeology and the Religion of Israel*, 3rd. ed. (Baltimore: John Hopkins Press, 1953).

Bauer, H. and Leander, P. *Historische Grammatik der Hebräischen Sprache des Alten Testamentes*. (Halle: Max Niemeyer, 1922).

Bewer, Julius A. *The Prophets*. (New York: Harper & Row, 1949).

Brockelmann, C. *Grundriss der Vergleichenden Grammatik der Semitischen Sprachen*, 2 vols. (Berlin: Reuther & Reichard, 1908-1913), 472-74.

de Vaux, Roland. *Studies in Old Testament Sacrifices*. (Cardiff: University of Wales Press, 1964).

Dronkert, K. *De Molechdienst in het Oude Testament*. (Leiden: Luctor et Emergo, 1953).

Eichrodt, Walther. *Ezekiel, a Commentary*. (Philadelphia: Westminster Press, 1970).

Eissfeldt, Otto. *Einleitung in das Alte Testament*, 3rd ed. (Tübingen: J.C.B. Mohr, 1964).

Ermarth, Margaret S. *Adam's Fractured Rib.* (Philadelphia: Fortress Press, 1970).

Geiger, Abraham. *Urschrift und Übersetzungen in ihrer Abhangigkeit von der innern Entwicklung des Judentums.* (Breslau: Hainauer, 1857).

Hennecke, E. and W. Schneemelcher, eds. *The New Testament Apocrypha,* trans. R. McL. Wilson. (Philadelphia: Westminster Press, 1963).

Herntrich, Volkmar. *Ezechielprobleme.* (Giessen: Alfred Töpelmann, 1924).

Jehiel, Nathan ben. *Sepher 'Arukh ha-shalem,* (ed.) A. Kohut, S. Krauss. (Jerusalem: Shiloh, 1969).

King, L. W. *Cuneiform Texts,* 24. (London: British Museum, 1908).

Kittel, G. *Theological Dictionary of the New Testament.* tr. G. W. Bromiley. (Grand Rapids: William B. Eerdmans, 1964).

Langdon, S. M. *Semitic Mythology.* (Boston: Jones, 1931).

Lohfink, Norbert. *Das Hauptgebot.* (Rome: Pontifical Institute of the Bible, 1963).

Maertens, Thierry. *The Advancing Dignity of Women in the Bible.* tr. Sandra Dibbs. (DePere, Wisconsin: St. Norbert Abbey Press, 1969).

Matthews, I. G. *Ezekiel: An American Commentary on the Old Testament,* (Philadelphia: The American Baptist Publishing Society, 1939).

McConnell, Richard S. *Law and Prophecy in Matthew's Gospel.* (Basel: Friedrich Reinhardt Verlag, 1969).

Smith, W. R. *Lectures on the Religion of the Semites,* 3rd ed. (New York: Macmillan, 1927).

Stendahl, Krister, *The Bible and The Role of Women.* (Philadelphia: Fortress Press, 1966).

Torrey, C. C. *Pseudo-Ezekiel and the Original Prophecy.* (New Haven: Yale University Press, 1930).

Trilling, Wolfgang. *Das Wahre Israel.* (Leipzig: St. Benno-Verlag, 1959).

Vos, Clarence J. *Women in the Old Testament Worship.* (Delft: N. V. Verenigde Drukkerijen Judeis and Brinkman, 1968).

Zerbst, Fritz. *The Office of Women in the Church.* tr. A. G. Merkens. (St. Louis: Concordia Publishing House, 1955).

Zimmerli, Walther. *Ezechiel.* (Neukirchen: Neukirchener Verlag, 1969).

ARTICLES AND PERIODICALS

Albright, W. F. "Molk als Opferbegriff . . . von O. Eissfeldt," *Journal of the Palestine Oriental Society,* 15(1935), p. 344.

Albright, W. F. "An Aramaean Magical Text in Hebrew from the Seventh Century B.C." *Bulletin of the American Schools of Oriental Research,* 76 (Dec. 1939).

Aliquier, J. and P. "Stèles votives á Saturne découvertes près de N'gaous (Algérie)" *Comptes rendus de l'Academie des Inscriptiones et Belles-Lettres,* (1931), 21-26.

Barth, Gerhard. "Das Gesetzverständnis des Evangelisten Matthäus," *Uberlieferung und Auslegung in Matthäusevangelium,* eds. G. Bornkamm, G. Barth, und. H. J. Held. (Neukirchen: Neukirchener Verlag, 1960).

Bea, A. "Kinder für Moloch oder für Jahwe? . . . ," *Biblica,* 18 (1937), 95-107.

Berry, George Ricker. "Was Eziekel in the Exile?", *Journal of Biblical Literature,* 49 (1930).

Brownlee, William H. "The Aftermath of the Fall of Judah according to Ezekiel," *Journal of Biblical Literature,* 89, (1970).

Brownlee, William H. "Ezekiel," *The Interpreter's One-Volume Commentary on the Bible,* (Nashville: Abingdon, 1971).

Brownlee, William H. "Ezekiel's Poetic Indictment of the Shepherds," *Harvard Theological Review,* 51 (1958).

Brownlee, William H. "Ancient Lore and Modern Knowledge," *Hommages a André Dupont-Sommer,* eds. A. Caquot and M. Philonenko. (Paris: Librairie d'Amerique et d'Orient, Adrien-Maisonneuve, 1971).

Cazelles, H. "Molok," *Supplément au dictionnaire de la Bible*, (ed.) L. Pirot, *et al.* 5. (Paris: Letouzey et Ané, 1957).

Charlier, R. "La nouvelle série de stèles puniques de Constantine," *Karthago*, 4(1953), 3-48.

Dhorme, Eduard. "Le dieu Baal et le dieu Moloch dan la tradition biblique," *Anatolian Studies*, 6(1956), 57-62.

Dhorme, Eduard. "Otto Eissfeldt, 'Molk als Opferbegriff'," *Revue d'histoire des religions*, 113(1936), 276-78.

Dossin, G. "Signaux lumineux au pays de Mari," *Revue d'Assyriologie*, 35(1938), 174-86.

Driver, G. R. "Ezekiel," *Biblica*, 35(1954).

Dussaud, R. "Précisions épigraphiques touchant les sacrifices puniques d'enfants," *Comptes rendus de l'Academie des Inscriptiones et Belle-Lettres*, (1946), pp. 371-87.

Eissfeldt, Otto. *Molk als Opferbegriff in Punischen und Hebräischen und das Ende des Gottes Molech*. (Halle: Max Niemeyer, 1935).

Fevrier, J. G. "Molchomor," *Revue de l'histoire des religions*, 143(1953) pp. 8-18.

Foerster, Werner "ҽxouoĩa" *Theologisches Wörterbuch das Neuen Testament*. ed. G. Kittel.

Goulder, M. D. "The Chiastic Structure of the Lucan Journey," *Studia Evangelica*, II, (ed.) F. L. Cross. (Berlin: Akademie—Verlag, 1964).

Gray, John. "Molech, Moloch," *Interpreter's Dictionary of the Bible*, 4. (New York: Abingdon, 1962), 422-23.

Harrelson, Walter J. "Molech, Moloch," *Dictionary of the Bible*. ed. J. Hastings; rev. ed. F. C. Grant and H. H. Rowley. (New York: Scribner's, 1963), p. 669.

Henninger, J. "Menschenopfer bei den Arabern," *Anthropos*, 53(1958), pp. 721-805.

Jensen, P. "Die Götter Kemosh und Melekh . . ." *Zeitschrift für Assyriologie*, 42(1934), pp. 235-37.

Kelso, James L., "Ezekiel's Parable of the Corroded Copper Caldron," *Journal of Biblical Literature*, 64(1945) 391-93.

Kelso, James L. "The Fourth Campaign at Bethel," *Bulletin of the American Schools of Oriental Research*, 164(Dec., 1961).

Kelso, James L. "Béthel la ville aux faux sanctuaries," *Bible et Terre Sainte*, 47(Mai, 1962).

Kornfeld, W. "Der Molech. Eine Untersuchung zur Theorie O. Eissfeldt," *Weiner Zeitschrift für die Kunde des Morgenlandes*, 51(1952), 287-313.

Kümmel, W. G. "Jesus und der Jüdische Traditionsgedanke," *Zeitschrift für Neuentestamentliche Wissenschaft*, 33 (1934).

Meyer, Eduard. "Molech (Moloch)" *Ausführliches Lexicon der Grieschischen und Römischen Mythologie*, ed. W. H. Roscher, 2:2. (Leipzig: Teubner, 1894-97) 2650-2652.

Michel, Otto. "Der Abschluss des Matthäusevangelium", *Evangelische Theologie*, 10(1950-51).

Michel, Otto. "Menschensohn and Völkerwelt," *Evangelische Mission Zeitschrift*, II (1941).

Moore, G. F. "Molech, Moloch," *Encyclopaedia Biblica*, (ed.) T. K. Cheyne, *et al.*, 3.(New York: Macmillan, 1902), cols. 3183-3191.

Poinssot, L. and Lantier, R. "Un sanctuaire de Tanit a Carthage," *Revue de l'histoire des religions*, 87(1923), 32-68.

Röllig, W. "Moloch," *Wörterbuch der Mythologie*, ed. H. W. Haussig, I. (Stuttgart: Ernst Klett, 1965), 299-300.

Schneider, N. "Melcom, das Scheusal der Ammoniter," *Biblica*, 18(1937),337-43.

Schceps, Hans Joachim. "Von der *Imitatio Dei* zur Nachfolge Christi," *Aus Früchristlicher Zeit.* (Tübingen: J.C.B. Mohr, 1950).

UNPUBLISHED

Brownlee, William H. *Major Critical Problems in the Book*

of Ezekiel. Unpublished Master's thesis. Pittsburgh-Xenia Theological Seminary, 1946.

Brownlee, William H. *The Book of Ezekiel—The Original Prophet and the Editors.* Unpublished Ph.D. dissertation. Duke University, 1947.

Thompson, John A. *Human Sacrifice among the Semites and the God Molech.* Unpublished Ph.D. dissertation, Johns Hopkins University, 1943.

PART II *THEOLOGY AND ETHICS*

BOOKS

Allen, E. L. *Guide Book to Western Thought.* (London: English Universities Press, 1957).

Altizer, Thomas. *The Gospel of Christian Atheism.* (Philadelphia: Westminster Press, 1966).

Barbour, Ian. *Issues in Science and Religion.* (Englewood Cliffs, N.J.: Prentice-Hall, Inc., 1966).

Bavinck, Herman. *Gereformeerde Dogmatiek.* (Kampen: Kok, 1928).

Beck, Robert N. and Orr, John B. *Ethical Choice.* (New York: Free Press, 1970).

Berger, Peter. *Rumor of Angels.* (Garden City: Doubleday, 1969).

Berkouwer, G. C. "Wat Is Theologie?", *Interfaculatire Colleges Aan De Vrije Universiteit Te Amsterdam, Curus 1949-50.* (Kampen: Kok, 1950).

Bonhoeffer, Dietrich. *The Cost of Discipleship.* (New York: Macmillan, 1959).

Calvin, Jean. *Institutes of the Christian Religion,* ed. John T. McNeill, trans. Ford Lewis Battles, Library of Christian Classics, Vol. 20. (Philadelphia: Westminster Press, 1960).

Cobb, John. *Christian Natural Theology.* (Philadelphia: Westminster Press, 1968).

Cobb, John, *God and the World.* (Philadelphia: Westminister Press, 1968).

deChardin, Pierre Teilhard. *The Appearance of Man.* (New York: Harper and Row, 1966).

deChardin, Pierre Teilhard. *The Future of Man.* (New York: Harper and Row, 1969).

deChardin, Pierre Teilhard. *The Divine Milieu.* New York: (Harper and Row, 1960).

Dooyeweerd, Herman. *In the Twilight of Western Thought.* (Philadelphia: Presbyterian and Reformed Publishing Co., 1960).

Drake, Durant. *Problems of Conduct.* (New York: Houghton and Mifflin, 1914).

Ellul, Jacques. *The Meaning of the City,* trans. Dennis Pardee. (Grand Rapids: Eerdmans, 1970).

Ellul, Jacques, *The Judgment of Jonah.* trans. G. E. Bromiley. (Grand Rapids, Eerdmans, 1971).

Ellul, Jacques. *Prayer and Modern Man.* trans. C. E. Hopkins. (New York: Seabury Press, 1970).

Ellul, Jacques, *The Theological Foundation of Law.* trans. M. Wieser. (New York: Seabury Press, 1960).

Fletcher, Joseph. *Morals and Medicine.* (Boston: Beacon Press, 1960).

Gilkey, Langdon. *Naming the Whirlwind: The Renewal of God Language.* (Indianapolis: Bobbs-Merrill, 1969).

Harnack, Adolph. *History of Dogma,* trans. Neil Buchanan. (New York: Dover, 1961).

Heisenberg, Werner. *Physics and Beyond: Encounters and Conversations.* (New York: Harper and Row, 1971).

Hordern, William. *A Layman's Guide to Protestant Theology.* rev. ed. (New York: Macmillan, 1968).

Jenkins, D. T. (ed.) *The Scope of Theology.* (Cleveland: Meridian Books, 1968).

Kelly, J.N.D. *Early Christian Creeds.* (London: Longman's, 1960).

Küng, Hans. *Infallible? An Inquiry,* trans. Edward Quinn. (Garden City: Doubleday, 1971).

Lehmann, Paul L., *Ethics in a Christian Context.* (New York: Harper and Row, 1963).

Lohse, Bernhard. *A Short History of Christian Doctrine,* trans. F. E. Stoeffler. (Philadelphia: Fortress Press, 1966).

Masters, R. E. and Houston, Jean. *Varieties of Psychedelic Experience.* (New York: Holt, Rinehart and Winston, 1966).

Ogden, Schubert. *Reality of God.* (New York: Harper and Row, 1966).

Outka, R. and Ramsey, P. *Norm and Context in Christian Ethics.* (New York: Scribners, 1968).

Pike, James A. *You and the New Morality.* (New York: Harper and Row, 1967).

Ramsey, Paul. *Deeds and Rules in Christian Ethics.* (New York: Scribners, 1967).

Rogers, Jack B. *Scripture in the Westminister Confession: A Problem of Historical Interpretation for American Presbyterians.* (Grand Rapids: Eerdmans, 1967).

Routley, Erik. *Creeds and Confessions: The Reformation and Its Modern Ecumenical Implications.* (London: Duckworth, 1962).

Roszak, Theodore. *Toward the Making of a Counter-Culture.* (Garden City: Doubleday, 1969).

Thielicke, Helmut. *Theological Ethics.* (Philadelphia: Fortress Press, 1966).

Thielicke, Helmut. *A Little Exercise for Young Theologians,* trans. Charles L. Taylor, (Grand Rapids, Eerdmans, 1962).

Tillich, Paul. *Courage to Be.* (New Haven: Yale University Press, 1952).

Tillich, Paul, *Systematic Theology,* I. (Chicago: University of Chicago Press, 1951).

Titus, H. H. *Ethics for Today,* (New York: American Book Co., 1957).

Torrance, T. F., *Theological Science*. (London: Oxford University Press, 1969).

Torrance, T. F. *God and Rationality*. (London: Oxford University Press, 1971).

Van Buren, Paul. *Secular Meaning of the Gospel*. (New York: Macmillan, 1963).

ARTICLES AND PERIODICALS

Bromiley, G. F. "The Church Doctrine of Inspiration," *Revelation and the Bible*, ed. C.F.H. Henry. (Grand Rapids: Baker Book House, 1958), 205-17.

Christy, Wayne H. "Truthfulness in All Things," *The United Presbyterian* (November 15, 1943), p. 11.

Fleming, John. "Theology as Scientific Inquiry and as Christian Commitment," *Bulletin of the Dept. of Theology of the World Alliance of Reformed Churches and the World Presbyterian Alliance*, 10:3 (Spring, 1970), 12-13.

Koop, C. Everett. "What I Tell a Dying Child's Parents," *Readers Digest* (Feb., 1968), p. 143.

Rogers, Jack B. "Van Til and Warfield on Scripture in the Westminster Confession," *Jerusalem and Athens: Critical Discussions on the Theology and Apologetics of Cornelius Van Til*, ed. E. R. Geehan. (Nutley, New Jersey: Presbyterian and Reformed Publishing Co., 1971).

PART III CHURCH AND MINISTRY

BOOKS

Allport, Gordon W. *Becoming*. (New Haven: Yale University Press, 1955).

An Advisory Study. Commission on Ecumenical Mission and Relations of the United Presbyterian Church in the U.S.A. (New York: nd).

Brenton, Myron, *The American Male.* (New York: Cow-ard-McCann, 1966).

Combs, Arthur W. and Snygg, D. *Individual Behavior.* (New York: Harper and Bros., 1959).

Cragg, Kenneth C. *Christianity in World Perspective.* (New York: Oxford University Press, 1968).

Erikson, Erik. *Childhood and Society.* 2nd ed. (New York: W. W. Norton, 1963).

Glasser, William. *Reality Therapy: A New Approach to Psychiatry.* (New York: Harper and Row, 1965).

Gordon, Andrew. *Our India Mission.* (Philadelphia, 1886).

Harris, Thomas A. *I'm O.K.—You're O.K.* (New York: Harper and Row, 1969).

Horney, Karen. *The Neurotic Personality of Our Time.* (New York: Norton, 1936).

Hulme, William E. *Your Pastor's Problems: A Guide for Ministers and Laymen.* (Minneapolis: Augsburg, 1966).

Jourard, Sidney M. *The Transparent Self.* (New York: Van Nostrand-Reinhold Co., 1971).

Jourard, Sidney M. *Self-Disclosure: An Experimental Analysis of the Transparent Self.* (New York: Wiley, 1971).

Loomis, Earl A. *The Self in Pilgrimage.* (New York: Harper and Row, 1960).

May, Rollo. *Psychology and the Human Dilemma.* (Princeton, N.J.: D. van Nostrand Co., Inc., 1966).

Ohlsen, Merle M. *Group Counseling.* (New York: Holt, Rinehart and Winston, 1970).

Reich, Wilhelm. *Character Analysis.* (New York: Orgone Press, 1948).

Rogers, Carl R. *Client-Centered Therapy.* (New York: Houghton-Mifflin, 1957).

Romig, T., and Crouch, A. *The Missionary.* (New York: World Horizons, 1965).

Seaver, George. *David Livingstone: His Life and Work.* (New York: Harper, 1957).

273

Tournier, Paul. *A Place for You.* (New York: Harper & Row, 1968).

van Leeuwen, Arend Th. *Christianity in World History.* (Edinburgh: Edinburgh House Press, 1964).

Walker, Daniel D. *The Human Problems of the Minister.* (New York: Harper and Row, 1960).

Warren, Max. *To Apply the Gospel.* (Grand Rapids: Eerdmans, 1970).

Webster, Douglas. *Yes, to Mission.* (London: SCM Press, 1966).

Whitely, John M. (ed.) *Research in Counseling.* (Columbus, Ohio: Charles E. Merrill Publishing Co., 1967).

ARTICLES AND PERIODICALS

Jourard, Sidney M., and Lasakow, P. "Some Factors in Self-Disclosure," *Journal of Abnormal Social Psychology* (1958), p. 56.

Niebuhr, H. Richard. "An Attempt at a Theological Analysis of Missionary Motivation," *Occasional Bulletin,* Missionary Research Library, 14:1 (January, 1963).

Seteloane, G. M. "The Missionary and his Task," *International Review of Missions* (January, 1970).

Contributors

ALL OF THE ESSAYISTS and the editor of this volume were students of James L. Kelso during their seminary training. Theophilus M. Taylor and Addison H. Leitch later were faculty colleagues of Dr. Kelso at Pittsburgh-Xenia Theological Seminary. Nine of the contributors also were students of Drs. Leitch and Taylor when the former was President of Pittsburgh-Xenia Theological Seminary, Pittsburgh, Pennsylvania.

THEOPHILUS M. TAYLOR is presently Secretary of the General Council of the United Presbyterian Church in the U.S.A. For nineteen years he was John McNaugher Professor of New Testament Literature and Exegesis at Pittsburgh-Xenia and Pittsburgh Theological Seminaries. Dr. Taylor received his Bachelor of Arts degree and an honorary Doctor of Divinity degree from Muskingum College, the Bachelor of Architecture degree from the University of Pennsylvania, the Bachelor of Theology degree from Pittsburgh-Xenia Seminary; he continued his studies at Yale Divinity School and at Yale University, where he earned the Doctorate in Philosophy in 1956. In addition to many other posts Dr. Taylor also served as Moderator of the United Presbyterian Church in the U.S.A. in 1958-59; was a teacher at Woodstock School, Mussoorie, India; and from 1954 he has been a member of the Commission on Faith and Order for the World Council of Churches. Dr. Taylor is internationally known as a leading American churchman.

WILLIAM H. BROWNLEE is Professor of Religion at the Claremont

Graduate School, where he has taught since 1959. Before that, he taught at Duke University for eleven years, nine in the Divinity School as Assistant and Associate Professor of Old Testament. A graduate of Sterling College (1939) and Pittsburgh-Xenia Theological Seminary (1942), he served as Pastor of the United Presbyterian Church of Newton, Kansas (1942-44). He subsequently obtained his Th.M. degree from Pittsburgh-Xenia (1946) and his Ph.D. degree from Duke University (1947). As a Fellow of the American Schools of Oriental Research, he studied at the American School in Jerusalem (1947-48), where he participated in the first study and translation of the Dead Sea Scrolls. An author of many publications, Dr. Brownlee is best known for his book *The Meaning of the Qumran Scrolls for the Bible*, New York: Oxford University Press, 1964. He has participated in three seasons of archaeological excavation, one with Dr. James L. Kelso at Bethel (1960), and two with Dr. Robert J. Bull on Mt. Gerizim (1966 and 1968).

JOHN ALEXANDER THOMPSON is presently a Special Secretary and Research Consultant for Old Testament with the American Bible Society. He received his education at Princeton University, where he was awarded the A.B. degree and was elected to Phi Beta Kappa; at Pittsburgh Theological Seminary where he earned the Th.B. and Th.M. degrees; at Johns Hopkins University, where he received the Ph.D. degree in Semitic Languages and Near Eastern Archaeology. Dr. Thompson was Professor of Old Testament at Biblical Seminary in New York for six years, and for nineteen years was Professor of Old Testament at Evangelical Theological Seminary, Cairo, Egypt. Dr. Thompson published *Major Arabic Bibles* in 1956 for the American Bible Society and wrote the introductions and exegesis to Joel and Obadiah for *The Interpreter's Bible.* In 1964 and 1967, he co-edited the two-volume *Arabic Dictionary of the Bible.* Dr. Thompson is an ordained minister in the United

Presbyterian Church in the U.S.A. and lives in Princeton, New Jersey.

KENNETH E. BAILEY, the son of missionary parents in Egypt, graduated from Monmouth College, Monmouth, Illinois (1952) and from Pittsburgh-Xenia (1955). He earned the Th.M. degree in Systematic Theology from Pittsburgh-Xenia, did graduate work in New Testament at Pittsburgh Theological Seminary, and earned the Th.D. degree from Concordia Theological Seminary, St. Louis, Missouri (1972). Dr. Bailey served the church in literacy work in Egypt for five years and as a seminary teacher of New Testament in Egypt for another four-year stint. From 1967-1970, Dr. Bailey was Assistant Professor of New Testament at Near East School of Theology, Beirut, Lebanon, the post to which he returned in August, 1972. During his years at Beirut, Dr. Bailey was preacher and lecturer-at-large for the Arab Evangelical Synod of Syria and Lebanon, conducting weekly radio broadcasts in Arabic. He has published four books in Arabic, one of which, a dialogic presentation of *The Doctrine of God,* has been translated into seventeen languages for world-wide distribution. Four of Dr. Bailey's plays for high school youth have been published by Westminster Press.

RICHARD S. McCONNELL is currently pastor of the John Knox Presbyterian Church in Topeka, Kansas. Previously he was Associate Professor of Religion and Chairman of the Department of Religion at Pikeville College, Kentucky. He received the A.B. degree from Wesleyan University, where he was elected to Phi Beta Kappa, and the B.D. degree from Pittsburgh Theological Seminary. His doctoral work was completed at the University of Basel in Switzerland under Oscar Cullmann and Bo Reicke. Dr. McConnell's published dissertation is entitled *Law and Prophecy in Matthew's Gospel.* He has also studied in the program of pastoral care and counseling at the

Division of Religion and Psychiatry of the Menninger Foundation in Topeka. Dr. McConnell is married and has three children.

JACK B. ROGERS is Associate Professor of Theology and Philosophy of Religion at Fuller Theological Seminary, Pasadena, California. A native of Lincoln, Nebraska, Dr. Rogers graduated from the University of Nebraska where he was awarded the B.A. degree and was elected to Phi Beta Kappa. He earned the B.D. and Th.M. degrees at Pittsburgh-Xenia Theological Seminary and studied at the Free University, Amsterdam, The Netherlands, with Gerrit C. Berkouwer, earning the Th.D. degree in 1967. From 1963-1971 Dr. Rogers taught at Westminster College, New Wilmington, Pa., serving for two years as Assistant Academic Dean. He is the author of *Scripture in the Westminster Confession*. Dr. Rogers is married and the father of three sons.

W. FRED GRAHAM, since 1966, has been Associate Professor at Justin Morrill College, one of the residential colleges at Michigan State University, East Lansing, Michigan, where he is Chairman of Religion. A native of Ohio and ordained in the United Presbyterian Church in the USA, Dr. Graham graduated from Tarkio College, Tarkio, Missouri (1952) and from Pittsburgh-Xenia Theological Seminary (1955). He earned the Th.M. degree at Louisville Theological Seminary, in Kentucky (1958) and the Ph.D. degree at Iowa University (1965). Dr. Graham served as pastor of the United Presbyterian Church, Waterloo, Iowa, for six years prior to his doctoral work. Dr. Graham recently authored *The Constructive Revolutionary*, a study of the social attitudes of John Calvin published by John Knox Press.

ADDISON H. LEITCH is currently Professor of Theology at Gordon-Conwell Theological School in Wenham, Massachusetts.

He is a widely-known lecturer and author, frequently writing the "Current Religious Thought" column in *Christianity Today*. Dr. Leitch has published several books, his last being *This Cup*, meditations on Holy Week. Dr. Leitch served as Professor of Theology and President of Pittsburgh-Xenia Theological Seminary, Pittsburgh, Pa. until 1962. Dr. Leitch was Distinguished Professor-at-Large at Tarkio College, Tarkio, Missouri, until assuming his present post in 1969.

WAYNE H. CHRISTY earned the B.A. degree from Westminster College, New Wilmington, Pa., the B.D. and Th.M. degrees from Pittsburgh-Xenia Theological Seminary, the M.A. degree in Ethics from Duke University and the Ph.D. degree from the University of Pittsburgh. He was on the staff of the Bethel excavation in 1960. Dr. Christy is currently Professor of Religion at Westminster College where he has been Chairman of the Department of Religion and Philosophy since 1950.

DONALD BLACK is General Secretary of the Commission on Ecumenical Mission and Relations of the United Presbyterian Church in the U.S.A. A native of Mercer, Pennsylvania, he graduated from Grove City College, Pittsburgh-Xenia Theological Seminary, and Temple University School of Theology. After serving pastorates in Oklahoma City where he organized a new congregation, and in Philadelphia where he served as President of the United Presbyterian Board of Foreign Missions, he was elected to the post of Executive Secretary of that Board. At the formation of the Commission on Ecumenical Mission and Relations in 1958, he became an Associate General Secretary, a post he held until he assumed his present responsibilities on January 1, 1971. He has been an active participant in ecumenical activities related to world mission, serving on committees and study teams of the National Council of Churches and the World Council of Churches. His writings have appeared in church magazines and papers related to the missionary movement.

BRUCE W. THIELEMANN holds a B.A. degree from Westminster College, New Wilmington, Pa., a B.D. degree from Pittsburgh-Xenia Theological Seminary, and an honorary Doctor of Divinity from Grove City College, Grove City, Pa. He has done graduate study at St. Mary's College of St. Andrews University, St. Andrews, Scotland, under a Rotary International Graduate Fellowship. Dr. Thielemann was ordained by the Pittsburgh Presbytery in 1959. Presently the Senior Minister of the Glendale Presbyterian Church, Glendale, California, he regularly preaches to one of the largest congregations in the Southwest as well as conducting Preaching Missions throughout the United States and in other nations. He was selected to give the lectures on preaching at the Presbyterian Celebration of Evangelism in 1971.

ROBERT M. URIE, born in 1930 in Glover, Vermont, attended Monmouth College, graduating with the B.A. degree (1958). He acquired his B.D. degree from Pittsburgh Theological Seminary (1961) and was ordained by the Presbytery of Northern New England, UPUSA, in that year. He earned the M.S. degree from the University of North Carolina at Chapel Hill (1965) and the Ph.D. degree from the same institution in 1972. His work experience includes several years as a self-employed dairy farmer, pulpit-supply preacher, and full-time counselor to high school and college students since 1961, the latter at St. Andrews Presbyterian College, Laurinburg, North Carolina. He holds memberships in professional counseling and rehabilitation associations and has published several articles in various professional journals. His present position is Director of Health and Rehabilitation Services at St. Andrews Presbyterian College. In 1950, he married Elsie Dean. They have five children, three girls and two boys.

JAMES A. GITTINGS is currently Associate Editor of *Presbyterian Life*. He attended the University of Pittsburgh, graduated from

Juniata College, Huntingdon, Pennsylvania, attended Pittsburgh-Xenia Theological Seminary and graduated from the Columbia University Graduate School of Journalism. Mr. Gittings, an ordained elder at the First Presbyterian Church, Pottstown, Pa., is active on the boards of the Pottstown Neighborhood House Inc., and the Interfaith Housing Corporation, Pottstown, Pa. A widely experienced and colorful journalist, Mr. Gittings published two books, *Life Without Living* (1964) and *Down Strange Streets* (1967). His articles and poetry have appeared in magazines and newspapers across the nation. Mr. Gittings was in Pakistan for five and one half years, in Indonesia for one year, and in Japan for three and one half years. While in Tokyo he founded *An Asia Notebook*, a monthly magazine of travel, business, entertainment, and religion and is still part owner. He married Garnet Sue Kellams in 1956. The Gittings have four children.

J. HARRY FISHER is currently pastor at Puckety United Presbyterian Church, New Kensington, Pa. Mr. Fisher graduated from Westminster College, New Wilmington, Pa. (1955) and earned the B.D. degree from Pittsburgh-Xenia Theological Seminary in 1958. He served as pastor of the Bethel United Presbyterian Church, Enon Valley, Pa., until he was called to his present position in 1964.

ROBERT A. COUGHENOUR has served since 1969 as Associate Professor of Religion at Hope College, Holland, Michigan. He graduated from Indiana University of Pennsylvania with a B.S. in Music and Pittsburgh Theological Seminary with the B.D. degree. Dr. Coughenour did graduate work in Biblical Studies at Pittsburgh Seminary, earned the M.A. in Religion, and the Ph.D. degree from Case Western University, Cleveland, Ohio. He served the Wallace Memorial United Presbyterian Church, Greentree, Pa., as Assistant Pastor, and for seven years was Instructor and Assistant Professor of Religion at Westminster

College, New Wilmington, Pa. Dr. Coughenour was a member of the Bethel Excavation staff (1960) and contributed to the published report of the excavation. He has written book reviews and articles for professional journals and is the author of *Enoch and Wisdom.*